The MBA Admissions Handbook

Everything you need to know to secure your place at business school

Sara Strafino and Balbir Guru

trotman t

The MBA Admissions Handbook

This first edition published in 2012 by
Trotman Publishing, a division of Crimson Publishing Ltd
Westminster House
Kew Road
Richmond
Surrey
TW9 2ND

Authors: Sara Strafino and Balbir Guru

British Library Cataloguing in Publication Data

A catalogue record for this book is available from the British Library

ISBN 978 1 84455 4 225

Text design by Andy Prior
Typeset by MacStyle, Nafferton, Yorkshire
Printed and bound in the UK by Ashford Colour Press, Gosport, Hants

Contents

Foreword

Association of MBAs

I started my Masters in Business Administration (MBA) after running three businesses and then went on to be involved in the start up of two more. I had friends and colleagues wondering why I felt the need for formal business education when I had lived and worked on four continents (Africa, Asia, Australia and Europe), sold into markets as diverse as China, Libya, Russia and Vietnam, and crossed sectors from oil and gas to Montessori pre-schools, to name but two.

I suppose I had always felt rather an "amateur" in the business world. I didn't have the right language, regarded success as by accident rather than design and did not know what I did not know! An MBA was a turning point and, as I have moved on in my own career to run the Association of MBAs and to mentor young entrepreneurs, I am perhaps more aware now of its value than when I was in the classroom.

I know from my own experience and that of the people I mentor, and from our research, that the MBA can open up a wealth of opportunities. It is an enabling tool for management and leadership. As well as propelling you within your current sector, it can also help you to change direction and go from a career in, for example, banking to the not-for-profit sector. It might even provide a good opportunity to live in another country. On some programmes you can choose to study all or part of your MBA overseas, thus enabling you to get international experience while simultaneously being introduced to new markets and building a rich international network.

There are many reasons why you may be planning on doing an MBA. The three main reasons I have come across are: first, the MBA is a way of moving from a speciality or profession into general management; second, it can provide a total change of career, for example shifting from the public sector to the private; and third, an MBA may be a way of getting out of a blocked career or restarting a career.

The view on MBAs has certainly changed from the dated 1980s perception that they only serve executive bankers and high-flying consultants. We come across MBA students and graduates from all backgrounds, for example nursing, the not-for-profit sector, and increasingly from the start-up sector. You don't even have to be in business to want to do an MBA – even ex-Olympians and actors do MBAs.

The 21st-century MBA is very diverse in the type of graduate it produces. As a result, the type of business school you choose will be very much dependent on where you want to study and what you want to do with your MBA. The vast range of accredited business schools and programmes throughout the world ensures that whatever your individual aspirations are, there is an MBA that is right for you.

While the MBA includes a huge amount of learning around core topics such as strategy, marketing, human resources (HR) and so on, you will also learn as much from your cohort as you do from your faculty. A typical MBA class would have an average of 40 nationalities from all different sectors partaking. The richness of the learning environment is incredibly unique, and that is what makes it such a valuable additional string to your career bow.

In addition, while the main MBA curriculum is obviously a very important consideration, so is the geographical location and style of business school. If your career aspirations suggest studying abroad, or if you have strong linguistic abilities, an accredited MBA offers an internationally recognised qualification that would enable you to pursue a career anywhere in the world.

MBAs are still very much in demand and valued at a strategic level in organisations. Their salaries have also reportedly increased, with a salary increase of over 30% immediately post-MBA, rising to more than 200% 6–10 years after completing the course. When you apply for a job with an MBA, you have a competitive edge. If an employer is looking at two people with the same experience, the MBA has that extra appeal.

We conduct a career survey to get an idea of the employment opportunities for MBA graduates. It shows that 42% of MBA graduates reported changing business or employer immediately after completing their MBA. It also showed that 68% go on to own their companies, and 26% of MBA graduates reported starting their own company/entrepreneurial venture.

The MBA programme itself has evolved to offer increasingly different modes of study from full time, part time, distance learning through to blended learning. This guide goes through them in detail. Interestingly, our research shows that more people have enrolled in part-time courses than full-time courses over the past two years. Naturally you want to consider your own priorities – such as time away from work, cost, flexibility, hours and location. The advantage of a part-time course is that it also gives you career security, as you do not have to quit your job to study. Over 60% of part-time students receive some kind of company support. However, you need to remember that holding down a job while studying for your MBA is not easy, as the course requires serious commitment of your time and is fast-paced and demanding.

There is the opportunity for even greater flexibility with distance-learning MBA programmes. This is now the single most popular form of study in the UK and accredited courses ensure that the student still receives a sufficient amount of engagement with the business school that includes face-to-face elements with access to academic and support staff, student feedback and pastoral care. Today's technology also offers opportunity for improvements in this area.

There are different indicators of quality of MBA programmes in the UK, such as rankings and accreditation, plus of course those business schools that have distinct brand names. Accreditation involves a quality assessment by a body independent of the school with the aim to set global standards in MBA education. The Association of MBAs accredits MBAs in 43 schools in the UK and in 146 across the world.

As an impartial authority on postgraduate business education and providers of an international accreditation service, the Association of MBAs' remit is to ensure that MBA programmes all over the world continue to improve and evolve. We work with the business schools and help them re-examine and refine their mission and commitment to continuous improvement, by looking at the design and content of their MBAs and defining the best ways to integrate analytical methods with the reality and complexity of modern leadership and management.

As with the MBA students themselves, it is important for the business schools to share knowledge and networks and bring the latest research into the classroom to ensure world-class teaching and learning. In uncertain, challenging times, we can ensure that there is certainty in the commitment of our accredited schools to developing tomorrow's global leaders.

This *MBA Handbook* will help clarify the MBA process and help you consider everything you need to know in your first step to furthering your career potential with an MBA. What is important to remember is that if you have done your research thoroughly, you should not make a bad choice. It will, rather, become a matter of choosing the most suitable school for you. Use our impartial online guide to MBA study at www.ambaguide.com for more information.

You are taking the first step to enhancing your career by reading this guide and considering which MBA programme to take. If you are considering taking the plunge I would definitely encourage you to go for it – it will change your life in a very positive way.

Sharon Bamford
Chief Executive, Association of MBAs

About the authors

Sara Strafino

Sara is an undergraduate and postgraduate admissions expert with extensive experience in student recruitment and selection within different organisations, including London Business School and QS Top MBA. She is passionate about management education and has a strong track record of success in coaching and guiding candidates through admissions processes with top schools around the world. More recently Sara has joined the Graduate Management Admission Council (GMAC).

Balbir Guru

Balbir is a seasoned recruitment and selection specialist in both undergraduate and postgraduate programmes with a strong passion for supporting education at management level. She has substantial admissions experience across top-ranked business schools including London School of Economics, London Business School and a number of partner programmes in the Middle East, US and pan-Asia region. Balbir has recently moved into a programme management role at London Business School.

Acknowledgements

We would like to thank those people without whose help this book would not have been possible.

First and foremost we would like to thank both our families, Guarav and Sagir. Without their support, understanding and words of encouragement, this book would not have been finished on time!

Athina Kafetsiou for her invaluable input, advice and guidance throughout the different stages of the writing process. Her background in psychology, coaching and interviewing along with her own experience of being a graduate of a top business school was fundamental to our research.

Michael Birdsall for his insights into the GMAT® and how to prepare for the test. Michael has extensive experience in providing GMAT® coaching to candidates who have successfully applied for top business schools.

Throughout the book we have tried to support our advice and concepts with the perspective of those that have been through the process. We have relied on the goodwill of numerous alumni and students to talk candidly about their experiences at business school.

This book includes a great deal of information from various schools and organisations. We are grateful to all of them for agreeing to use the data while also providing us with quotes.

Introduction

"Once we accept our limits, we go beyond them."
Albert Einstein

The MBA is one of the most coveted postgraduate degrees. It is normally chosen as the degree that will furnish a candidate with the knowledge and skills that can be applied to a variety of real-world business situations. This is why the MBA is seen as a post-experience degree that boosts professional careers as well as a key qualification for significant career promotions within global businesses. Many eminent and contemporary business leaders and entrepreneurs alike are MBA holders; schools such as Harvard, Wharton, London Business School and INSEAD are some of the modern centres that have nurtured generations of global leaders.

This handbook will give you an insight into the application and admissions process for business schools based on the combined and shared experience of professionals who have participated in admissions committees, graduated from top business schools and provided executive and admissions coaching to MBA candidates. The guide will take you through the various stages of your journey towards the right MBA for you – from choosing the school and the programme to preparing your Graduate Management Admission Test (GMAT®) and application package, accepting your offer or dealing with disappointing decisions. You will be able to learn everything you need to know about MBA admissions in a few days of focused reading.

Who is this book aimed at?

This book is for anyone who is planning to apply to a top MBA programme. In an ideal world you should allow yourself between nine months to a year to prepare your application to a business school, and certainly additional time if you are applying to more than one business school. However, you may be working on a shorter timeframe. In such instances, this guide will be particularly useful as it will help you fast-track your preparation.

How will this book help you?

There are no secrets, hard and fast rules or shortcuts in this book to help you secure a place on an MBA programme. However, what it does provide is a framework and concepts which you can apply to your decision-making process. The concepts will assist you when putting together a compelling and competitive application, increasing your chances of successfully securing a place on a programme at the top of your list.

When reading this book, think critically about why you want an MBA and what your alternative choices are. Once you start the process of researching schools and programmes, your thought process will crystallise. You will be investing a great deal of time in preparing for an MBA, and it is crucial that you make sure it really is the right step to take for you and your career.

A typical MBA candidate usually has an undergraduate degree and anything between three to five years of work experience; candidates thinking about alternative MBA programmes on average have more experience to offer. In any case, what you as a candidate are trying to showcase in your application is that within that timeframe you have achieved a great deal. Your objective as a candidate is to convince the admissions committee that, armed with the knowledge from an MBA, you will continue on the path of success and achievement.

Alternatively, you may realise after reading this book that you are not yet at the right level to apply for an MBA. We would therefore suggest you focus on consolidating your experience and revisit your MBA plans in the not-too-distant future.

What is covered in this book?

This guide offers you a realistic, step-by-step overview of the following:

- identifying what an MBA is and the different programmes available
- typical reasons why you want to do an MBA
- deciding on which schools to apply to, taking into consideration the reasons behind your motivations
- financing and the associated costs of undertaking an MBA
- understanding the admissions process around getting an MBA and developing a strategy to help you secure a place
- practical tips on how to complete an MBA application form and an insight into essay questions and how to approach them
- advice on the GMAT®, what it is, how to prepare for it and sample GMAT® questions
- how to prepare for interviews and what to expect at an MBA interview
- application decisions and what they mean
- rankings overview to give you a heads-up on what schools are offering top MBA programmes.

When you are researching schools and programmes, the alumni service offered by schools is something you need to consider carefully. Although in this book we talk about alumni, we do not go into detail about life as an alumnus at business school but will direct you to bear this in mind during your research.

Ultimately, within this book we aim to demystify the MBA process by helping you with your research to choose the right programme and school that fits with your personal and professional aspirations. We wish you good luck!

1

What is an MBA?

The MBA is a postgraduate degree in general management designed to equip its graduates with theoretical frameworks and functional knowledge of all the core areas of business (corporate finance, accounting, marketing, strategy, operations). Besides the core knowledge, nowadays an MBA aims to nurture leadership by focusing on a wide range of "soft" skills that facilitate leadership development.

Who is it for?

MBA programmes target professionals who have significant work experience: in fact, most business schools usually require or expect at least three years of postgraduate professional experience. There are a few notable exceptions in the US: for example, Harvard and Stanford consider final-year university students and also offer deferred admission to a future class, based on the condition of gaining approved full-time work experience. Despite this, they recommend that prospective students have had exposure to the work environment before applying.

If you are a fresh graduate, you should consider either waiting a few years before applying for an MBA, or take a pre-experience master's in management (MSc in Management), which will prepare you for graduate entry level positions in the corporate world. Most business schools offer MSc in Management as part of their business degree portfolio.

There are different types of MBA, which suit different people. In Chapter 3 we will examine the different programme types in detail, but some of the options include: part-time MBA (PT MBA), executive MBA (EMBA), global MBA, distance-learning MBA (see p.40).

How it started and evolved

The MBA model was created in the US at the beginning of the 20th century to respond to the needs of industrial and economic development. It was purely a full-time academic programme which aimed to give graduates background understanding of business functions. At that time students could enrol for an MBA immediately after completing their undergraduate degree.

In the US, the MBA went through a major crisis at the end of the 1950s, when it was criticised for being too vocational and lacking academic depth and breadth (The Economist Intelligence Unit, "The MBA – some history", *The Economist*, October 2003). American schools addressed the criticism by introducing more rigour in the selection of both students and faculty. They set higher entry requirements and improved the quality of academic research and teaching. This led to the two-year MBA model in which students dedicate their first year to the core business and management discipline while choosing electives in more specific areas in their second year.

MBAs came to Europe in the late 1950s, when the first MBA was launched by INSEAD, followed a few years later by a number of other business schools. Some institutions in Europe (such as London Business School and Manchester Business School) adopted the American two-year MBA model. Others (for example INSEAD and IMD) opted for more intensive and shorter programmes.

In the 1990s, MBA programmes, especially in the US, again received fierce criticism, this time for being too theoretical, academic and research focused, and failing to address the practical needs of business. It was felt that managers needed not only analytical and numerical skills but also leadership attributes which MBAs were not delivering. Following this debate, leadership and soft skills modules were integrated into build in the MBA curriculum of both US and European schools.

The MBA formula has evolved through crises and changes to become a global phenomenon and the MBA is today the most familiar and popular business qualification worldwide. An MBA is considered a must to achieve general management positions in certain sectors.

The MBA curriculum and content

The MBA curriculum is comparatively consistent across different business schools: no matter which MBA you take, you can always expect to study strategy, corporate finance, accounting, marketing, leadership, etc.

The MBA curriculum has been designed with the aim of giving you a broad understanding of the fundamental and functional areas of management. As an MBA graduate you will not be a technical expert in any specific discipline (although you can specialise in particular areas by choosing specific electives or concentrations in the second year or second part of the programme), but you will be able to identify and analyse the links between issues affecting different functions of the business.

For EMBAs and PT MBAs the curriculum is more compact than in their counterpart full-time programmes. The basic idea permeating a business school's curriculum is giving course participants the fundamental insights that will enable them to make meaningful and efficient decisions in the short and long term alike.

Business schools review their MBA curriculum on average every five years to respond to new trends and issues in business. However, the key components of the MBA curriculum have been consistent throughout the various updates. Often what has changed is the teaching or delivery methods for those elements of the programme.

In addition, the core elements of the MBA curriculum in business schools tend to be the same because of the impact of the MBA accreditation systems that assess the academic curriculum against a set of established quality criteria (see p.78 for an overview of the main MBA accrediting bodies).

The key components of any MBA programme are the core courses, the electives and the skills portfolio. Also, depending on the type of MBA, the curriculum may include in-company projects, placements and international assignments. The MBA student experience can be enriched through international exchange programmes, which enable students to spend a term in a partner business school overseas. Especially for the FT MBA, business schools include foreign languages in the core or elective curriculum.

Core modules

Regardless of the programme type and format and the different names used by business schools, the key areas that should be included in any MBA curriculum are:

- accounting
- business ethics
- economics
- finance
- managerial statistics
- marketing
- operations management
- organisational behaviour
- strategy.

Business schools may cover the same disciplines from different angles or place stronger emphasis on particular aspects of the subject. This also depends on the specific strength of faculty in one or more subject areas. Most business schools have a core group of resident faculty along with a number of visiting faculty from other universities and business schools of global standing.

We recommend that you read the description of each course to gain a clear idea of the content that will be covered and the expected learning outcome on completion of the module. Sometimes this means that you will have to contact each school to obtain a more detailed syllabus: you will be surprised to discover that many descriptions published on websites can be unhelpful and leave you wondering what the course is about!

In a two-year FT MBA or EMBA, you will typically dedicate your first year to the core modules, while if the programme is shorter you will study the core modules in the first term or part of your MBA.

In some business schools, students who have postgraduate degrees or professional qualifications in accounting, economics, finance or marketing may obtain an exemption or waiver for the subject they have already studied. However, given that most schools' ethos is based on contribution and collaborative learning, the rules on exemptions are very tight: students are expected to share their knowledge and contribute to the learning of others who may be less strong or experienced in those areas.

Accounting

Accounting is the discipline that focuses on recording and reporting of the costs, transactions and financial information regarding a business. If you want to be an effective business leader, you need to be able to plan and manage costs and read and interpret corporate financial statements and information. Most MBA programmes split accounting into two core modules.

1. Management accounting, which focuses on reporting costs and financial information to people within the firm for decision making, planning and control purposes.
2. Financial accounting, which concentrates on the process of producing financial information – in particular the company's financial statements – for external purposes (shareholders, investors, auditors, government, etc.).

Business ethics (or corporate social responsibility)

Managerial decision making must take into account complex ethical and legal implications of business decisions. In general, schools aim to provide students with some analytical frameworks and practical tools to identify and deal with ethical issues in organisations. Often they investigate the link between personal values, business goals and ethics. Some ethics modules explore the role of government and regulation in promoting and implementing corporate responsibility.

Corporate social responsibility has become one of the core business school modules to be explored as part of the fundamentals in business.

Economics

Economic competence and awareness are essential qualities for any leader who needs to think strategically to achieve the business goals. MBA programmes adopt a focused and practical approach to economics, teaching what is relevant to the needs and goals of general managers. You will gain a good understanding of how markets function and an overview of the key drivers that influence economic growth at national and global level. These forces shape the environment in which companies operate. Some schools split economics in two modules.

1. Microeconomics: analyses concepts such as market supply and demand, pricing theory, cost. It enables you to understand the conditions under which markets work efficiently and how firms decide on the type and quantity of products or services they want to provide.
2. Macroeconomics or global macroeconomics: looks at the external economic environment and how it affects the business. It investigates factors such as unemployment rate, national income, price level, inflation and gross domestic product. It also gives an overview of the tools (for example, monetary policy and fiscal policy) used by governments and central banks to stimulate economic development.

Finance

Corporate or managerial finance enables you to develop quantitative and qualitative tools for the analysis of the financial operations and decisions of the business. On one side, corporate finance investigates the balance between assets, which are the resources owned by the company (including cash, building, equipment, land), and liabilities, which are debts or anything that the firm owes to other people. The assessment of the balance sheet information provides grounding to understand the principles of budgeting decisions. On another side, corporate finance regards all transactions in which capital is raised. As an MBA student you may learn how to analyse capital markets and risk; you may also develop the ability to organise data for capital investment decisions.

Managerial statistics (or management science or decision science)

These modules teach you how data analysis and quantitative models can be used to evaluate issues, assess risk and make decisions. They also help you understand how to critically use and interpret business statistics. Some of the basic business decision making tools explored are Game Theory and Monte Carlo simulation, which are two of the most versatile ways for understanding and analysing global, fast-moving environments of intense competition.

Marketing (or marketing strategy)

Aspiring business leaders require critical awareness of the role of marketing in creating value for the company and its customers, together with a good understanding of how this function fits and interacts with the other business operations. Usually a core marketing module within the MBA curriculum, it aims to provide you with analytical tools to identify and assess target markets, or customers within them and place the company's products or services effectively and profitably. It also teaches about the challenges of developing and executing marketing strategies in specific markets. You will become proficient in discussing the marketing jargon (marketing mix, pricing, market segmentation, branding, positioning, distribution channels, etc.) with several stakeholders.

The MBA Cambridge

UNIVERSITY OF CAMBRIDGE
Judge Business School

Ranked as the top 1-year programme in the UK by both the *Financial Times* and *BusinessWeek*, Cambridge is a unique place to study for your MBA.

The Cambridge MBA offers:

IMPACT: an international, general business qualification from the world renowned University of Cambridge will make an impact with global recruiters, and make a dramatic impact on your career trajectory.

TAILORING: through our "concentrations", and with more variety of courses and practical consulting projects than most other business schools, you can build your MBA experience to suit your own career goals.

PEOPLE: our MBA class is smaller than most, with around 150 students. This allows for close-up interaction with your highly talented and diverse classmates. Your new network, which will include top-class faculty and a wide range of external practitioners, will be your springboard to great things.

RETURN ON INVESTMENT: a 12-month programme, intensely practical and anchored in the real business world, our MBA delivers results for graduates, fast. With 88% of our graduates employed three months out with an average base salary of £62,000, you'll make a quick return on your investment.

Programme highlights:

- four practical projects (two of which are live consulting projects)
- eight concentrations (cultural, arts and media management, energy and about 45 elective courses to choose from, including environment, entrepreneurship, finance, health, international business, strategy and marketing)
- Summer activities phase: includes opportunity for internship, individual project, language courses, study abroad programmes, career development projects
- Cambridge Judge Business School is part of the University of Cambridge.

Overview figures for the class of 2011	
Size of class	149
Average GMAT score	684
Mid 80% GMAT score	630–740
Nationalities	40
Female	29%
Average age	29.6
Average work experience	6.5 years
Average number of languages spoken	3

Want to know more? Visit our website: www.theCambridgeMBA.com

Case study

Dima's story

From political analysis to business

I was born in the Ukraine and moved to Israel as a child. My interest in current affairs and politics led me to pursue a BA in Political Science and International Relations, and to start working as a political analyst for the Israeli defence ministry and government. As I progressed in my organisation, I discovered my interest in management and business. An MBA was then a natural decision for me.

Journey to the Cambridge MBA

I started my MBA research based on practical measures: ranking, size, location, curriculum, faculty, and career outcomes. The Cambridge MBA interested me because of its small size, its location at the heart of one of the world's oldest and greatest universities, and its location in the UK. However, it was only after visiting the programme that I experienced the genuine uniqueness of the programme – it simply felt like the perfect place for me and I immediately felt I belonged in the programme, the university and the city. This feeling, I discovered, was what the programme calls its collaborative nature.

Practical experience and personal growth

What I valued most about the programme were the student body, the faculty and the practical experiences. I can honestly say that the profound personal experience of the Cambridge MBA made me a better person and a more perceptive businessman. The faculty was highly professional, but also supportive and friendly. Also, the practical experiences were key in grounding academic content in reality and providing an invaluable business education.

Support for a new career in consulting

The Cambridge MBA team provided me with many opportunities to pursue my interest in consulting, especially by putting me in touch with alumni who enthusiastically and truthfully assisted me in my research.

Working with the Cambridge MBA careers team

Having made my decision I received wholehearted support from the careers team, who helped me make the right choice of company, translate my skills and experiences to the business world, and prepare for the interview process. Eventually I ended up with my dream job – associate at McKinsey's London office.

Dima Podpolny, McKinsey
Cambridge MBA alumnus

Visit our website to read more career pathways from our Cambridge MBA alumni students.
www.theCambridgeMBA.com

Operations management

Operations management is concerned with how the company produces its products and services and aims to increase the company's profitability and performance. Most operations management modules have a practical and applied nature and are designed to teach you analytical techniques and conceptual frameworks for evaluating the operational aspects of the business and the potential issues that might arise. In an operations management course you are likely to: study the process that the company follows to manufacture products or provide services (product or service development; process analysis and flow; quality management); discuss how the company may become more competitive by leveraging the flexibility of its supply chain (supply chain management) and by managing the supply chain; and evaluate how technology can assist the business in optimising its performance. Other topics within the operations management module may include inventory management, project management and management of services.

Organisational behaviour (or leadership and organisational behaviour)

Successful leaders need to be aware of what motivates different people to achieve excellence in their performance. Organisational behaviour focuses on the human dimension of business: it aims to understand and explain how individuals and groups behave in organisations. Besides teaching theoretical frameworks, this module normally includes the discussion of case studies and experiences on managing and developing people within organisations. Among the topics of an organisational behaviour module you may study how to manage and motivate individuals and teams and how to design and lead organisations through change. You may also discuss how the organisation culture and different management styles influence people's performance. Human resources themes are commonly explored within organisational behaviour modules; however, sometimes human resources management is a distinct subject in the curriculum.

Strategy (or strategic management)

Strategy is about identifying organisational objectives and planning the most efficient ways of pursuing and achieving them. The focus of this subject area is the long-term performance of the company against its competitors and the study of how the company maintains or improves its competitive position in the sector or sectors in which it operates. Strategic management refers to the direction of the company and the process through which the firm decides on its objectives and priorities.

Strategy modules normally aim to give you analytical tools and models to assess the company's internal resources and external environment to identify the key challenges that organisations face and the possible options to overcome them and ensure sustainable success. Business schools usually look not only at strategic decision making, but also at its implementation. The topics that you are likely to study in a strategy module include themes such as: strategic analysis of the company's internal resources and external environment; strategy formulation and execution plan; and anticipating and managing change.

Additional core modules

Other core modules may include entrepreneurial management. Often business schools which place a strong emphasis on entrepreneurship may decide to have a dedicated module in their core curriculum. Entrepreneurial management courses explore the issues in setting up and managing entrepreneurial ventures, providing you with the analytical tools to explore, evaluate and start up entrepreneurial opportunities and turn them into successful businesses. Students usually learn also how to carry out a feasibility study and develop a business plan.

Especially in FT MBA programmes, it is also common to find core modules that look at the current political, legal and economic environment in which companies operate and how political events or government regulation influence global markets, trade and impact on business profitability and performance. These types of module have significantly increased since the latest financial turmoil of 2008.

Elective modules

In the second year or second part of the programme, the MBA curriculum gives you the opportunity to specialise in one or more areas of interest, building and integrating the functional skills and knowledge developed in the core modules. FT MBA programmes usually allow greater choice and time than EMBAs for the elective curriculum. If you are looking at US MBA programmes, you are likely to find the expression "concentration" or "major", which refers to the subject area (accounting, finance, strategy, etc.) in which electives are grouped. By selecting electives you can tailor the programme to your learning needs and career objectives. Students who have clear career goals generally decide to focus on specific disciplines which will help them access those industries or become more effective in their future roles.

- If your ambition is to work in investment banking or other financial institutions, you may want to choose electives from the finance, accounting and strategy areas.
- If you are an engineer hoping to make a shift to commercial roles in your industry sector, marketing electives will give you the knowledge and tools to complement your technical knowledge.
- Students who aim to set up their own business will pick electives from the dedicated entrepreneurship curriculum, which is now being offered by most schools; or they may mix modules from different areas to prepare themselves for general management.

The electives portfolio is updated regularly to take into account new business trends, academic interests and student demand. Sometimes MBA students are allowed to take electives taught by faculty from non-business subject areas or from other partner institutions: for example, London Business School (LBS) FT MBA students can study some electives in technology and life science business at University College London (UCL). As elective modules may help build your knowledge for your next career move, you should check if the subjects of interest to you are part of the elective portfolio of the school and the chances of being able to pick those electives. Sometimes for courses in popular subjects (or taught by a popular faculty member) schools cannot guarantee a place to all interested students.

Other components of the MBA curriculum

Foreign languages

A competency in foreign languages is a key attribute for global leadership, therefore business schools have included language learning in the core or elective curriculum of the MBA. You are more likely to find foreign language modules if you study an FT MBA which is longer than one year, as this enables schools to build these modules in the portfolio; it also gives students more time to develop language skills. If you take your MBA in a non-English-speaking country, the business school will normally give you the opportunity to study and become competent in the native language. In addition, for these schools it is not uncommon to offer tuition in the national language before the programme commences. As the majority of MBA students are fluent in at least two languages, the foreign language offer is very diverse and in tune with global business developments: besides European languages such as Spanish, French and German, Asian languages (such as Mandarin, Japanese, Russian) and Middle Eastern languages (Arabic, Turkish) have become very popular.

Leadership skills

Leadership skills modules were introduced in the MBA curriculum in the 1990s in answer to the criticism regarding the excessive focus of business schools on functional knowledge ("hard" skills) and their inability to develop well-rounded leaders. Leadership or soft skills modules are designed to enhance those attributes or techniques which will make you more effective in liaising with internal and external stakeholders and achieving business objectives. Leadership skills modules can be attached to the core curriculum or offered as an elective within the organisational behaviour subject area. Occasionally, they are taught as a stand-alone element of the MBA curriculum. They are usually organised through thematic workshops (influencing, negotiating, presentation skills and public speaking, stress management and conflict management, etc.), which last one or more days and are taught by faculty, career services or external consultancies. You can choose effectively the themes which are more helpful for your leadership development by referring to formal and informal feedback from your managers, peers and faculty. Formal feedback includes performance reviews and psychometric tests, which sometimes are administered by current or prospective employers, or business schools within their organisational behaviour modules.

Internships

Internships are typically a feature of FT MBA programmes and may help you gain skills and experience in a sector and role you want to switch to in your post-MBA career: in fact, many internship are followed by job offers. In addition, internships may be a way to earn while studying, as in most schools you would be taking paid placements. Although not mandatory, internships are obviously popular. Similarly to in-company placements, students find internships through career services, faculty, alumni or personal contacts and initiative.

Intercultural experiences during your MBA: exchange programmes

Most MBA programmes, regardless of their full-time or part-time mode, offer exchange programmes which give students the opportunity to experience life in another country and to expand their network. You will spend an academic term at a partner business school abroad, taking a number of electives. Business schools have exchange partners in many regions around the world. Participating in an exchange programme in a specific geographical area can be helpful if you are planning to seek career opportunities in that region. Moreover, if you have been admitted to a mid-tier school with a strong network of exchange partners, you could still have exposure to a top business school through the exchange programme. However, given the high demand for exchanges, participation in these programmes may be allocated by schools according to competitive criteria based on academic merit.

> *"My exchange with Goizueta Business School in the US will allow me to broaden my network yet further and gain exposure from an American perspective alongside a new group of students."*
> Alamelu (Preethi) Narayanan, ESADE MBA class of 2012

Teaching and learning methods

As postgraduate management education aims to connect theory with practice, the teaching in any MBA programme is always directed to the implementation of the conceptual models and analytical tools of the various management disciplines. Faculty at business schools combine interest for academic research with corporate experience. Some members of faculty are often practitioners and act as advisers for boards of directors or governments, feeding the latest business thinking and insights into their teaching and research.

Business schools use a wide range of methods and technologies to teach the MBA curriculum and deliver a stimulating learning experience to their students. Teaching methods include case study discussions, role-plays, workshops, simulations, field visits, business leaders' talks and team projects, which complement faculty lectures. Business schools decide on the most suitable methods to teach each subject and most modules combine at least two teaching and learning approaches.

Case study method

If you are an international student and have studied outside the UK or US, you may not be familiar with the case study method, which was initiated by Harvard and is today used in most business schools in combination with other approaches. It consists of presenting students with a scenario or "case" based on a real company (whose name is often concealed) and business life. Case studies always involve problems that raise complex business questions without a straightforward answer. Students are, first, split into small teams to analyse the situation, identify the causes of the problem and come up with possible solutions. With the direction of faculty, they later share their views and findings with the class, comparing alternative options and recommending the best course of action for the company.

Case studies are typically used for modules such as operations management, organisational behaviour, marketing and strategy. Some business schools such as Harvard use case studies more heavily than others. This methodology has been subject to criticism from various sources (Geoff Gloeckler, "The case against case studies", *Bloomberg Businessweek*, January 2008) and has led schools to use a more diverse range of methods to teach the MBA modules.

One of the critiques which have been raised against the prolific use of case studies in the MBA class is that this does not leave time for the ground work and the conceptual frameworks that are necessary to assess business situations. Others have argued that case studies are narratives which give a general overview of business problems and therefore are not always effective in preparing students to tackle the real management experience. In addition, for a long time, case studies have had a strong emphasis on North America due to the main sources of case studies (for example, Harvard Business School and Stanford Graduate School of Business in the US and Richard Ivey School of Management at the University of Western Ontario, Canada are very active in writing case studies). This has changed more recently as European and Asian business schools have started developing their own case studies.

Group work

Group work and collaborative learning play a key role in business schools: no matter which type of MBA programme you choose, you will work in a team to analyse case studies, to prepare presentations and to deliver projects or essays. Where it is necessary to work remotely in virtual teams, schools provide platforms and technologies to facilitate communication. Programmes for more experienced professionals tend to place an even stronger emphasis on teaching methods and activities which enable students to share their knowledge in business practices and learn from each other.

Through group work, business schools aim to replicate the challenges of the workplace and give students the opportunity to practise skills such as negotiation, influencing, intercultural awareness and conflict management. Study groups are usually formed by programme managers or members of faculty by mixing together five or six students from diverse industry sectors, job functions, education and cultural backgrounds. In some schools you may work with the same study group for the entire core curriculum; in others, there is a rotation based on modules or academic terms. Regarding study groups for elective modules, you will normally work with a different study group for each of them. Sometimes study groups for elective modules are assigned by faculty; at other times students can choose whom they want to work with.

When you speak to people who have completed or who are studying an MBA, you will hear all kinds of stories regarding study groups that they have enjoyed or absolutely hated. It is very uncommon for business schools to accept a request to be reallocated to a different group; they expect that you learn to work with personality clashes, conflict or sluggish attitudes. However, even on the very rare occasion in which study group members end up never talking to each other after the end of the project, most MBA graduates would agree that this was one of the most helpful developmental experiences for their career.

In-company or management projects

In-company projects have become a common feature in MBA programmes as they facilitate the practical application of the conceptual frameworks and skills learnt through the modules. In-company projects can feature in different components of the curriculum and have various length and structure. In FT MBA programmes students undertake one or more consulting projects within an organisation as part of their electives. Consulting projects evaluate particular strategic and/or operational issues (for example, preparing the business case for a new product; conducting an audit of the supply chain) and aim to deliver a report and set of recommendations for the company's senior management and the school. They are usually supervised by faculty and contribute to your academic assessment.

Business schools often give the opportunity to decide whether you want to carry the consulting project on your own or as part of a small team. The business contacts are normally sourced by the school through faculty, career services or alumni network and include a wide range of organisations: global corporate, start-ups and charities. You can also contribute your contacts, or take personal initiative to identify and develop relationships with companies that operate in the areas of interest to you. It is not uncommon for regular corporate sponsors of a school to remunerate students for these projects and to use this as a recruitment tool: in fact, many projects lead to job offers for the majority of the students who have been involved.

PT MBA or EMBA students usually undertake in-company projects within their organisations in the second part of the programme, choosing, researching and assessing a business problem of particular relevance to senior management. If you are approaching your employer to obtain approval for your PT MBA or EMBA, the in-company project supervised by faculty can be presented as one of the key tangible benefits that they will obtain from your MBA (see p.95).

In some instances in-company projects are carried out within not-for-profit organisations or social enterprises as pro-bono work to give students an opportunity to contribute to commendable schemes and learn about the so-called "third sector", which some of them consider among their career options.

Typical contact and study hours

The number of contact and study hours required to complete an MBA vary depending on the school and the type of programme. However, anyone who has completed or is completing an MBA will tell you that it requires a lot of work and puts you under a lot of pressure. For an FT MBA programme you will normally take around five modules in each academic term and have 15 contact hours per week on average. In addition to classroom lectures, as an MBA student you will need to allocate time to team-based work and individual study or research, requiring at least between 15 and 20 hours per week. The time for these activities cannot be exactly quantified, as it also depends on your academic achievement objectives and team dynamics, if you have a group assignment. Most programmes are more intensive in their first year or first part.

For PT MBAs and EMBAs contact hours are less consistent as they depend on the structure and format of the programmes. Regarding number of study hours, most business schools say that 15 hours per week is a good indicative figure.

Assessment and grading systems

Each academic module is assessed using at least two different tools to evaluate your progress at distinct points of your learning progress. The assessment is designed to give constructive feedback which will help you address any weak areas and improve your academic performance. Unless you have intentionally planned to fail, it is highly unlikely that you are unable to graduate for poor performance: MBAs are academically demanding; however, faculty will give you support and every opportunity to fill gaps in your preparation.

Assessment methods include a mix of formal exams and individual or team-based projects (such as essays, presentations and reports) and are outlined in the module description that you will receive before you start the programme. In most business schools class participation contributes to the grades of some modules. Class participation refers not only to attendance, but also, more importantly, to the ability of the student to take an active part in class and group discussions. In team-based projects participants are assessed as a group and they receive the same mark.

MBA courses are usually graded using letter-numerical or letter systems. In letter systems grades are expressed with a letter from A to F, with A corresponding to the top 10%. Some schools have different grading systems: for example, at Harvard Business School, the grading system is based on four categories corresponding to different levels of academic performance, in which the lowest is a fail. At Yale School of Management, student performance is graded according to a four-point scale (distinction, proficient, pass and fail). Students must obtain a majority of "proficient" in their courses to complete the programme.

In terms of the final grades for an MBA degree, you will normally obtain either a distinction or a pass (some also grant merits). The distinction is awarded to a very small percentage of students and it is often only given in your degree certificate. In calculating your final MBA grade, some schools may use the Grade Point Average (GPA) system, in which your final score is calculated as the average of your grades weighted by the number of course credits. Others may use a curving system in which your academic performance is compared with the performance of the other students in the class and, after using appropriate statistical methods, the school assigns distinction to a specific top percentage.

Disclosing your marks?

At the end of the 1990s, among the top US business schools there was a debate on the disclosure of grades to employers and its impact on collaborative spirit. Some schools (Harvard Business School, Yale School of Management) thought that this had led to a competitive environment which was detrimental to the team learning which they were trying to foster; they decided to adopt "grade non-disclosure" policies, which prohibit the discussion of grades during the recruitment process and prevent prospective employers requesting academic transcripts from students. The only exception was made for students who achieved a distinction. Other US schools such as Wharton gave students the freedom to disclose any information regarding their academic performance to prospective employers or other interested parties. European schools were also influenced by the dilemma regarding the effect of grades on collaborative spirit. However, today in Europe the majority of business schools grade their MBA students.

Other key features of the MBA experience

Careers services

Careers services departments have a crucial role in driving the post-MBA success of their graduates. Careers services provision in top schools is generally of a good standard, as they tend to invest heavily in ensuring that their MBA students obtain well-paid jobs and contribute to keep up rankings. In mid-tier schools the scenario can be mixed; some schools are much better than others in fostering relationships with prospective employers and developing useful careers resources for their students. Information on placement statistics and post-MBA salaries is easily accessible through programme brochures and school websites. The rankings also measure and publish this type of data. Researching prospective employers' websites, speaking to MBA recruiters and to MBA alumni will also give you a sense of the effectiveness of particular schools in opening up opportunities in certain sectors.

Workshops on writing CVs, cover letters, interviewing skill training, career counselling, seminars on specific careers (finance, consulting, etc.), alumni mentorship programmes, mock interviews and job portals are some examples of careers service provision. The careers services teams also organise campus recruitment fairs and visits, or milk rounds as they are more popularly known, for companies that are interested in recruiting MBA students.

Given the level of positions available through these recruitment channels, these types of event are usually less suited to experienced professionals taking PT MBA or EMBA programmes. However, if you can take time off from work (most of these events are still during office hours), on-campus presentations and recruitment fairs may still be a good way to learn more about specific companies you are targeting. It is likely though you will obtain more helpful insights from alumni who are working for those companies: it should be easy to have access to the alumni network through the school's intranet. You can also enquire with your career adviser, programme or admissions manager, who can usually recommend some names.

Often experienced executives can benefit from dedicated career management resources such as one-to-one career coaching and workshops on career strategy.

Outside the classroom

An MBA is not just about academic work. Business schools offer a lively social life and are usually within easy reach from the artistic and cultural scene of vibrant cities. They have a programme of internal and external social activities for the academic year and encourage participation in student associations and clubs, which are an important and integral part of the education experience. Clubs are not only about sports and cultural interests: some focus on specific sectors such as finance, consulting, energy, media, private equity. Others gather students and alumni who want to promote networking and business opportunities in specific regions. Most schools also have a "partners club", which generally aims to engage in the school community spouses and partners who sometimes may have relocated to another country. Another typical club is the "women in business", which addresses the need to promote women's participation in leadership positions.

Typically clubs apply for funding from the business school to carry out their activities, which include inviting business speakers, organising conferences, fact-finding visits to companies or fundraising events for charities as well as wine tasting, barbeques or belly dancing classes.

A word of advice: social activities are a powerful networking tool but can be expensive. When you budget for your MBA, take this into account too.

What a good MBA needs to include

There are several variations in the way MBA programmes are structured and delivered; however, the right MBA for you should at least include the following elements:

- core modules in accounting, business ethics, economics, finance, managerial statistics or management science, marketing, operations management, organisational behaviour and strategy
- a choice of electives in the areas which are relevant to your career objectives, or alternatively viable alternatives which will enable you to build the knowledge that you need
- a good soft skill portfolio
- group projects and assignments to challenge your ability to work in teams
- one management or consulting project in which you will apply the learnt conceptual and analytical tools
- exchange programme opportunities with a range of schools that could add value to your MBA student experience
- a solid careers service provision which will help you connect with employers in sectors of your interest
- an active student community with a track record in creating a rich social life and networking opportunities for its members.

The Open University Business School

Institution: The Open University
Faculty: The Open University Business School
Duration: 3–7 years
Entry requirements: Bachelor's degree awarded with honours from a recognised UK university or the equivalent PLUS a minimum of three years' experience in a managerial, professional or technical role. Please visit our website to see open entry options.
Course fees: £14,000–£16,000
Start months: May, November
Course type: MBA

The Open University Business School is among the top 1% business schools in the world and the only non-campus-based business school to achieve triple accredited status from AMBA (UK), EQUIS (Europe) and AACSB (US). You can be confident your MBA will be recognised wherever you go in the world, and we have produced 22,000 of the world's finest MBA graduates.

Our MBA students get an experience like no other – we are one of the top three UK universities for overall student satisfaction (National Student Survey 2010/11). Wherever you are, we are close by with our support network of 13 national/regional offices and many study centres near you. If you are in Scotland, Wales or Northern Ireland, you can visit your National Open University Campus.

Top tier quality and reputation

- Rated 4th in the UK and 9th in the world by *The Economist* (2010).
- It takes your career to a new level – the average salary increase post-OU MBA is by 40%.
- 75% of FTSE 100 companies have sponsored students on OU programmes which shows the practical focus and effectiveness of our MBA.

Flexibility and affordability

Our MBA has been designed flexibly to integrate with the demands of your day job and lifestyle, backed up with our cutting-edge online teaching technology, to study where ever you are.

Practical and applied

Our unique learning method of "work-based action learning" brings your MBA into life at your workplace. What you learn today, you can apply tomorrow.

To find out more, visit www.open.ac.uk/business-school; Email oubs@open.ac.uk; Call us on 0845 366 6035; Post-Student Registration & Enquiry Service, The Open University Business School, PO Box 197, Milton Keynes, MK7 6BJ

Case study

Roberta Thomson, OU MBA student of the year

Roberta Thomson completed her Open University MBA in 2010 and upon completion she won the highly acclaimed MBA Student of the Year award from The Open University.

Her motivations for doing the MBA were initially focused on career development; however, as she got into her studies this was replaced with something deeper. She explains: "I think my main reason initially was that I wanted to use the MBA to help me progress in my career, but that quickly developed into something a little bit more meaningful. I really wanted to study the MBA in order to give me the practical knowledge, experience and skills to equip me to do a more senior management role effectively."

When Roberta considered where to study her MBA, the key benefits that set The Open University apart from other academic institutions was the flexibility of the study and the quality of support that it offers students who are often trying to juggle work, study and family life.

The innovative content of The Open University MBA really impressed her. "I wanted something that combined classical management theory; coverage of those very, traditional themes with content that focused on what it means to be an effective organisation in the modern world. Plus I wanted to look at more forward looking, future-thinking areas of study as well. I felt that The Open University offered a combination of the traditional, the good, solid grounding but also that, very dynamic forward looking way of thinking."

Her conclusion is that the MBA is serving her very well in her working life and in her own words, "I think overwhelmingly it has been an incredibly rewarding, positive experience. I've applied a range of different aspects from the course in many, many different ways," and she further concludes: "Like using some of the theories and strategies in the workshops that we're holding within my organisation and applying some of the techniques around creativity and innovation in my day-to-day thinking."

Would you like to know more? Contact us on 0845 366 6035 or go online www.openuniversity.co.uk/mbas.

2

What can an MBA do for you?

An MBA is a massive undertaking, requiring immense self-discipline. In addition, the extensive monetary and time commitment is considerable. But, with this in mind, there are numerous very good reasons why doing an MBA – putting in the time, effort, and money – is worth it. In this chapter we will take a closer look at the different reasons for wanting to undertake an MBA, and what the qualification can bring to your career. Some may be relevant to your motivations; others may not. The key thing is to think critically about your career plan – where you want to be in the future, and whether an MBA can get you there.

Introspection – checking if an MBA is right for you

Before embarking on an MBA you need to be clear about the benefits to you personally and professionally and you need to ensure that undertaking an MBA is the right choice for you. You may be looking to get an overview of general management or you may want to enhance your knowledge of particular areas of business; however, before you make a final decision it is imperative that you look at the alternative options.

For example, if you are looking to become a finance specialist, a one- or two-year Master of Science (MSc) in Finance may be a better option than an MBA. There are different types of MSc in Finance and many of them are taught by leading business schools. If your focus is to develop knowledge in one specific area only (such as accounting, marketing, operations or organisational behaviour) there may be professional or short courses that will give you an overview in a shorter time period and at a much lower cost.

This book is designed to give you a real insight into the MBA qualification, and equip you with the information you need to make this decision for yourself.

MBAs are not a "one degree fits all"; however, there is an element of flexibility which gives you the possibility to either learn the fundamentals of general management or allows you to specialise in a particular area, for example marketing or finance through the elective choices.

Not only do MBAs provide an insight into general management but an MBA from a top-tier business school will enhance your marketability in an increasingly competitive market. It will provide you with a broad range of skills, access to a wide alumni network and a strong brand for your CV, opportunities that you may not otherwise have.

An MBA will not necessarily benefit all, but for those wanting a traditional career in a particular industry such as investment banking, strategic management consulting or finance it is a pre-requisite. People from non-traditional industries are also opting to take an MBA to broaden their skills set.

Let's look a little more closely at some of the benefits of undertaking an MBA, and things to consider to ensure it is right for you. We'll also touch on how to make sure that doing an MBA will bring you the career you want.

The reasons listed below are not given in any particular order of importance. These are dependent on you as an individual, the stage you are at in your career and your own personal objectives and motivations for wanting to do an MBA.

Career shift to different function or industry

The desire to change your career path is seen as one of the most important reasons for wanting to undertake an MBA. The MBA will certainly assist you to facilitate a career change either from one industry to another or from one function to another.

However, as an aspiring career-switcher, it is strongly advisable to first of all discuss your plans with someone already doing the job you aspire to and ask them their advice. Key questions you should be asking are:

- are there others who have already made a similar shift?
- what where their experiences?
- was it a particularly difficult or challenging move?

Be armed with the right questions and research thoroughly. Before embarking on an MBA for this particular reason you need to be assured that the transition you wish to make is a viable option.

A business developer or a technology manager who wishes to move to management consulting will certainly find an MBA a useful tool to accomplish his/her goals within relevant areas of professional services. If you are an information technology (IT) manager and you wish to become an investment banker, you need to be aware that in most cases this transition will be unrealistic or extremely difficult.

Making a transition from one industry to another, keeping the same role, or switching from one job function to another within the same industry sector is certainly more viable than trying to shift both industry sector and job function at the same time. A similar principle applies if you are trying to change both industry sector and country at the same time: double transitions are always more complex and tricky to achieve at once in the same role.

Contact the admissions team of the business school you are interested in and ask to be put in touch with alumni who have made a similar transition to ensure that the switch you want to make is still feasible and discuss how you should go about it. Their advice and guidance will

Alumni case study

Gaurav Sharma, London Business School, MBA 2009
Pre-MBA: Consultant at Microsoft, London, UK
Post-MBA: Management Consultant at Boston Consulting Group, Canberra, Australia

After graduating from university, I really didn't know what I wanted. Armed with a software engineering degree, I didn't subscribe to working for large corporate behemoths. I was more intrigued by start-ups, where I could invest my energy in creating something tangible. As it turned out, graduating in 2001 wasn't a great time for start-ups globally and I was forced to park my start-up aspirations to follow the rest of the sheep in joining a large consulting firm where I was just another cog in the machine. Surprisingly, it turned out to be quite a good stint. I worked with many different clients in various geographies and really fine tuned my core analytic skills. After six years of consulting, what worried me most was that my career path was mapped out ahead of me. There was no uncertainty. There was no sense of adventure. With this realisation, I talked to senior people from various disciplines to see how they had sculpted their careers. A recurring theme that unfolded was how a good-quality MBA can open doors and really lets you do whatever you aspire to. With some introspection and much research, I chose an MBA programme that would not only plug my skill gaps, but also surround me with high-calibre individuals that would challenge my thinking and give me a truly global perspective.

The LBS MBA programme delivered on all these counts and more. It's given me the confidence and self belief that the world really is my oyster and anything is achievable. I have a global network of friends, contacts and resources that I can leverage. But perhaps most importantly, post-business school, I can finally understand the *Financial Times*. I hoped to work in a start-up but as luck would have it, 2009 was amidst the global financial crisis (*déjà vu* I know) where access to start-up funding was scarce to say the least. As an interim measure, I joined a prestigious management consulting firm where I worked with business leaders across Fortune 100 companies to define blue sky strategic vision, target operating models, market entry strategies and the works. It's given me invaluable insights on the challenges corporate CEOs face when running their company and equipped me with the tools and analytical frameworks to address these challenges. Ten years since graduating from university, I'm finally pursuing my dream of working in a start-up, the only difference being, this time it's my own.

stand you in good stead. Sometimes it is even a good idea to use a career coach to obtain some guidance regarding the shift you would like to make with an MBA.

Once you are on the programme, you will need to use all the resources available to you. Speak with the careers advisers; they are the experts and will give you realistic advice. Factors to take into consideration when thinking about making a transition include economic climate and industry changes. It may be the case that you need to readjust your plans slightly – be prepared for this eventuality. An important way of making the transition successful is using the summer internship. This is a safe and fantastic opportunity to try out a new industry or job function.

In order to facilitate a switch you need to look closely at the skills you do not have and take elective courses to fill in those gaps. Look at the elective offerings that are most likely to broaden your knowledge in the chosen area.

Finally, connect with people in the desired line of work. There will be plenty of opportunities to do this on campus. For example, the school will hold networking and organised speaker events. This is a great chance for you to talk with those who have exposure in the area you wish to move to. There are a plethora of clubs for you to participate in; you just need to find the one most suited for your industry or functional interest. This will keep you abreast of developments and help you to make new contacts.

Career enhancement

An MBA can fast-track your career and give you promotional prospects which could be difficult to achieve otherwise. An EMBA or PT MBA in particular will enhance your skills and knowledge in your own industry or function so that you can gain additional managerial responsibility and seniority while providing you with job security.

Alternatively you may have hit the glass ceiling or feel like you need to expand your knowledge and skills set. Whatever the reason may be, you may be finding it difficult to progress. An MBA will help to give your career a push in the right direction, for example, making the path easier to move from middle to upper management.

By studying part time and working full time, you will have the opportunity to immediately put into practice your learning from the MBA. Your company will be able see for itself your operational effectiveness and the impact it has on the business. Furthermore, it is not uncommon for PT MBA or EMBA students to change jobs and move up the career ladder while still on the programme.

As part of the core curriculum, some schools will ask you to carry out a company project. You can use this opportunity to investigate a current issue or problem within your organisation, applying your learning from the MBA. You will have access to research facilities and faculty who will provide support and guidance to help evaluate the issues and find solutions.

Alumni case study

Jannine Griffiths, Cranfield School of Management, EMBA part-time 2009
Pre-EMBA: Chartered Accountant, BOC Gases Ireland
Post-EMBA: Finance Director, BOC Gases Ireland

Having worked as a chartered accountant in industrial gases with BOC for a number of years, I felt I needed a better understanding of the wider business world for my personal development to increase my opportunities as a senior manager.

I chose Cranfield because of the practical teaching methods and the focus on personal development and they certainly didn't disappoint. I learnt a lot about myself and how to deal with others through working with excellent academic staff and fellow students. This has greatly improved my confidence and influencing skills. Working in small learning teams allowed me to operate in a safe environment and form strong bonds with people who have become lifelong friends.

Cranfield not only provided me with the toolkit to use in almost every business situation, but a strong network of people with different backgrounds and experiences that has helped make me a more informed manager. The lively debates made learning new subjects interesting, often carrying on outside the classroom. The enthusiasm and willingness to learn from the cohort was refreshing.

Although managing a full-time job and the MBA was challenging, I benefited from the part-time EMBA format by going to Cranfield every other weekend. This kept my focus on studying and allowed the learning teams to work and socialise together.

During the final year of my MBA, I was promoted to finance director, and I have been able to call on many of the skills learnt at Cranfield to add value and become a valued business partner.

Obtaining functional knowledge in the core areas of business

Whether you want to progress along the same career path or shift to a different industry sector or job function, you will always need to gain functional knowledge of the core areas of business. An MBA is designed to give you a broad understanding of the different functions of general management: corporate finance, accounting, marketing, operations, etc. You will be able to critically analyse, evaluate and discuss business trends and issues and make informed decisions.

Ashridge Business School

Ashridge Business School is an independent, not-for-profit organisation just outside of London in the UK. Its activities include open and tailored executive education programmes, MBA, MSc and Diploma qualifications, organisation consulting, applied research and online learning.

Business leaders from all over the world come to Ashridge to renew and refresh their thinking. Its atmosphere is one where tradition meets innovation – in one of the most beautiful locations in England.

Ashridge faculty comprises both business professionals and consultants, who bring academic rigour, in-depth industry experience and the latest management practices to the design and teaching of executive education.

Programmes offered

Ashridge offers a one-year full-time MBA and a two-year EMBA, both starting in September and an additional intake in March (EMBA only). Both take an integrated view of business, rather than teaching functional subjects in isolation, and provide thorough grounding in all the disciplines required to lead a business.

Key features

Great connections with organisations – Ashridge is one of the best business schools worldwide for its corporate links and students learn through live case studies, project work and direct corporate involvement.

Dual location provides the ultimate study experience – Students benefit from the wide opportunities provided by a London location through developing business contacts, implementing study knowledge and through company interaction, attending additional events and the cultural experience. They will also benefit from the reflective study environment at Ashridge with access to personal development tools and information.

Flexible start points – Three programme starts per year allow flexibility to suit finances, job and personal circumstances.

International diversity – Accelerated and executive students share modules to enable them to benefit from many different backgrounds and nationalities, gaining a rich cultural understanding of the global business environment.

Academic rigour with practical focus – Real insight offered by the experienced Ashridge faculty through live case studies, projects and group work to enhance employability and commercial awareness.

Quality and credibility – Ashridge is one of only 1% of business schools worldwide to be approved by US, European and UK MBA accrediting bodies providing increased global recognition.

Contact details: Ashridge Business School, Berkhamsted, Hertfordshire HP4 1NS, UK
Tel: +44 (0) 1442 841061; Email: mba@ashridge.org.uk; www.ashridge.org.uk/mba

Case study

Grace Yang is now Vice President (Investment Banking Audit) at JP Morgan

Why an MBA?

Having worked for a number of multinational companies in China, I was keen to find a new role overseas. My ticket to achieving this was further education and in particular an MBA.

I chose Ashridge for a number of reasons, including its consistently high ranking with *The Economist* and the *Financial Times* educational league tables. Smaller classes with more experienced participants and being taught by faculty members who have many years working in industry made an MBA at Ashridge very appealing.

What did you learn?

It was an intense experience – well structured, with an emphasis on leadership, strategy and CSR. I learnt how to solve conflicts and find solutions within tight time constraints which was very challenging but invaluable as it is a true reflection of business life, particularly in an international environment.

Before doing the MBA, people found me quite shy. Having to constantly present to the group was very good for me and I've gained a huge amount of confidence in my ability to present and interact with others.

What were the highlights?

Supported by my Ashridge tutor, I carried out strategic research for a top insurance broker. I was working directly with the Deputy Chairman, reviewing their international strategy and identifying opportunities concerning Chinese energy companies. They implemented many of my recommendations.

My knowledge of China combined with the MBA gave me the skills and language advantage to deliver. It felt good to add value to an organisation.

How has your career changed post MBA?

Ashridge has an excellent track record of promoting its MBA alumni and as a result I walked straight into a well-paid risk management job with Standard Chartered in Hong Kong. I don't have a finance background but the Ashridge MBA gave me the confidence and skills set to change sector.

A couple of years later I moved to the UK after being hired by JP Morgan. Again, I changed function from risk in front office to an audit role specialising in credit risk. It's a dream role for me as it involves leading a team on a variety of projects, interacting with senior people across Europe, Africa, the Middle East and Asia, and it is very well paid.

Without the MBA I would never have such a high-level job. It was an excellent investment and an unforgettable experience.

Increase in salary

Numerous surveys have been carried out which indicate that if you undertake an MBA, your salary will increase exponentially. Although this is a key motivation, it should not be the most important reason for applying – or if this is your key motivation to pursue an MBA you should avoid being very candid about it when you speak to the school representatives. Hopefully, by the end of your MBA, you will have discovered that there are so many other gains and benefits from this experience than just the salary increase.

While the argument for the financial return on investment is strong, there are other factors that you need to take into consideration. For example, the industry you decide to enter post-programme, your level of experience, your geographical location and the prestige of the school you attend will all play an important part in the position you take and the remuneration package offered to you. It is more likely that you will see the largest growth in your salary two to three years after graduation. Make sure you factor this into your plan.

Access to a powerful network

Networking or access to a powerful network is another reason why people decide to do an MBA. The relationships that you make, the exposure to industry contacts and, more importantly for some, the friendships that remain long after the programme has ended are all powerful reasons for undertaking an MBA.

One of the key selling points of any business school is the alumni network. The alumni network is a powerful tool for students and alumni alike. The alumni play a pivotal role in building the school brand, attracting the right calibre of candidates and marketing the school.

Of course you may already have access to a large network through friends or your work; however, the influence of a school network can span far and wide around the globe. Typically the top-tier business schools have alumni in over 50+ countries, allowing you to be a part of a global community. All schools have a directory, typically accessed online, which lets you search and contact alumni.

The University of Pennsylvania Wharton School, for example, says "Our alumni empower you at every stage in your career" – a powerful statement. There is a long-term value of having these contacts, you can draw on it at any stage, especially if you are thinking of changing jobs, industry or sector or to expand your business in a new country.

The MBA will give you access to a network; however, be mindful – it does not guarantee you a job. What it will give you is advice and guidance, the opportunity to get a foot in the door, maybe a conversation with the right person or even a recommendation, but what it does not do is guarantee a job. The rest is up to you.

Educational experience

If you are intellectually curious, an MBA can help to satisfy your need to stretch your mind. Your thinking will be challenged, especially if you come from a non-business background. An MBA provides you with an overview of the various functions of management and gives you the understanding and confidence to speak convincingly about these functions. Through the interactive classroom environment, you are given the opportunity to absorb new ideas put forward by faculty and your culturally diverse peer group. You can challenge existing perspectives and experience new opportunities.

For EMBA students who may have been away from academia for over five years, the MBA can prove to be an intellectually stimulating experience. Some MBA programmes also have a research element where you are required to complete a project or dissertation as part of the core curriculum.

Alumni case study

Alessio Ghignone, ESCP Europe, EMBA 2010
Pre-EMBA: Director, International Project Management Team, TI Sparkle
Post-EMBA: Sales Director, TI Sparkle

After more than 11 years of senior management and coaching experience, I decided in 2009 that it was time to take my career to the next level. An MBA seemed like the qualification I needed to fulfil my expectations of professional progress, and I eventually decided to pursue ESCP Europe's EMBA.

ESCP Europe's programme stood out from all the others because of the range of modules and the individual subjects therein. I also liked the prospect of the international seminar, something I hoped would allow me direct contact with high-profile speakers from around the world, and the participation of the school's alumni association.

After spending 18 months on the EMBA, I can vouch for the quality of the teaching and the value of the opportunities to work alongside fellow participants; the programme has an authentic international culture, something definitely enhanced by the opportunity to travel while studying. I was able to meet high-profile people from a variety of countries, all with vast professional and life experience.

The methodology taught on the ESCP Europe EMBA is something I am now using with my current team. And the success of the programme is more than evident in my career progression: before the EMBA I was the director of the international project management team at TI Sparkle; since graduating from ESCP Europe I have been promoted to the position of sales director.

Enhancing your personal brand

Having an MBA from one of the top business schools will give you additional credibility when you liaise with prospective employers or business stakeholders. In fact, your credibility will not only be enhanced with MBA recruiters and head-hunters, but clients and business partners are also aware that MBAs at top business schools are competitive and intensive programmes. A strong brand on your CV will show that you have the intellectual power and the ability to draw resources from a strong network. If you are competing with other candidates for a senior position or to win some business, an MBA from a top school will be noticed and considered with your track record of achievements in your area.

If you are someone who lacks a strong educational background, you may have found that this hinders your ability to secure senior roles against other candidates with good academic and career record. A good MBA could persuade employers that they have what it takes to succeed.

Relocation

The world has become a much smaller place and the pursuit of a global career is becoming a more common objective. By undertaking an MBA you will certainly have more options open to you. If you are lacking international experience, then try to get as much exposure as possible while on the MBA. If relocating to another country is your main objective, there are a number of things you can do to help facilitate a move.

- **Take an MBA with a global focus.** There are MBAs designed specifically to give students a more global perspective. For example, the TRIUM is a global EMBA offered by three schools, New York University Stern School of Business (NYU Stern), London School of Economics and Political Science (LSE) and HEC School of Management, Paris (HEC Paris). The INSEAD Global executive programme is taught in France, Singapore and Abu Dhabi. At Duke, The Fuqua School of Business students have the choice of two global programmes: the Cross Continent programme, a full-time programme, and The Duke MBA–Global Executive programme, which is aimed at executive students. On both programmes, students are taught in China, UK, United Arab Emirates, India and Russia. While providing you with the broad overview of management, the format of these programmes requires you to study in different locations. This will give you exposure to the region, which you may not otherwise have had, an opportunity to study with a more diverse student base, and, in some cases, a degree qualification and the alumni networks of more than one school.
- **International assignments or field trips.** An excellent opportunity to gain exposure to a different region. You can therefore make your selection decisions based on where you would like to relocate. These types of assignments broaden your global perspective. You could be working in teams as consultants on a particular project and presenting your findings to real organisations. Furthermore, you will build your network by attending guest speaker events and meetings with senior industry heads.
- **International exchange programmes.** MBA programmes usually have an international exchange programme where you spend around one semester taking elective modules at another business school.

An opportunity to relocate to another country or region is an option if you have an MBA. However, this is only ever realistic if you have had prior international experience. Language barriers or cultural differences can make it more difficult to make the shift, but the main reason is that companies are unlikely to recruit an MBA who has no experience of working in an international context. Take into consideration the economy of the country you wish to relocate too; if it is going through a bad phase, competition will be fierce with many local candidates competing with you for the same role.

Filling gaps in your skills set

An MBA is not just about teaching you the hard skills such as strategy or financial analysis. In the past having a complementary skills set would have been seen as a useful addition to a candidate. However, given the current economic climate, companies are now looking for MBA graduates who are well-rounded individuals and have the ability to work in challenging environments. A good MBA will help you develop several interpersonal or soft skills.

- **Strategic thinking and decision making.** It is important for organisations to stay one step ahead of their competitors. If you want to have a competitive advantage over others then the ability to think strategically is essential. How you understand a situation, and anticipate and act upon it, can have a long-lasting effect on a project or organisation. An MBA will teach you how to think strategically and plan ahead for different eventualities. You will become more adaptable to changes and look at the bigger picture from different perspectives.
- **Communication and confidence.** In any given situation you will need to communicate your ideas in a persuasive and authoritative way. The MBA will help you develop these skills through specific classes and coaching sessions and give you the confidence to communicate effectively with senior management.
- **Group work.** You may have spent your entire life developing relationships; however, the MBA will help you to identify the best ways to interact with others and develop relationships in a variety of situations. As part of the MBA, you will be placed in a study group of four to six people from culturally diverse backgrounds where you will work on assignments together. Learning to respect your fellow group members' opinions even if you disagree is crucial to working successfully in a collaborative environment.
- **Leadership.** One of the most, if not the most important, skills you will learn on the MBA is how to become a good leader. As mentioned above, you will be working in a study group. All group members will have the opportunity to lead the team at some stage. This will give you the real-life experience of leading culturally diverse teams, meetings and projects and help you develop your leadership style. During the programme you will explore the skills and attributes needed to become an effective global leader, such as listening, delegating and motivating others. You will also learn how to become more self-aware and act on the feedback given to you. Advice from experts such as executive leadership coaches and faculty on how to improve your leadership

style will equip you with the knowledge and tools that are crucial to manage employees effectively and, most importantly, run a company in a global business environment. With these skills you will be well positioned for future leadership roles.

- **Creative problem solving.** The MBA promotes creative problem-solving skills. You will face many challenges and problems throughout the programme and in your career. This could be in a team situation or as a leader. The MBA will help you to improve your critical analysis and problem-solving skills. Discussing problems with classmates from different industries and backgrounds will help you think outside the box. On an EMBA or PT MBA this will be more evident as you can come up with a range of solutions that you can implement straightaway. You will quickly realise that some solutions work better than others, and you will have the ability to bring this learning back into the classroom and discuss it further.

Having a combination of hard and soft skills is important to recruiters. By demonstrating that you have both core knowledge and strong interpersonal skills you are showing them you are a strong candidate for them to consider.

"My MBA is an experience of a lifetime. This one year has changed the way I look at the world around me. It has helped me learn in a highly intellectual environment and enhanced my skills, through interaction with my fellow classmates from various backgrounds and some of the top business leaders. Attending classes, submitting the assignments on time, preparing for examinations, brain-storming for club activities, participating in Global Case Challenge and 'Masteriadi', searching for internships and enjoying the enriching social gatherings and 'aperitivos' make it an experience which I will treasure. This course provides a great launch pad for a life with limitless possibilities."

Partha P. Ganguly, SDA Bocconi School of Management MBA, Class of 2011

Entrepreneurial opportunities

Many MBA candidates pursue an MBA to accomplish their dream of becoming a successful entrepreneur. The economic climate of the past few years has stimulated more and more MBA graduates to pursue their entrepreneurial ideas rather than joining the corporate world.

There is a school of thought that believes entrepreneurship is inherent. Although some business schools state it is something that can be taught and developed. Becoming an entrepreneur is what many people want to do at a certain point in their life and certainly some of them are incredibly successful without an MBA.

If you have an entrepreneurial spirit, going to business school can help shape and test your ideas, providing you with knowledge, skills and contacts that you will not have access to otherwise. At the same time, you will receive a lot of feedback on the pitfalls of your venture or your business plan, and this will give you the opportunity to assess the risks and address issues before implementation. If you have an entrepreneurial idea in mind, an MBA can help nurture your skills, such as creativity and innovation, to help develop your business plan or to think entrepreneurially in your current organisation. It can also enhance your ability to identify opportunities that you may not have considered previously.

At business school you will have access to events and clubs specifically aimed at starting your own business. By taking specific electives in entrepreneurship you will have the opportunity to look at real-life business ideas through the study of business cases. For example, at Harvard Business School, you can choose from over 30 electives on entrepreneurship. You will attend lectures with likeminded individuals who also share your passion and are looking to develop an idea. At London Business School, you have the opportunity to attend an entrepreneurial summer school. You are given the chance to test the feasibility of your idea in a safe environment, assigned a mentor and offered guidance and support to help you develop your concept. You are able to discuss your ideas with faculty who have already had exposure to start-ups or input from angel investors (individuals who provide capital for a start-up in exchange for ownership equity) to try to secure buy-in for your idea. The MBA will allow you the time and space to articulate your vision. You will be the person driving the vision forward; you will be at the helm of the ship – and others will look up to you. An MBA will help you develop a leadership mindset and get people behind you.

However, having a business plan is not enough. Most importantly, an MBA will develop your skills in functional areas such as marketing, finance, operations, which are vital to get your idea off the ground.

In this chapter we looked at the various benefits that an MBA can deliver and also discussed the various reasons for wanting to do an MBA: you may have felt that one or more of the above motivations apply to you. When applying to business school you need to be clear about the specific aims you are hoping to fulfil and why an MBA at a particular school is the best tool to achieve your goals. Most schools will expect that you have also explored other viable options before concluding that the MBA is definitely what you want to do. Once your objectives and motivations are clear to you, the research and decision-making process will become more straightforward. Look carefully at what each school has to offer you to help you achieve your objectives. In Chapter 4 we will look more closely at how to choose the right business school for you.

Kingston Business School

Gain your MBA at Kingston Business School

Why an MBA?

The past 20 years have seen rapid and dramatic changes in the conditions within which business operates – globalisation has been the dominant force. Today's MBA students need both a strong theoretical and practical basis for understanding what changes are occurring in the contemporary global political economy, and why and how these might affect their strategic business policy formulation.

The subject matter of the MBA, while providing the basics for senior management, will need to adjust accordingly to include not only issues of developing new markets, products and competitiveness, but also responsibilities and relationships between business, both public and private, on the one hand, and society, technology, culture, ecology and equality internationally on the other.

Why a Kingston MBA?

The Kingston MBA offers an intensive, stimulating and challenging learning experience that will provide you with a broad foundation of knowledge in the main management disciplines. In addition, the Kingston MBA will allow you to reflect on your professional practice and personal development, and lay the foundations for assuming a senior strategic role in your organisation.

Organisations will benefit from the constructive and creative input that successful Kingston MBA graduates can contribute in terms of their ability to implement company-wide decision making through their improved understanding of business strategies.

The Kingston MBA is one of the few UK and international MBAs accredited by the Association of MBAs. Successful completion also confers eligibility for membership of the Chartered Management Institute.

Successfully complete the programme and you will be able to:

- critically appraise a range of business management theory and knowledge and apply it to the solution of business problems
- be proficient in the analysis and interpretation of business data
- synthesise cross-disciplinary knowledge and apply it to the analysis of complex business issues in a rapidly changing international business environment
- demonstrate the key personal and interpersonal skills required for effective leadership and implementation of solutions at all levels inside and outside your organisation
- show a critical appreciation of the significance of recent advances and theoretical developments in business, and their strategic implications.

Case study

One of the key attributes of the Kingston MBA is the diversity of its student community. Students come from a variety of business and non-business backgrounds, bringing a range of skills and knowledge to enhance the learning experience on the MBA.

Our students and graduates attest to the significant boost the course has given them, both in their professional lives and in their personal development and level of confidence.

"In my pre-MBA days I remember hoping for promotions at work, a company car and the benefits that promotion would bring, but no matter how much I tried my employers always recruited for the top jobs from the outside. Often feeling rejected and having to accept that my bosses' way was right, I thought up excuses that made me feel better about the way things were at work. Eventually I decided that this was wrong – I had to stop blaming myself and others and start doing something positive with my career. I decided to take charge.

"I graduated with my MBA from Kingston and my life has changed. I run my own company, I do business around the world, I drive nice cars. I've moved on. Ultimately it's all down to my Kingston MBA, which gave me confidence and proved that I could do more and could look after myself. I feel like I wasted a lot of time waiting for things to come my way, but I don't have to make up excuses anymore. Now I'm in charge of what happens to me."

Martin Brighty
Kingston MBA Graduate
Managing Director, Hunters Partnership Ltd, UK

Hunters Partnership Ltd sells luxury, handmade silk ties from its Harley Street headquarters in Central London to businesses and individual clients around the world.

3

The different types of MBA programme: choosing the format that is right for you

Once you have decided that you want to do an MBA, the next challenge you will face is deciding on the type of MBA you wish to apply for.

Nowadays, the types of MBA degree have increased together with the number of schools offering them. You can find MBAs that match all needs and preferences in terms of content, length, delivery and learning methods. However, greater choice also means greater confusion: PT MBA, global MBA, accelerated MBA, EMBA, or global executive MBA, online or distance-learning MBA (DL MBA), dual MBA and a lot of other names may appear in the business school literature.

To choose the right programme for you it is important first of all, that you understand what all these names and acronyms indicate. This chapter is designed as a guide to help you cut through all the jargon. A word of warning: business schools are quite creative and have introduced various types of programmes to satisfy the demand from specific groups. Occasionally in the MBA world, there are some courses which do not exactly fit with definitions, or perhaps are creative hybrids.

Full-time MBA (FT MBA)

Who it is for?

FT MBAs are normally aimed at professionals who want to accelerate or change their career, or aspire to become entrepreneurs. Most business schools require at least three years of postgraduate work experience as an entry criterion. Typically the average work experience in an FT MBA class is between five and six years. Normally, class profiles of FT MBA tend to be younger than their part-time or executive counterparts. However, a few business schools target more experienced candidates by increasing the required work experience or establishing that management experience is mandatory for entry into their MBA (for example, Henley Business School recruits students with at least five years of postgraduate work experience). As part of the curriculum, FT MBA will include internships or in-company projects that are designed to enable the students to apply the frameworks and tools which they have learnt, and prepare them for the next career move (see p.14).

The full-time study mode will enable you to benefit from total immersion in the student learning experience. While undertaking an FT MBA, you will have the opportunity to live and enjoy student life to the fullest, taking advantage of all the social and networking activities that business schools offer. Students taking part-time or executive programmes and juggling study with their career and private life may not have the time to dedicate to clubs and other business school initiatives. Most FT MBA programmes are nowadays scheduled to fit with MBA recruitment cycles of prospective employers and you will always be in a position to make the most out of all the on-campus recruitment events.

Format and length

The length of an FT MBA can vary from one to two years. FT MBA programmes in the US are typically two-year programmes (or just under two years). They are structured into academic periods of different length: North American schools usually have semesters (two in each academic year, for a total of four) and sometimes shorter periods (trimesters or quarters). In Europe, FT MBAs tend to be more "compact" or "accelerated" and usually last around 12–16 months, apart from a few notable exceptions which seem to be either more aligned with the US model or oriented to find a middle ground between the accelerated and the two-year programmes. Core modules are taught in the first year or first part of the programme, while electives take up the second part of the curriculum. One-year programmes are intensive and usually offer a more limited number and selection of elective modules compared to their two-year counterparts. In schools following the two-year model the summer between the two academic years is dedicated to internships. Students taking a one-year FT MBA take the internship at the end of the programme.

> *"The FT MBA at ESADE has an innovative format: our participants enjoy great flexibility in defining their MBA experience by customising the length of study in 12, 15 or 18 months."*
>
> *Olaya García Lancha, Director, Full-time MBA, ESADE Business School*

Part-time MBA (PT MBA)

Who it is for?

PT MBAs normally satisfy the needs of professionals who want to progress their career without leaving their jobs. Career changers can also succeed in their aim through a PT MBA; but as most part-time courses do not provide internship periods, career transitions may require more time and become more of a challenge to achieve. In addition, if you are working full time and taking an intensive academic programme at the same time, you may not have much time to invest in attending career fairs and networking events. On the other hand, you will study with like-minded professionals who are also juggling work with studies; you may have the opportunity to meet people already working in the area or company you are interested in and who have fresh contacts and insider knowledge they can share.

In many cases for people who cannot afford giving up work to complete an FT MBA, taking a part-time programme is a good way to obtain the degree without impacting on personal or family finances. In the past, most PT MBA students were sponsored by their employers; however, this trend has been on the decline in recent years and nowadays the majority of PT MBA students are self-funding.

In terms of required work experience, most business schools have similar criteria for both FT and PT MBA. However, as business schools have become more experimental and innovative with part-time programmes, the only thing you can be sure about when you hear or see this expression is that they are not full time! Regarding format, delivery, length and entry requirements, you will need to check that the programme fits with your level of experience and your preferences in terms of time commitment. In fact there are PT MBAs designed for professionals who have a similar profile to that of an FT MBA (three years of experience and above); while some others target or prefer more experienced candidates with managerial responsibilities.

Format and length

Some part-time programmes are taught weekly in the evenings or during the weekend (Kellogg PT MBA and Chicago Booth evening and weekend MBA in the US; Vlerick Leuven Gent PT MBA in Belgium); some others are delivered in block modules once a month or less (HEC Paris PT MBA and St Gallen PT MBA in Switzerland). Regardless of their modular or weekday format, all PT MBA programmes will have some residential weeks on campus, typically at the beginning and the end of the course.

Occasionally, PT MBA have an element of online or distance learning. In most cases you can complete the degree in two to three years minimum and you will have a lot of flexibility in the upper limit by which you can complete the degree. Of course, bear in mind that you may be charged tuition fees for each year in which you are enrolled, so make sure that you check the fee details before you apply. The other aspect that you may want to consider is the impact of the MBA (and the time it takes you to complete it) on your future career. Although most business schools award the same degree to both full-time and part-time students, if you want to make the most out of it, you will need to complete it within a reasonable time to impress prospective employers.

Alumni case study

John Gordon, Australian National University PT MBA 2010
Pre-MBA: Team Leader
Post-MBA: Senior Engineer

As an engineering graduate I joined an early stage start-up company and developed my career in the navigation/telecommunications field. My experience growing into more senior positions within the small company both necessitated and inspired me to focus on broadening my skills and growing outside of the technical areas I was comfortable in. In a company with limited time and resources there were limited opportunities for formal development and mentoring internally and so I decided to pursue these goals by enrolling in an MBA at the Australian National University. The ANU was an attractive choice, as (while not well known for MBAs) it is a highly prestigious university and offered a well-structured degree with some major project work and a range of elective options. Another important consideration for me was that choosing a local university would allow me to attend lectures, facilitating the networking and shared learning that would help me get the most out of the experience.

Like much postgraduate study I believe that what you get out of an MBA programme depends on what you put into it. I didn't have any strong expectations going into the MBA but formed these as I progressed, shaping the experience as I worked in new areas and explored the subject matter. Two key benefits of my experience were the broadening of my knowledge and skills, and also the gaining in confidence through working with a mix of people in a range of disciplines. I found the opportunity to apply myself and use my skills in new areas empowering and helped drive a sense of achievement and increased confidence tackling the unknown. I took the opportunity to involve myself in the programme where ever possible which provided further growth such as international travel as part of a team representing Australia in the Global Management Challenge corporate strategy competition.

Having completed my MBA I considered moving into management consulting and interviewed with large firms. I came to realise that I wasn't passionate about the change (and what it would mean for my young family) and decided to engage with technical work again in another promising small start-up company. As time has passed I'm confident that I made the right decision and that my decision was partly that I'd rather develop entrepreneurship skills from the trenches in a small firm than as part of a team of hired help in the big end of town. Though I've returned to much the same field as before my MBA, I know that I now have the confidence, knowledge and drive to pursue opportunities that I'm passionate about going forward.

Newcastle University Business School

A new perspective: An MBA for complex times

The MBA programmes at Newcastle University Business School have been designed to bridge the gap between academic theory and professional experience, and to meet the increasing demands placed on managers to adapt in the ever-changing global business environment.

We live in an age of unparalleled uncertainty with global shifts in economic and political power, immense environmental challenges, and natural and human-created disasters.

Our MBA is designed to boost your performance in today's fast-moving world by enhancing your success in a management or leadership position. At Newcastle University Business School our MBA programmes offer our future leaders an education that equips them to apply their learning in practice with the highest level of competencies and capabilities necessary for professional practice.

Our programme is supported by some of the world's leading academics, underpinned by real-life cases and innovative teaching methods. This programme is complemented by international experience programmes, an exemplary professional and personal development programme, and a mentoring programme.

Students benefit from a dedicated MBA club lounge and state of the art facilities, all within a brand new building in the UK's best university city (MSN Travel, 2011).

The MBA at Newcastle University Business School not only offers a new innovative perspective on education, it offers a new perspective on managing in a global context.

Case study

Mark McKenzie MEng, GUITARGUITAR, Head of eBusiness, MBA class: 2010–12

Benefits of undertaking an MBA

The "actual" academically rooted, practically applicable, managerial education – you won't find that on your typical five-day management course.

It is a source of competitive advantage for an organisation that provides students with personal business connections and endless networking opportunities.

Myths busted as a result of studying an MBA

20+ years of business experience is not required! The MBA is suitable for someone operating in a small business as well as large organisations.

Key benefits of the MBA programme

Everyone takes something different from each session (from both the lecturers and the cohort). This has been key in enabling me to round out my business experience with exposure to other industries that I don't see on a daily basis. This course has been a key enabler in my ability to help significantly grow and develop our business to its full potential online

How has the MBA programme aided your career progression?

Sometimes I think individuals get too caught up in career progression as the primary focus of an MBA; you see people split between two camps, the "personal progressors", and the "business progressors". I fall into the latter. So has the MBA helped progress our business? **100% yes.**

How has the MBA aided your personal progression?

Very quickly you start to think about things differently and gain a wider appreciation for real business opportunities. I don't look at the world the same anymore. Something as simple as a bar of soap is no longer an item you use daily, your brain, *by default*, starts to analyse the product, the company, the industry and the opportunities ... you get the idea.

Main reason for studying an MBA

In the cut-throat world of business, we don't always take the time-out to review our educational needs or even like to admit the requirement for it; however, as we all face new challenges, a little help is not such a bad thing! This realisation led me to seek further education, initially looking at areas such as business strategy and operation optimisation; however, as I dug deeper, and looked at how I wanted to develop as a person, I realised that an MBA was the best fit for me.

Anything else you would like to promote about the MBA programme

If you're reading this far ... your next step should be applying!

Executive MBA (EMBA)

EMBAs are often confused with PT MBAs. The confusion in prospective students' minds is absolutely understandable and it is due to the multiplication of both PT and EMBA programmes which have been designed and launched by business schools to appeal to different needs and segments of the MBA market. In terms of level of work experience, the overall profile of a typical EMBA class tends to be more senior than a FT or PT MBA class, with exceptions due to the PT MBAs becoming more sophisticated and varied.

Who it is for?

EMBA programmes are aimed at middle and senior managers who want to earn an MBA qualification without leaving their positions. Entry requirements for the EMBA programme include management experience and responsibilities over an extended period of time. Most schools target candidates with around seven or eight years of postgraduate work experience; however, some programmes are directed at managers with at least 10 years of professional experience (for example, IESE Business School Global EMBA; IE Business School, Georgetown-ESADE EMBA).

Mid-career and senior managers and executives are normally eligible for both PT and EMBA types of programmes. If you have a wealth of experience and achievements and you are looking to gain an MBA degree while working, you will probably prefer to study with classmates who have a similar level of responsibilities and leadership. Therefore EMBA programmes will be more aligned with your objectives.

One of the key features business schools emphasise for this type of programme is the ability for the EMBA students to immediately transfer business and management knowledge and frameworks gained in the classroom to their jobs. In addition, given their level of seniority, EMBA participants have the opportunity to learn from their peers as well as from faculty. During case study and classroom discussions faculty act as facilitators to enable EMBA students to share and contribute their experiences. The exchange of views and experiences also takes place in a PT or FT MBA class, but if you are an experienced manager you will benefit and learn more from the interaction with professionals who are decision makers in their roles.

Like the PT MBA, EMBA programmes are particularly suited to mature or fast-track professionals who have already achieved a good level of managerial experience and responsibilities and aim to advance their career without having to leave their positions and losing their income. Career changers can also benefit from EMBA programmes, but if you are planning to make a specific transition it is useful to have a reality check with a career coach or MBA alumni in your network before applying. Most schools will also give you the opportunity to discuss the programme with an alumnus. You will also be able to meet members of the alumni community at the schools' information sessions, which provide an ideal context to informally discuss your career objectives and motivation for doing the EMBA.

Another aspect that may be less favourable to career changers is the intensive work and study schedule, which does not leave EMBA students a lot of time to dedicate to job hunting. Entrepreneurs or aspiring entrepreneurs also find the EMBA a very good formula to obtain their business degree and make good contacts to launch or grow their venture.

Business schools place a lot of emphasis on the team-based learning, which takes place in the EMBA class, and aim to create groups with diverse background and experience. As EMBA students are at a more advanced stage in their career than FT MBA students, they do not compete in milk rounds (university recruiting events attended by recruiters from large companies) and are more collaborative: their career strategies rely heavily on exchange of contacts, information and networking with fellow classmates and alumni.

From an academic point of view, EMBA programmes have the same rigour and standing as the full-time degrees, but their modules as well as coursework are more compact. An EMBA requires a strong focus, commitment and discipline, as participants need to find at least 15–16 hours a week study time besides attending lectures.

In the past, most EMBA participants were company sponsored; the trend has considerably decreased in recent years and more EMBA students are self-funding. If you are unable to obtain your employer's sponsorship, you should aim to obtain at least paid time off for training (or time support as most business schools would say) while you are doing your EMBA. Business schools do not recommend using your annual leave to attend classes or to take exams.

Format and length

When comparing the format, the main distinction is between weekend EMBAs and those in which the programme modules are taught in week blocks (the majority). Weekend EMBA classes tend to start on Fridays or Saturdays and last for two full days (some schools have longer weekends from Friday into Monday). The length and frequency of weekend and block week formats vary a lot from school to school: some programmes require monthly attendance while others schedule contact hours at every other month. The number of months required to complete this type of degree varies between different institutions but is typically less than two years. Calculating the exact amount of time out of the office is crucial to fit your professional and personal commitments with the EMBA schedule.

Global EMBAs: multi-campus and multi-school approach

Who it is for?

Global EMBA programmes are a spin-off from the standard EMBA. They have been designed to respond to the career needs of executives working in a global business environment. There are two main models of the global EMBA programme: some schools have opened their own campuses in different geographical locations to deliver global EMBA programmes (INSEAD, Chicago Booth and Duke are a few well-known names); some others have forged institutional partnerships to offer a multi-school approach (Kellogg/Hong Kong University of Science and Technology – HKUST; Columbia/London Business School – LBS; Trium EMBA; Kellogg/WHU EMBA): participants are taught by faculty from all partner schools and travel to different campuses for the lectures. Some global EMBAs award a dual MBA degree where participants receive an MBA qualification from each of the partner schools: for example, Columbia/LBS EMBA Global. The entry requirements in terms of professional experience and the learning dynamics in the class are very similar to that of a standard EMBA. However, schools usually seek candidates with a very clear international outlook for their global programmes.

Global EMBAs require a heavier financial commitment than the regular EMBAs, both for the tuition fees and the cost of international flights and accommodation. You will normally arrange and cover the cost of international flights to attend classes. Regarding accommodation, sometimes it is covered by the tuition fees for the programmes and arranged by the business schools; in other cases the school facilitates the search of suitable accommodation but you will need to pay an additional cost. It is always worth checking and making sure that your budget is accurate.

Format and length

Global EMBAs are modular and taught in block weeks over a period of time varying between 13 and 24 months. Like the EMBA, the length of global EMBA programmes is not consistent but it is always less than two years.

Alumni case study

Natacha Dagneaud, Kellogg-WHU EMBA 2009
Founder and Managing Director, Séissmo

The EMBA provided me with a framework that deepened my understanding and interpretation of daily professional activities as an entrepreneur. Personal growth and leading skills development were an integral part of the programme as I learned to cope with and thrive under the challenge of professional and cultural diversity in study groups. Through the personal development component of the curriculum, I became aware of my own management patterns and discovered how to use this blueprint to manage and motivate teams and individuals. Thanks to the extremely high quality of this programme, I gained knowledge and experiences for every aspect of life.

Distance-learning MBAs

The popularity of distance-learning courses has grown substantially in recent years, and while in the past there was a certain scepticism towards DL MBA compared to the traditional FT MBA, more recently the attitude towards this type of programme and the general perception has changed. Similarly to what has already happened for EMBAs, recruiters have started noticing the self-motivation, discipline, focus and ability to juggle different tasks required to complete an academic programme on top of a full-time job, family and personal life. More and more reputable business schools have started adding DL MBAs to their course provision.

Several different titles are given to DL MBAs: "online MBA", "e-learning MBA", "blended learning MBA". Given the absence of clear consistency between different programmes using similar terminology, it is impossible to provide hard and fast definitions here. In general, however, you need to be aware that courses which are completely "online" and do not involve any attendance are very rare. Most DL MBAs require students to be on campus for the residential parts of the course, which could be a couple of weekends or weeks throughout the academic year. When you look at the various distance-learning options it is important to check that you are able to commit to the face-to-face lectures, seminars and tutorials required to complete the programme.

Pros and cons of DL MBAs

The key reason why people choose DL MBAs is flexibility. This format allows working professionals to take the programme from different locations and to study in their own time at their own pace, taking out a minimum amount of days from their work schedule. In addition, DL MBAs usually have more intakes and starting dates throughout the academic year. Another advantage is the reduced financial impact as distance-learning students not only keep their jobs and income, but usually pay lower tuition fees for their degree than standard FT MBAs or EMBAs.

The other side of the coin is the minimum face-to-face interaction with other students, you need to work harder to get to know the school community and benefit from the networking opportunities it offers. Most MBA alumni state that one of the most valuable pieces of learning was the class experience and interaction. Working at your own time and pace also means that you need to have strong determination and willpower to prioritise and regularly complete the coursework. If you are interacting with your globally dispersed classmates in a virtual place, you will need to make sure that you are active in the online chats and forums.

DL MBAs have not yet been ranked by the *Financial Times* or *BusinessWeek*. Choosing an accredited course (see p.78 for more information regarding MBA accreditation) offered by a well-recognised business school with experience of delivering the standard MBA will ensure that you are taking a programme whose curriculum has been carefully designed and assessed. A good DL MBA will have the same academic rigour of an FT MBA or EMBA and require a similar level of commitment and workload. Opting for programmes that look very easy will not give any added value to your background or experience: recruiters will not pay any attention to an MBA qualification that people can simply buy from money-making schemes.

Specialist MBAs

In recent years the already complex landscape of MBA programmes has been populated by various specialised or specialist MBAs designed by business schools who want to combine the general management frameworks and theories with the comprehensive knowledge and practical understanding of a specific industry (Francesca Levy, "The spread of specialized MBA programs", *Bloomberg BusinessWeek*, July 2008). Today, you can find MBAs focusing on many different industry sectors including aerospace and aviation, healthcare, hospitality and tourism, luxury brand management, real estate and sports management. In some cases the specialisation is part of the degree and students receive an award with a clear reference to the specialist area, for example, MBA in Healthcare Management. In others, students receive a second certificate or award in the specialist subject together with the degree, or business schools offer dual degree programmes that require a longer study period.

Debate on specialist MBAs

There has been a long debate in the business school community between supporters of the generalist MBA and the enthusiasts for the specialised models. Those who champion the standard generalist MBA tend to consider the specialist one as an unnecessary dilution of the content that a general management programme should have. They also argue that students who want to specialise in a particular area can do so by choosing relevant electives, in-company projects or internship in that subject. In addition, it is often highlighted that the MBA is a life-changing and eye-opening experience, which often makes students discover new interests or re-think their career objectives. The risk of a specialist MBA is to limit the available post-MBA choices.

Supporters of the specialised MBA emphasise that, like the standard MBA, these programmes cover all the core business and management functions and at the same time enable students to specialise in a particular area. Some of these degrees also require a longer period of study to complete. They refer to the need for companies to hire managers with knowledge and expertise in their sector as they already know the key issues facing them and are able to grasp the job quicker.

Originally, a specialist MBA seemed to be the prerogative of second-tier schools which were seen as trying to appeal to specific segments of the MBA market. However, over time, a number of specialist MBA programmes have also been introduced by business schools in the top tier, or very close to the top tier. Among the best known, Haas School of Business at the University of California Berkeley gives students the opportunity to specialise in real estate and to obtain an additional certificate in this area. Through the Lauder Program, Wharton awards a joint degree integrating its MBA with an MA in International Studies. MIT offers a Global Operations MBA, which is a dual degree combining the MBA with a master's from the School of Engineering; and the Biomedical Enterprise Programme, a dual degree in partnership with Harvard Business School and which is currently under reassessment.

Top-tier European schools do not seem to follow the trend of specialised MBAs; although a number of reputable institutions have recently launched specialist MBAs: for example, the Healthcare MBA at Imperial College in London and the MBAs in Luxury Brand Management and Hospitality Management at ESSEC Business School in France.

Specialised MBAs may be an option if you have a strong and clear focus on a certain industry, career and geographical location. When you consider this type of format it is important that you make sure that the school has well-established ties with your target sector and the main recruiter in that area. The better of these programmes have been designed to respond to real needs of employers in specific areas and may offer opportunities equivalent to those from an MBA from top-tier schools.

"At SDA Bocconi MBA students have the opportunity to focus their path on subjects related to general management in luxury business. We approach these businesses from 360°, from strategy to finance, from operations to legal issues. This track has been introduced to respond to the needs expressed by our international students who wanted to specialise in an area most global Italian brands are best known for. Bulgari provides us the

perfect partnership to ensure a unique interaction between theory and practice. The Track in Luxury Business Management is an opportunity to apply the frameworks learnt on the MBA programme to a specific theme and industry: our students still need to take all the core modules of their MBA."
Proffessor Luana Carcano, SDA Bocconi School of Management, MBA Track in Luxury Business Management

Dual MBAs

As already mentioned, some business schools offer specialised MBAs which are awarded as a dual degree combining the MBA with a different subject. In these cases, to complete the curriculum students spend a longer period of time than in a standard MBA and receive the double award. Occasionally, dual degrees are granted by the same university; in other cases they are based on a partnership between two different schools.

Dual degrees can be a good option if you have clear career objectives that can be satisfied by these degrees. You need to take into account that this type of degree requires a bigger financial commitment and time investment. The time you spend in education and out of work is considerably longer.

A slightly different option is the dual MBA degree awarded by business schools that have created partnerships to deliver MBA programmes. Students taking these programmes earn two MBA degrees, one from each participating school: for example, the dual MBA offered by the Chinese University of Hong Kong with HEC or RSM; the EMBA-Global programmes offered by Columbia-LBS and Columbia –University of California Berkeley, which demonstrates that sometimes there are overlaps in the terminology as an EMBA can also be a dual degree if two qualifications are awarded.

All these definitions and classifications demonstrate that the MBA landscape is very crowded: when you check the website of any particular business school, sometimes you may find at least four or five different MBA programmes. On a positive note, this also means that you have greater opportunity to choose an MBA that fits with your needs and goals. There are a number of aspects to consider when you are deciding on an MBA and the next chapter will provide you with a framework to evaluate schools and programmes.

Summary: how to choose which format is right for you

Consider your level of experience

- If you are in your early career, most likely an FT MBA is the right fit for you. A limited number of PT MBAs may also be accessible to you but you will need to demonstrate that you are a high flyer who has moved very quickly up the career ladder.

- If you are a middle manager or an experienced executive or entrepreneur, you will probably benefit more from sharing your business knowledge with other senior professionals. An EMBA or PT MBA may offer you the ideal learning environment. However, there are also a number of FT MBA programmes that are geared towards more experienced students.

Consider your objectives

- If you are planning to make a feasible career transition, an FT MBA is usually more suitable as you will have the opportunity to do an internship, take more electives or carry out a number of projects which you can use to gain relevant knowledge and exposure. In addition, an FT MBA will give you time to attend all on-campus recruitment events.
- If you enjoy your area of work and want to accelerate progression without interrupting you career momentum, a PT MBA, EMBA or DL MBA may be more suitable.
- Aspiring entrepreneurs can explore FT and PT MBA or EMBA depending on a series of other circumstances including their level of experience, the type of networking they want to gain exposure to and the entrepreneurship tools that specific programmes offer.

Consider your learning style and preferences

- If you want to enjoy student life to the fullest and take advantage of all the social and networking opportunities that business school offers, an FT MBA is the right choice for you. PT MBA and EMBA students need to juggle their studies with their jobs and private life, which does not leave them much time to dedicate to on-campus recruitment events and other business school initiatives.
- If you are a pragmatic person and enjoy using and experimenting immediately what you have learnt in the classroom, a PT MBA or EMBA may be better suited to your learning style.
- If you are looking for maximum flexibility, a DL MBA will usually allow you to study at your own time and pace, taking out a minimum amount of days from your work schedule. However, if you need face-to-face interaction to keep engaged and motivated in your learning, this is not the right format for you: you need to have strong determination and willpower to prioritise and regularly complete the coursework when you are working at your own pace.

Consider your budget and funding options

- The choice of one format or the other may also depend on your budget: if you have limited funding options and a tight budget, you may find that the PT MBA, EMBA or DL MBA are the most affordable options as they enable you to keep earning while studying.

Ultimately, make your final decision on which format is the most appropriate for you after balancing all the pros and cons of each programme.

The Edinburgh MBA at University of Edinburgh Business School

UNIVERSITY OF EDINBURGH
Business School

The Business School

The University of Edinburgh Business School enjoys a long tradition of teaching and research. The School offers undergraduate, postgraduate and executive education programmes in business and management and provides a platform for research, discussion and debate on a wide range of business issues. The School has a world class faculty of over 70 members. The 2011/12 student population is close to 1,400 (with 499 students pursuing postgraduate studies). Part of the University of Edinburgh, one of the world's top 20 universities with a rich heritage of delivering education for over 400 years, the Business School has an international student body typically representing more than 88 countries.

The Edinburgh MBA has been taught for more than 25 years and stresses teamwork in a collaborative learning environment. The programme is reviewed and refreshed on a regular basis. Recently the team introduced a unique week-long leadership module situated in the Scottish Highlands. Also new is a specialisation route for students looking for more focused pathways through the programme.

Ranking and accreditation

The School is accredited by EQUIS and AMBA and consistently ranked in the *Financial Times* and *The Economist MBA* Rankings – reflecting not just a long history of business teaching but also the substantial experience of a faculty that comprises more than 70 teaching staff.

A new home for business

Recently, the School relocated to a new building in Buccleuch Place, located at the heart of the University campus. This state-of-the-art space features eight lecture theatres, multiple syndicate rooms, an executive education suite, a student study centre and online resource, a cafe and significant flexible space for staff and students. The building has been designed to meet the current and anticipated future needs of the School's portfolio of activities and represents an investment of £17 million by the University.

Why Edinburgh?

As one of Europe's leading financial centres, Edinburgh uniquely combines a dynamic business community with its status as a World Heritage Site. Located in the heart of Edinburgh, the Business School is perfectly placed to engage with the local, national and international business community. As a city of culture and a city for business, Edinburgh has a real sense of dynamism. Several major global financial institutions have their headquarters in Edinburgh. A compelling blend of history and cutting edge modernity, it is the second largest financial centre in the UK with a thriving, diverse economy and a highly educated and motivated workforce.

Case study

The University of Edinburgh Business School enjoys a long tradition of teaching and research. The school offers undergraduate, postgraduate and executive education programmes in business and management, and provides a platform for research, discussion and debate on a wide range of business issues.

Part of the University of Edinburgh, one of the world's top 40 universities, with a rich heritage of delivering education for more than 400 years, the Business School has an international student body typically representing more than 25 countries.

One of these international students was Yoni Titi, the Co-Founder of Coyne Titi Business Evolution and an MBA graduate in International Business. Reflecting on her experiences with the University of Edinburgh Business School, Titi said:

> "Edinburgh is a truly amazing city with such incredible beauty that it was a joy to study there. I learned much about other cultures with 30 different nationalities in the class. I made many new friends from every continent and these friendships are still important to me and have proved highly beneficial, even a year after completing the MBA. Following two semesters in Edinburgh, I had the opportunity to undertake an exchange programme to Schulich School of Business at York University in Toronto. Being such a diverse city, this gave me a further opportunity to learn about other cultures and to learn from the best. I was then accepted onto the United Nations' New York internship programme. Here again I experienced so much that was new and inspiring.
>
> "I returned to South Africa after the MBA and have embarked on a business venture of my own which is proving to be rewarding as it seeks to make a significant contribution to skills development and the upliftment of many South Africans – a cause close to my heart."

The School's teaching and research covers six main subject areas – accounting and finance, entrepreneurship and innovation, management science and business economics, marketing, organisational studies and strategy and international business. An emerging area of expertise for the Business School is carbon management, through an innovative partnership with the School of GeoSciences.

Many members of faculty at the Business School are active in research and consultancy. Core to the School's philosophy is a close interaction with the corporate world through industry-based research and consultancy.

Please visit our website for more information: www.business-school.ed.ac.uk.

4

Choosing the right school and programme for you

With a wide range of MBA programmes available, you may find it hard to decide which one is right for you. The search for the right MBA can often be a time-consuming task. Most prospective students will start their research by looking at rankings as their only criteria to select schools. Rankings are certainly one of the indicators to consider when you are choosing your MBA; however, they should not be the only pointer in your decision making. If you are applying to top-tier schools, you need to be realistic and consider that the competition for places is very high and inevitably you may be disappointed if you are not accepted into the top schools on your shortlist. A thoughtful candidate will usually think about different options to cover situations; if your plan A does not materialise, you should have a plan B at hand. It is not uncommon for FT MBA candidates to apply to at least five or six different schools. Although there is no limit to the number of schools you can apply to, we would advise against applying to more than five schools. While undertaking your research, you should make a shortlist of schools that you are seriously considering. As a PT MBA or EMBA candidate your choice will depend on the logistics of attending the MBA while in employment. PT MBA and EMBA candidates normally apply to two or three schools.

Where should you start?

When you are choosing an MBA the best way to start is by clarifying your objectives and needs, then look for schools and programmes that are best placed to match them. In addition, it may be helpful to benchmark your profile to compare and contrast against the entry requirements and class profiles of your target schools to see where you stand in terms of your professional experience. This analysis will also help you market yourself to the schools (see p.111). Admissions committees will evaluate your candidacy on the basis of your professional experience, academic abilities and soft skills. They will also assess you against the applicant pool and the previous class profiles; their objective is always to recruit the most competitive candidates. The schools' website and programme literature will contain information on the entry criteria and key class statistics regarding work experience, Graduate Management Admissions Test (GMAT®), etc., and usually admissions teams are happy to clarify the key elements that are assessed through the application and interview process.

Checklist of your needs and objectives

Short-term goals	To enhance your knowledge of a particular function or gain an understanding of general management.
Medium-term goals	First job after graduation. Career acceleration, career transition (industry sector, geographical area, job function), entrepreneurial, sectors in which you want to work
Long-term goals	What is your ambition – what do you want to achieve within the next 10 years? Run your own business, etc.
Funding	Availability of loans and scholarships
Time you want to invest	One or two years if FT MBA; evening, weekend or block week format if PT MBA or EMBA
Main areas of interest	Finance, strategy, marketing, operations, entrepreneurship, etc.
Study experience preferences	Large or medium city; availability of exchange programmes and overseas trips, etc.
Learning style	Full immersion in the student experience; learn and apply immediately
Class size	Small or large class

With a clearer picture of your own needs and objectives, it will be easier for you to read and critically evaluate the programme information provided by the schools.

Based on our experience in advising prospective MBA candidates, we recommend that you consider 10 key areas when you are deciding between different programmes and/or schools. These areas are not listed in any particular order and the weight of each factor will depend on your individual preferences.

- Faculty
- School culture
- Student/alumni profiles and alumni community

- Rankings
- Accreditations
- Career services track record
- Programme type and format
- School facilities
- Location
- Tuition fees

Type and format of programme

In Chapter 3 we discussed the broader elements of the different types of MBA. When making a shortlist of schools it is important to look at your motivations, learning style and your lifestyle. The type of programme that you choose will depend largely on your experience and how much time you wish to commit to a programme – either one or two years or whether you wish to study full time, part time, distance or online.

Consider your experience

If you have 10+ years of experience in management, an EMBA may be more suitable, since it is aimed at senior executives. Similarly, if you are at the start of your career and want to get exposure to general management then a two-year MBA may be more suited. Alternatively, you may want a programme that will give you specific industry knowledge or gives you the opportunity to choose a specialist area such as marketing, economics, finance entrepreneurship or technology. Another factor for you might be selecting a programme that requires an internship or offers an international exchange.

Duration of the course

Most European MBA programmes such as IMD, SDA Bocconi, INSEAD and SAID Business School often take one year to complete, but there are others such as London Business School, IESE Business School and Rotterdam School of Management that are designed to take 15–24 months. While many American MBAs take two academic years (typically 16–20 months), there are others that require anything in between one year to a year and a half.

Some MBAs give you the option to accelerate your MBA degree by taking more courses at once and finishing a few months earlier than expected. Distance-learning programmes can vary from anything between three and eight years; on the distance-learning MBA at Imperial College Business School there is a four-year registration period for completion. Many distance-learning courses offer the option to finish later than originally planned which helps to balance work and family life.

The skills you are looking to gain

There is an array of programmes available globally, all differing in one aspect or another. When choosing a programme think about what you want in terms of your aims and objectives. You can then select the school that will give you the experience and skills set to help you meet your objectives. Think about how the school will help you to gain the experience you are looking for; does it provide the opportunity to take an internship or international trips? What opportunities are available to network to secure an interview or a job? These are vital questions to think about before deciding on a school.

Your learning style

Another factor to take into account is your learning style. Are you someone who interacts better in a classroom environment or do you prefer to work alone. If it is the latter you might want to choose an online or distance programme. If you are better at learning face-to-face, enjoy being in group settings and enjoy classroom interaction, then a campus-based degree programme will be ideal.

You may prefer the style of learning in which you take courses with a small group of MBA students for the duration of the course, or you may prefer a learning environment in which you have different students in all your courses. The advantage of being in a larger cohort means that you will have a larger peer group from a diverse background. The experiences and knowledge will enhance discussions and learning opportunities from your peer group.

Facilities

The high-quality facilities a school has to offer will no doubt add to the overall experience while studying for an MBA. Most business schools in the US with their large endowment funds have the resources available to create outstanding facilities, such as Harvard Business School and Wharton University of Pennsylvania. As a minimum requirement the schools on your shortlist should offer a library and extensive online services.

A well-stocked library with books or services specifically for MBA students is not uncommon at schools. Online services are crucial if you are considering an online, PT MBA or an EMBA programme. Having access to reading materials, research papers, databases, the school's intranet and communication systems becomes an important factor to consider if you are not there full time.

Some schools expect or strongly advise students to bring a laptop with them, which has resulted in wireless access typically becoming more prevalent at schools. Lecture theatres and study rooms either have access points or have wireless access for laptops.

Recreational facilities

When undertaking your research on school facilities also consider the sports and recreational facilities on offer. Does the school have a gym on campus or nearby, places to eat and the opportunity to socialise with others? Undertaking an MBA is not just about studying; it is also about building relationships and making new friends and contacts. Having the facilities available to make it easier to connect with others is important.

Accommodation

Finding suitable accommodation can be a challenge at the best of times. Many schools are part of a bigger university, therefore students will have access to on-campus accommodation. Typically universities have their own accommodation offices and will provide support and guidance in looking for suitable accommodation at one of their halls of residence. You can then look for accommodation, depending upon how much you are willing to spend and how far you wish to travel. Compare prices and availability of off-campus accommodation, you may find a better alternative but be sure to check out the safety of the area and transportation links. If you are looking at a school in a different country, it is strongly advisable to visit the campus and see the accommodation for yourself. You will then get a good idea of the location and quality of accommodation available. If you are moving with a partner or a family, their needs should also be taken into account.

Some schools such as London Business School do not offer campus accommodation or have an accommodation office; the onus is on its students to arrange accommodation for themselves. This can be a daunting experience for someone who is new to the UK. However, what London Business School does offer is an informal network opportunity to enable their students to find other like-minded individuals looking for accommodation and to make contacts before classes start.

Location

Location is a very important factor to consider when making your shortlist of schools. However, selecting the right location for you is dependent on various criteria. Ask yourself some critical questions that are related to your post MBA objectives. For example: what are your reasons for undertaking an MBA; a change in industry or job function, enhancing your career, gaining international exposure or career acceleration? If post programme it is to gain international exposure or wanting to move to a particular region or country then it makes sense to choose an MBA in the region or country you are targeting. You should also assess carefully the placement or job opportunities post programme to ensure that the school you choose will help to make the transition to another country.

Even if your objective post-programme is not to move country, think about where the school is located: is it in the city or on the outskirts? A school located in the city will no doubt offer more diversity in terms of social and cultural activities. Furthermore, it will be easier for schools to attract visiting professors, keynote speakers who are passing through an international hub or city rather than a school that is located in the outskirts of a city or in a smaller town. INSEAD Business School, for example, is located in Fontainebleau, about 65km from Paris. It is well renowned for its scenic Forest of Fontainebleau, as well as for the historical Château de Fontainebleau, which attracts groups of locals and tourists alike. Its location means that it is close enough to Paris but also located far enough to get a sense of the French countryside.

Your personal considerations should also be a factor when choosing schools, and perhaps more importantly the needs of your partner and family. The school's location will have an impact on your partner if they are in employment. Similarly, if your children are of school age then finding a relatively good school nearby will be a factor to take into account.

On the other hand, if you are planning on taking a PT or an EMBA programme you will most likely select schools that are within relatively easy travelling distance from where you are already based; otherwise you will spend a considerable amount of time travelling to and from classes rather than studying and enjoying the experience.

Costs

The financial costs involved in undertaking an MBA will vary significantly depending upon the school you choose. When assessing the tuition fees you need to take into account what exactly is covered in the tuition fees and what constitutes as extras, such as living expenses, computer costs and books. Unless you have the money to pay for an MBA upfront, it is highly likely that you will have a student debt after the MBA. For planning purposes, you should account for long-term costs of repayment of student loans with interest.

Campus-based and online MBA programmes will have different fees. For example, online or distance-learning MBAs will include a technology fee in addition to costs around interactive tutoring, online careers service and virtual academic advising. Some schools will include textbooks in the tuition fees while others will not. Some will include textbooks for the core component of the MBA and not for the electives part of the course – it is worthwhile investigating this further.

If you are looking at an MBA in another country, not only will you have to consider relocation costs but also the cost for applying for the necessary visa(s). For instance on a global programme such as the EMBA Global Americas and Europe at London Business School and Columbia Business School, students need to account for flight costs every month. In addition, those who require a visa to enter the UK will have to pay the cost of applying for a student visitor's visa every six months. So if the programme duration is 20 months, students will need at least two visas for the core courses in the first year.

How do you decide which MBA and school to attend?

Nunzio Quacquarelli, MBA from Wharton and Director at QS Ltd, gives his top tips on choosing the right MBA for you. QS organises major MBA events around the world, including the QS World MBA Tour and Connect 121.

1. **Make a realistic self-assessment:** You need to make a realistic self-assessment of your experience, abilities and skills base. This will save you a great deal of time and energy and help you make a more focused selection of schools.

2. **Analyse your motivations:** Analyse your personal motivations for taking an MBA. Don't undertake an MBA just because you have recently graduated and can't find a job. If you have lost your job you may choose an MBA to ride out the economic storm. But for most, an MBA is a more strategic decision. Perhaps you see that in a year or two a recovering economy is going to need more business leaders of your profile, which is probable, and an MBA will equip you to take advantage of these opportunities. Next, try to narrow down the types of career you might like to pursue. Are you geographically mobile? Do you have a strong first degree and a successful track record? Do you have a vision of how you can progress within your current industry or function? Or are you just hoping an MBA will help you do something completely new? Talk to HR managers and MBA alumni at target companies to gain their input.

3. **Consider budget and study mode:** Consider your budget and your preferred study mode. The FT MBA is still by far the most popular programme in terms of candidate numbers. EMBAs target more experienced professionals and allow modular study periods while you carry on working. Part-time and distance-learning MBAs are also growing in popularity.

4. **Identify which criteria matter to you the most:** With so many schools to pick from, you need a rational approach to your selection. Decide what criteria matters to you and aim to identify six schools which match your criteria. Only select those schools for which you believe you can meet the entry criteria. With so many rankings, all producing different results, today's applicants are becoming increasingly sceptical and seeking alternative selection criteria. According to QS Top MBA Applicant Research, the most popular selection criteria, in order of importance are: career placement record, return on investment, reputation of the school, quality of academic staff, specialisations, student profile, rankings, scholarships, location.

5. **Meet the schools face-to-face:** When making such a major personal investment it is important to meet school representatives. Ideally visit the school campus. You can also visit an MBA event around the world – most leading business schools run their own events and attend those organised by QS. Strong candidates will develop a personal link to the admissions manager, who may ultimately be the person making the decision to admit, or a key influencer in the admissions process. Talking to alumni will make sure the cultural fit is right and confirm your school selection.

Listed below are some of the costs involved in attending an MBA. When researching, you should find out whether these are covered in the tuition costs:

- accommodation
- meals
- relocation costs (if moving to another region/country)
- supplies and laptop
- course materials and course textbooks for core courses
- course textbooks for elective modules
- flights for any required international assignment
- accommodation for any required international assignment
- meals during any required international assignment
- printing
- photocopying
- internet access
- student association (SA) subscription
- pre-programme preparation materials (online support)
- healthcare costs
- travel costs.

The most important thing is to ensure that you can afford the costs before you start the MBA and that the return on your investment with an MBA justifies the costs involved.

We'll go into more detail about MBA course fees and sources of funding in Chapter 5.

Faculty credentials

One of the factors to consider when you are deciding which MBA to apply for is the quality and credentials of the faculty at the school of your choice, particularly the faculty teaching those subjects that are relevant to your end goals and aims. The MBA is different from standard academic degrees, and its focus is on equipping students with all the skills required to achieve success in demanding roles across the global business domain. Faculty is one of the key aspects of the MBA experience, not only in terms of their breadth and depth of knowledge and business exposure, but also in relation to their ability to teach large groups of international professionals coming together to learn and exchange experiences.

A superb learning environment can be delivered only by academics who know their subject really well, are high in demand by business schools around the world, and have the opportunity to travel across countries and cultures teaching diverse audiences. They have developed a more facilitative teaching style beyond the stern and dry traditional "talk at" style. The main purpose of wanting to undertake an MBA is to have the opportunity to be exposed to knowledge and information from various sources and in particular from your classmates. The seasoned and high quality faculty will be building a perfect platform to share their knowledge and expertise in doing business or running organisations across sectors, industries, geographies and companies.

Business schools typically have their resident members of faculty and an array of visiting professors who fly in and out of various business schools across the world to teach their subjects. The calibre and credentials of members of faculty will vary significantly depending on their discipline, age, career and business schools they are sought by. A typical MBA member of faculty in top-tier business schools will have had at least 5–10 years of experience in teaching MBA students and others taking different degree and non-degree courses, including EMBA programmes and executive education courses.

Executive education courses

Executive education courses are short programmes that business schools offer to professionals who do not wish to go back to school and study for a degree but desire to be exposed to the most advanced lessons in business and leadership. Business schools offer two types of executive education courses: open programmes, which have a set curriculum and are aimed at participants from different companies and sectors; and bespoke programmes, which are built exclusively around the needs of one particular company. Academics chosen to run these high-intensity, high-profile and highly priced programmes – ranging from £5,000 to around £30,000 – are the most accomplished faculty in their fields. If obtaining a degree is not your priority, a good executive education programme could give the knowledge and tools to apply immediately to your workplace, as well as the exposure to a network of talented professionals.

Faculty at top schools feature highly in public speaking and business consulting assignments across the world. They are flown in and paid very high fees by companies, governments and other organisations for their expertise and experience in understanding sophisticated business landscapes. These academics would also normally be involved in research or practice centres around their subject area, which reinforces their stature and gives them exposure to projects usually involving large numbers of data sourced from companies across the world. Top MBA schools recruit the big names who are the experts in their field as well as upcoming talent, whom they groom and develop through their versatile academic ranks. The big American schools choose their faculty well and retain them even better, honouring their initial investment. They set the tone as well as having a pool of academics that are highly sought after around the world. The credentials of these high-calibre faculty members are usually as follows.

- Under- and postgraduate degrees acquired at top schools around the world.
- Long and substantial lists of publications in recognised and highly respected journals (for example, *Harvard Business Review* and the *Journal of Finance*) in their area of expertise and subject matter.

- Collaborations on articles with top brand names in the universities where they studied or top schools around the world.
- Level of engagement and recognition in the business community: leading business school faculty sit on companies' boards or are consultants for world-class business leaders, who draw from their expertise to inform their strategic decisions.
- Good teaching experience and engaging teaching style.

You would expect all faculty members at business schools to have a PhD, which is the necessary standard prerequisite to become an academic across the world. However, because business is more an applied subject than an academic one, it is often the case that you will find some practitioners in the school lists of faculty members. Some top schools (mainly the American ones) have high-profile entrepreneurs and senior executives who are experienced in business teach their students; the typical MBA case studies that students discuss in class are built on the experience of these people. Of course this is a great added benefit of any MBA programme, since students have the amazing opportunity to hear it all "from the horse's mouth" and not second-hand only.

The vast majority of business schools ask students to evaluate faculty members at least once if not more, typically at the end of the academic term and/or end of the course. These evaluations are instrumental to provide constructive feedback regarding choice of curriculum and delivery style; they also play a key role towards schools' decision making on whether and how to continue deploying their faculty members. Some faculty may be much better suited for some audiences than others and students' feedback assists them with this type of assessment. For example, students on EMBA programmes who have full-time jobs and experience of 5–10 years and who often have to fly in from other countries or locations usually enjoy being taught in a way that engages them, i.e. in a more interactive and experience-focused manner. The diversity of experiences within the classroom fits smoothly with the academic knowledge communicated by the faculty.

When you choose an MBA programme, it is important that you gather students or alumni's feedback on the overall teaching style of faculty and the level of interactions within the class. We'll look at gathering students and alumni feedback later in this chapter.

School culture

One of the key differentiators of business schools around the world is their culture, which translates as "the way we do things around here", the way we treat our students and each other, and how we like to measure and evaluate our results.

This is a "soft" indicator of choosing business schools; however, it is a critical one, since if your personal style of learning and achieving does not match the school's culture, your learning experience will be more difficult and less enjoyable. Similar to top companies, top-tier business schools look at the candidate's personality and style while assessing their potential match with the school. For example, a top school that is renowned for its open learning style and empowering way of approaching the student's experience will need to recruit highly committed and motivated individuals who can learn fast and integrate themselves within a group of strong achievers.

Although the MBA programme will put a basic structure and organisation around the programme, it is up to the students to organise their learning and achieve highly on their own as well as in a group environment. Students who do not command the natural ability to assimilate, integrate and learn fast, stretching themselves to achieve the highest standard, or students who lack the self-discipline to commit to such an intensive course will find themselves being left behind very fast, causing detrimental effects to their individual and study group performance. The typical MBA programme (whether FT MBA, PT MBA or EMBA) is organised around three types of learning.

- Individual learning initiated by the student as per the requirements of each MBA module, which is typically evaluated through exams and/or individual assignments.
- Group learning through participation in study groups that are required to work together for finite periods of time and deliver joint results for the study group assignments.
- Class participation, which involves student interaction and contribution towards group discussion within a classroom environment with the faculty.

Each school will have a different set of generic expectations of their students that will generally permeate throughout the MBA programme and the way members of faculty run their courses too.

Culture also has a lot to do with the school's reputation for certain specialisms which influences the teaching approach and the types of student it attracts. This also impacts on what students expect the school to deliver for them in terms of added value of their course in their professional careers.

A school's course structure and delivery can give good hints about its culture. There are schools that have a very strict and detail-driven curriculum built around areas of expertise like finance and delivered in highly concentrated block weeks where students are expected to take in-depth exams after the end sub-modules of the core courses. These schools are more traditional in their ways of teaching and attract students who are looking to specialise through being put under a lot of direct pressure and robust structure.

Although culture is not one of the tangible factors when choosing the right MBA, there are some key pointers for identifying a school that is a good fit for you.

- **Visit the school's website**. What does it tell you about the school? Is it a place you would like to join? Do you like the feel of the place as communicated on the website, what type of success stories come through? Most importantly, what types of people will your classmates be and what value has the MBA added to their lives?
- **Attend the school's open day**. We cannot stress enough how important this step is towards identifying your match to the school(s) of your choice. Start interacting with the school and see how its people respond. Arrange to visit the

school for an information day and see how it feels like to you – the place as well as the people. Does it inspire you to be part of this campus? Do you get a nice feel when you are there? What about the people you meet – members of staff, students and alumni? Are they your "cup of tea", do you manage to engage them into meaningful conversations? What do they have to say about the course? Can you see yourself part of this student and alumni community? Most importantly, do you get the sense that they can too? What types of transition have alumni achieved? Does this match your vision and career path?

- **Gather as much information as possible** about how courses are organised, the teaching method, the expectations and the commitment required as well as the application process. How are you going to be evaluated before, during and after? How intensive is the course and how strict are the criteria for success? How connected is the school to industry? Can you see a clear indication of a link between the school and top companies around the world? Are organisations sending their employees there for full-time or part-time courses? Does the school have a wide recognition as a brand name for the culture it nurtures and promotes throughout its courses?
- **Think carefully** whether what you see, hear, read about is aligned with where you see yourself going in the next 5–10 years. At the same time, think carefully about whether you will be able to commit to delivering the types of results the school is requiring of its student body. It is of utmost importance that you have a "Socratic dialogue with yourself" in a clear and honest way, evaluating your real match with the school's expectations. Every school sets subtle signals about their culture and the people that fit that profile. Carry out your research in a comprehensive and exhaustive manner so that you are absolutely certain that you have done your best to see which types of people this school is selecting and equally importantly, why this school would fit your profile and learning requirements. It is only natural among highly ambitious and motivated people to aspire to attend the best possible school; however, this is sometimes neither realistic nor possible. A school more suited to your learning pace and style will give you much more instead of a school that will stretch you in ways you are not ready to commit to or deliver yet. And most importantly, the frustration and disappointment of committing your heart and valuable resources to a school that ends up rejecting you is an experience to be avoided at all costs.

Student and alumni profiles

It really is all about people, people, people. It is vital that you carry out a comprehensive research on student and alumni profiles. You need to use this information in order to make the best decision of which business school is right for you. Contact the admissions teams to put you in touch with student and alumni contacts. These teams will help source contacts for you in a particular industry or function if you request this.

Looking at the profiles of current and past students can give you a very good indication of your chances of being accepted as well as what you will be able to achieve after graduating.

This is the second critical reason for getting as much information as you can about students and alumni profiles as early as possible in the process; so that you can evaluate whether this is the school that will furnish you with the right skills, qualification and experiences which, post-graduation, will enable you to make the critical next steps in your career.

Each business school, according to its vision, culture and ranking position will be in a position to select – and equally reject – large numbers of applicants. It is critical that you check the profiles of the people accepted in this particular school. Ask yourself and the people you talk to – whether members of staff, students and alumni – about the following.

Pre-MBA

- What were students doing before the MBA?
- Were they working for large companies in a particular sector, or were they more regionally focused in companies without an extensive reputation and catchment area?

During the MBA

- What were they doing during the MBA?
- Has the school empowered these people to build the skills and competencies they needed to excel in global business? What has the experience of these people been while doing the MBA? There are numerous forums and discussion boards (for example, the *BusinessWeek* forum is popular) on the MBA experience as well as a plethora of information on what different MBA schools offer their students in terms of skills portfolios, internships, career services, peer and faculty support, networking events, clubs and groups of interest that fit your mission and vision.
- Has the MBA been a meaningful experience that has satisfied their learning objectives as well as their career goals?
- Has the student body been of the calibre and quality you want to be exposed to, and have the classmates been able to contribute to the learning experience in the best and maximum possible way?

Post-MBA

- What have these people achieved with their MBA experience and degree?
- What change has their careers seen, comparing careers before and after?
- Has there been a clear progression in terms of either ascending the career ladder or changing industries and sectors altogether?
- In a nutshell, has the MBA worked as a platform of substantial, advanced and concentrated learning that boosted their personal and professional development in ways that would not have been possible, or would have taken much longer otherwise?

It is of vital importance to understand through your research the profile of people who are accepted and achieve the maximum in the business schools of your choice. Joining an MBA programme is a commitment for life, and you need to decide the group of people you want to belong to, which should tie in with your vision in the next 5–10 years.

Once accepted on an MBA programme you will find yourself surrounded by people who share some basic characteristics – depending on the school you choose and get accepted into. Ask yourself whether this is the space you want to find yourself in and why. It is a commonly accepted fact that one of the most important differentiating factors across tiers of MBA schools is the quality and diversity of the students they attract, which translates into the power of the network of the people you are connected to during the programme and after graduation.

The other set of questions to ask yourself is:

- Do I want to be part of this group and an ambassador of this school's brand?
- How diverse and international is the student and alumni body?
- Is it a school with a high concentration of one nationality, or can you see a clear diversity within both the student and alumni communities in terms of culture, ethnic identity and levels of exposure to international business?
- Does the school diversity match your career goals and objectives either within a specific locality or across the global terrain?
- Upon graduation, will you have developed not only the right skills and competencies required to run exciting businesses and organisations, but also have tapped into the culture and way of doing things in the geography of your choice as well as into networks of recruiters and people in your preferred location, which is a significant head start when having ambitious career plans in mind?
- Look at the experience as a whole.

After ascertaining the benefits and advantages of the MBA degree for others who have been through it, you also need to be looking at the more general MBA experience.

An MBA is an atypical degree compared with most other academic qualifications. It is definitely a master's degree in terms of the knowledge and skills targeted and acquired; however, it is at the same time a very practical endeavour structured around experiential learning and exposure to case studies, simulations and significant amounts of group work.

This is exactly the point of the MBA – to connect and interact with large groups of people interested in learning more and developing themselves personally and professionally in order to excel in the global business terrain. The exposure to a very diverse and largely international student group engaged in various activities such as clubs, conferences, business competition for consulting and entrepreneurial projects, sports competitions, profit and not-for-profit or social enterprise focused businesses across the world is an invaluable part of the whole MBA experience.

When choosing your school and programme this is one of the factors that *needs* to weigh highly towards making your final decision.

Rankings

Through surveys and analysis of various indicators, rankings or league tables aim to quantify the quality of the business education provided by different schools and the impact of higher education programmes on career development.

One of the first MBA rankings was developed by *Bloomberg BusinessWeek* in 1988 and since then numerous journals and other media organisations have published their own rankings. Ranking critics, including business schools, often have reservations on the methodologies used by media and research companies; for example, rankings make a wide use of surveys but surveys are not always able to ensure a large number of responses or an appropriate level of checks to avoid multiple or false entries. There is also the well-known objection that league tables are simply a way to sell papers and attract advertising space.

Rankings are usually the starting point for most candidates when choosing an MBA and are certainly are a good way to quickly gain an overview of the global business schools and wide range of available programmes. Obviously you are keen on having on your CV a brand that recruiters will immediately recognise and associate with quality and talent. However, rankings are not a perfect science, and different methodologies put different schools at the top; you should consult rankings with critical awareness of how data is collected and presented and identify what is helpful to your needs. In addition, rankings tend to classify programmes according to the school's home country and do not benchmark those that are taught by the same school at overseas campuses against those delivered in that region.

We are aware that ranking methodologies are not always easy to read and digest. We aim to give you a good overview of the most well-known MBA rankings and their methodology; we will also provide you with advice on how you can use the rankings to make an informed choice.

The most known well-known rankings

Besides *BusinessWeek*, the rankings you may be most familiar with are those by *The Economist*, the *Financial Times* (*FT*), *Forbes*, *U.S. News & World Report* (*US News*) and the *Wall Street Journal* (*WSJ*), which are discussed below in alphabetical order.

The popularity of these rankings varies according to the geographical area in which you are; for example, the FT rankings are commonly used in Europe, while *BusinessWeek* and *US News* have a stronger following in North America because of their emphasis on US schools.

When you compare how schools have performed in different rankings, it is immediately obvious that the programmes at the top are not the same throughout each ranking system. This is due to the use of different criteria and the weighting assigned to each indicator. However, you will also notice that a group of schools will consistently appear in the top 20–30 spots in the majority of these publications.

HEC Paris

The HEC MBA programme offers participants a unique experience of being immersed in a student body of highly diverse nationalities, academic and professional backgrounds. Teamed with exceptionally talented peers from 50 countries, participants push each other to achieve, realise their full potential and ultimately develop and sharpen their leadership skills.

The 16-month programme is divided into two phases. During the *fundamental phase* participants develop comprehensive management knowledge and techniques in 11 core subjects. In the *customised phase*, participants can concentrate on finance, entrepreneurship, marketing or strategy, or carry out one of 40 exchanges available. They also select from a range of electives or gain corporate exposure through an individual or group fieldwork project. Additionally, we have 12 double degree programmes available with partner schools around the world. Our ideal programme duration and structure gives participants the time to gain a solid grounding in core business, *and* the time to tailor the MBA in line with individual career goals.

Leadership is a transformative process enhanced through hands-on, practical experience and experiential learning initiatives: integrated into our curriculum are seminars and student-run events. For example, the MBA sports tournament is a participant-run event which HEC MBA participants not only organise but also compete in as they welcome around 1,500 MBAs from some of the best business schools in Europe. Another example is the Situational Leadership Seminar, which exercises participants' leadership skills during a stay at St Cyr military training camp as they learn to manage their teams. Such experiences give our participants the opportunity to transfer the knowledge that they learn in the classroom into real-life situations.

The HEC MBA Career Management Centre offers training in adapting job search skills to differing geographies. Participants receive customised job-search advice from consultants, coaches, peers and from our alumni network of over 44,000. We provide individual coaching and counselling to help smooth navigation through the programme and, ultimately, pave the way to a fulfilling professional life. The careers approach is customised to the individual, whether the aim is to advance in their current career path or to make a radical career change.

Case study

When I think of HEC MBA, I think of people, challenges, opportunities, excellence and innovation.

Diversity is a distinctive characteristic of HEC MBA: this translates in a truly multicultural environment, as demonstrated by the 50 nationalities represented on campus, and diverging backgrounds both in terms of professional and personal experience. All this constitutes an amazing opportunity of sharing, learning, discovering and understanding different cultures and leadership styles. The uniqueness of HEC MBA is that the class size, length and structure of the programme allow you to truly get to know each of your peers.

The programme integrates a first-class education with a strong focus on soft skills, especially on leadership development. From this point of view there is a wide range of opportunities based on a hands-on approach. This means that at HEC leadership is not simply taught, but is practised in real situations. As a general coordinator, I directly ran the organisation of MBA Tournament (MBAT) in 2011. During this thrilling experience, I reinforced my belief that leadership has two dimensions. It is certainly about inspiring, taking initiative, driving changes, delivering results and following a vision; but at the same time, it is about being inspired, learning, sharing and exchanging. It is about doing things together.

A very important element of my MBA experience has been the HEC Alumni Association. Clearly, this is a very valuable resource for networking and gaining deep knowledge in almost every industry. Furthermore, another element also struck me: the more I knew about the association, the more I realised how strong the sense of belonging to the HEC community is. The passion and dedication of my peers and all alumni instilled in me the pride of being part of this community and the commitment of making it bigger and stronger.

HEC MBA provided me with the tools and knowledge to define and expand my objectives, and enhanced my skills and motivation to reach them. Most importantly, I shared all this with truly exceptional people.

Michele Cantanzariti, HEC MBA 2012

Advice on how to use the rankings

- Do not stop at the headlines and the overall rankings, read carefully how they collect and weight data and represent results (ranking methodology).
- Choose the methodology and rankings that best match your needs and objectives. Use your critical analysis to break the rankings into different elements and select those that are more meaningful and relevant to your goals.
- Check how business schools have performed over a number of years (ideally, three to five years) and across a few of these sources.
- Look for consistency in how schools have performed in different rankings.
- Remember that reputation and recognition within specific business communities sometimes go beyond rankings. If you want to work in a particular country or niche sector, you may find that some local business schools which perhaps are not at the top of the lists are able to offer better connections with your target sectors than global business schools. Check the rankings of local media players in the country in which you are planning to work, and research the school contacts in the industry sectors or regions in which you want to obtain your post-MBA job.
- Rankings should not be the only indicator or source of information for choosing your MBA. It is important to look at the other factors discussed in this chapter; for example, the school culture is absolutely vital to your MBA experience and it is not helpful to choose an institution whose environment, vision and community are not a good fit with what you are or aim to be. Equally, if you want to specialise in a particular area you need to ensure that the MBA curriculum offers relevant electives.
- You also need to be realistic about your possibilities to obtain a place in one of the top-ranked schools. It always helps looking at the entry requirements and class quality indicators (years of work experience, GMAT®, academic qualifications, etc.) and draw up a list of "second bests" besides your dream schools.
- You need to do your own research by visiting schools where possible and talking to admissions and programme staff, students and alumni.

BusinessWeek

BusinessWeek publishes FT MBA, PT MBA and EMBA rankings based on the opinion of students and recruiters or programme managers as collected through surveys. When its first MBA ranking was launched, this approach was innovative as other existing tools mainly considered academic data. *BusinessWeek* set a number of eligibility criteria that schools must satisfy to be included in the rankings; for instance, age of the programme, enrolment number and programme accreditation.

The majority of the ranked schools are US based (only US schools are ranked for PT MBAs); FT MBA rankings show two separate league tables for US and non-US schools. *BusinessWeek* provides a lot of details on the methodology that has been used to compile the rankings.

BusinessWeek FT MBA rankings

When

BusinessWeek FT MBA rankings are published in late October or early November in even-numbered years. Prior to 2010, only 40 FT MBA programmes were ranked and all the others were placed in an unranked second-tier group. Since 2010, *BusinessWeek* ranks all FT MBA programmes whose surveys have provided the required response rate. Programmes at US schools are ranked separately from non-US programmes.

Methodology

The main sources used to compile the FT MBA rankings are the student and employer surveys and an intellectual capital rating, which is not survey based. The student survey is conducted online through a site and participants are identified through the contact details provided by the target schools. Students answer 45 questions and score areas such as teaching, career services and alumni network. For the employer survey, *BusinessWeek* chooses recruiters from lists supplied by the schools. Recruiters must indicate which schools they actively recruit MBA students from and the number of MBA hires in the previous two years. They also rank the top 20 business schools according to the quality of their MBA graduates in areas such as analytical skills, communication and teamwork.

BusinessWeek carries out the intellectual capital rating by assigning points to articles published by faculty in 20 renowned academic journals and book reviews written by faculty and published in *BusinessWeek*, *The New York Times* and *WSJ*. Each survey contributes to 45% of the final ranking, while the intellectual capital score counts towards 10% of the final ranking.

Pros and cons

The advantage of this methodology is that it measures the satisfaction rate of students and employers, who are the main users of business education. Clearly this advantage is also its limitation, as the results from these rankings are mainly based on surveys rather than hard data.

BusinessWeek EMBA and PT MBA rankings

When

EMBA and PT MBA rankings are published in November in odd-numbered years. *BusinessWeek* generally ranks schools; however, you can also find separate entries for EMBA programmes taught by the same school.

Methodology

EMBA and PT MBA rankings are based on two surveys; one for graduates and one for programme managers. The former contributes to 65% of the overall rankings, while the latter counts for 35%. Graduates answer questions and score their programme on different areas, including teaching, curriculum, career services and the calibre of their classmates. Programme managers are asked to list the top 10 programmes they are most familiar with. *BusinessWeek* attributes points to the top 10 schools of each programme manager and adds up the points received by each school to calculate the programme manager rank.

Pros and cons

Same as FT MBA rankings.

Access the most up-to-date rankings at www.businessweek.com/bschools/rankings.

The Economist FT MBA rankings

When

The Economist launched its first *Which MBA?* rankings in 2002. They are usually published in mid October.

Methodology

The Economist's FT MBA rankings are based on data from two surveys, one for business schools and one for current students and alumni who graduated within the most recent three years. The school data count towards 80% of the rankings, while the student and alumni survey contributes to 20%. Schools can be included in the rankings only if they provide minimum thresholds of data and obtain a minimum number of responses from the student and alumni survey. The top 100 schools are included in the overall rankings, while the remaining ones are considered for the regional rankings only. The rankings consider four main indicators: new career opportunities, which counts towards 35% of the score; personal development and education experience (35%); salary increase (20%); and networking opportunities (10%). Each school receives a unique score and no schools occupy the same spot in the rankings, although the differences between them may be small.

Pros and cons

The Economist's rankings include a wide range of institutions worldwide. It considers four key indicators when choosing an MBA. The main critique regards the results inconsistent as there are schools that go significantly up or down from one year to another.

Access the most up-to-date rankings at www.economist.com/whichmba.

FT rankings

When

FT launched its first FT MBA rankings in 1999. Today, *FT* ranks all the main postgraduate degrees in management and finance: FT MBA, EMBA, pre-experience master in finance and master in management (which are degrees designed with graduates with less than one year of work experience) and post-experience master in finance (which are postgraduate degrees designed for experienced professionals). The FT MBA ranking is published every year in January, while the EMBA ranking is published in October. The FT also ranks the top European business schools based on the results from the other rankings.

FT MBA and EMBA methodology

FT considers for rankings all the business schools that have obtained accreditation by AACSB, AMBA or EQUIS. Programmes must have run for at least four years and produced its first graduates at least three years before the publication date. In addition, for the FT MBA programmes there is a minimum enrolment requirement of 30. The methodology for the ranking of both programmes is based on data collected through online questionnaires from business school and graduates who completed the degree three years before: the main focus in the *FT* rankings is the impact of the degree on salary and career. Schools must achieve at least 20% of responses from their graduates to be included in the FT MBA and EMBA rankings.

FT MBA

Regarding the FT MBA, the information from the questionnaires is used to determine the schools' position with regard to 20 indicators in three key areas: graduates' salary and career impact; internationalism of the school and of the programme; and research quality. Eight of these criteria are based on the information collected from the graduate survey, while 11 (such as "women faculty" and "international experience rank") are based on the questionnaire completed by the school. The FT considers data collected in the surveys from the previous three years. The information from the most recent survey weights 50% towards the calculation of the score in these areas, while the two previous ones carry 25% each. If only two years of data are available, the recent survey accounts for 60% and the second one for 40%.

The salary components (weighted salary and salary percentage increase) are those that contribute the most towards the overall rank of the participating schools (40%). *FT* excluded from the salary calculations the data of graduates in full-time studies or working for the public or not-for-profit sectors. Looking to convert salaries expressed in different currencies into dollars, *FT* chose to use the purchasing power parity rates provided by the International Monetary Fund. These rates take into account the cost of living in different countries. The "research rank" criterion is calculated by *FT* according to the number of publications published by faculty within the most recent three years in 45 journal titles. Each school receives a number of points for each publication and the score is adjusted by the size of the faculty. The research rank contributes to 10% of the final ranking.

The final rank of each school is calculated by considering the differences in the scores achieved by schools in each indicator and the spread of scores between the two schools that have the highest and lowest score (Z-scores).

EMBA

The data from the school and graduate surveys are used to determine the school's rank according to 16 indicators in three key areas: graduates' salary and career impact; internationalism of the school and of the programme; and research quality. Like in the FT MBA rankings, *FT* collates three years of data to determine the school's rank in the 16 indicators: while data from the most recent survey contributes to 50% of the score, questionnaires collected in the previous two years weight 25% each. If only two years of data are available, the recent survey accounts for 60% and the second one for 40%. The indicators regarding the salary and career progression of the EMBA graduates contribute 50% of the final score.

FT excluded from the salary calculations the data of graduates in full-time studies or working for the public or not-for-profit sectors. To compare salaries expressed in different currencies and convert them into US dollars, *FT* uses the currency conversion rates provided by the International Monetary Fund through the purchasing power parity rates. *FT* then calculates the average salary for each school after excluding the highest and lowest value. The salary increase percentage is calculated by considering for each school the difference between the average salary of the students before they started the programme and three years after completing the degree. Other indicators that weight significantly in the final ranking (25%) are those which measure the diversity of faculty and students and the internationalism of the programme (for example, women faculty, languages). The "Aims achieved" indicator contributes on its own to 5% of the total score for the schools. The "research rank" criterion is calculated by *FT* as explained for FT MBAs.

Pros and cons

One of the key positive aspects of *FT* rankings is that they include a wide range of schools from different countries around the world, so they have a global rather than a US focus. These rankings are based on many different criteria – some are more objective (for example, salary increase), others such as "aims achieved" are subjective. Critics of *FT* rankings do not agree with all the elements that are measured, the way in which they are assessed or the weight assigned to each of them.

Access the most up-to-date rankings at: http://rankings.ft.com/businessschoolrankings.

Forbes rankings

When

Forbes launched its first FT MBA rankings in 1999 and publishes them at odd-numbered years in August. It has three different sets of FT MBA rankings: top US schools, top non-US one-year business schools and top non-US two-year business schools. Only two-year FT MBAs are considered for the US school rankings. There seems to be a stronger emphasis on US schools.

Methodology

Forbes' methodology focuses on the return on investment (ROI), which MBA graduates achieve five years after attending business school. *Forbes* calculates the five-year gain by considering the earnings of MBA graduates in those first five years after graduation, minus tuition fees, other fees and forgone compensation (pre-MBA earnings which students gave up when they started the programme). Figures are also adjusted for cost of living expenses and the time value of money. In a few words, these rankings look at the payback from the MBA investment and assign the top spots to schools that are able to deliver bigger and faster returns.

Pros and cons

Forbes' methodology is quite straightforward and totally based on ROI, which makes it easy to understand. It does not include other aspects of the MBA experience, which may perhaps be important to some candidates. In addition, as these rankings capture what happened five years after graduation, the main critique is that they are not helpful in understanding the more immediate gains from an MBA.

Access the most up-to-date rankings at www.forbes.com.

US News

When

US News publishes FT and PT MBA rankings each year in March.

Methodology

US News considers for their survey all the business schools that are accredited by the Association to Advance Collegiate Schools of Business International (AACSB International), which at the time of writing number 437. The methodology is based on multiple surveys of graduates, recruiters and business school deans and looks at three indicators: quality assessment; placement success; and student selectivity. The quality is determined by the peer and recruiter surveys. In the peer survey, business school deans and directors are asked to rate other programmes on a scale from one to five, where five is the top score. The peer questionnaire weights 25% in the overall ranking. Recruiters are also asked to rate programmes using the same scale and this score weighs 15% in the overall ranking. The placement success component looks at mean starting salary, and bonus and employment rates, which contribute to 14% and 21% of the overall ranking, respectively. Student selectivity is based on the average GMAT® score, the average grade-point average (GPA) from the undergraduate degree and the acceptance rate of the class. Student selectivity weights 25% in the overall rankings.

PT MBA and EMBA rankings

PT MBA and EMBA rankings are considered as "specialty" rankings together with finance, marketing and others. Specialty rankings are based exclusively on peer ratings by business school deans and directors who receive a list of programmes in each specialty and are asked to nominate up to 10 programmes in each of the listed area. Schools must receive seven or more nominations to be included in the rankings and are ranked based on the number of nominations and points that they have gained.

Pros and cons

One of the key positive aspects is that it is based on the views of all major stakeholders involved in business education. It also tries to measure indicators that are helpful when considering MBA programmes. The weight assigned to each component clearly attracts criticism: for example, the peer questionnaire weighs more than the employers' survey. Regarding the EMBA ranking, clearly it is only based on a survey of business school deans and directors, which appears to be a subjective and limited way to assess the quality of a programme.

Access the most up-to-date rankings here: http://grad-schools.usnews.rankingsandreviews.com/best-graduate-schools/top-business-schools.

WSJ EMBA rankings

When

WSJ launched its first EMBA rankings in 2008 and it continues publishing them in even-numbered years. This EMBA ranking is based on the scores from two surveys: one for the most recent graduates and one for companies that employ EMBA graduates. The school score contributes to 40% of the overall ranking; the recruiter survey contributes to 40%; and the score from the rating of the management and leadership skills by graduates and recruiters is weighted 20%. Schools are considered for the rankings if they are accredited by one of the international bodies and if they meet specific eligibility criteria: their EMBA programmes have produced at least four previous graduating classes; 25 enrolling in the graduating class; their EMBA students have had at least nine years of professional experience, including two years of management experience, and commuted at minimum of 45 miles to attend the EMBA classes. Schools can submit different programme entries if they meet the eligibility requirements.

Methodology

The graduate survey consists of questions in which participants are asked to score different aspects regarding two main areas: the quality and applicability and its ability to teach practical skills in key management or leadership areas. For the recruiter survey, the *WSJ* selects companies out of a list of names identified by graduates and schools: companies with fewer than 75 employees, firms which do not have a qualified HR executive or those where an EMBA student is in the senior management team are excluded. Recruiters have to rate at least two schools they are familiar with in a number of skills. They also have to rank the three schools they felt were the best and express how familiar they were with these schools.

Pros and cons

The main advantage of this ranking is its focus on graduates and EMBA recruiters' opinions and management and leadership skills. One of the critiques is that it is mainly based on qualitative rather than quantitative elements.

Access the most up-to-date rankings here: http://online.wsj.com/public/page/business-schools.html.

Accreditation

When you are choosing your MBA, it is important to check that the programme or the school is accredited by at least one of the internationally recognised independent bodies, which are: Association of MBA (AMBA); the Association to Advance Collegiate Schools of Business (AACSB International); European Quality Improvement System (EQUIS), run by the European Foundation for Management Development (EFMD). Accreditation ensures that the programme meets quality standards in a number of academic and non-academic areas.

Like many other quality assurance systems, in earlier stages accreditation was subject to critique: there were doubts about the reliability of these schemes in which schools paid to be accredited. However, the rigour and thoroughness in the approach and practices of the above accrediting bodies overcame the initial resistance. Today, accreditation by the AMBA, AACSB and EQUIS is widely recognised as a commitment to deliver quality in MBA education. These accrediting bodies have certainly introduced some quality benchmarks that all schools felt they had to comply with when coming up with new MBA solutions to respond to the market trends.

An overview of the accreditation criteria and processes developed by the three institutions will help you gain a better understanding of why accreditation ensures that you are choosing a good programme. A number of programmes worldwide have achieved triple accreditation. However, there are a number of the world's top business schools which are not triple accredited. Typically these business schools will have accreditation from their national body and are not concerned with international accreditation. In general, when undertaking your research, you should be looking at schools with at least one of the accreditations mentioned below.

AACSB

Founded in the US in 1916, AACSB International is the oldest internationally accrediting body and provides accreditation for undergraduate, postgraduate and research degrees in business and accounting. It is a membership organisation and has around 1,200 members globally – from educational institutions to corporate and public sector or not-for-profit organisations. Membership of the AACSB does not guarantee accreditation.

To obtain accreditation from AACSB International, schools must satisfy a number of eligibility requirements and standards. One of the eligibility requirements is that the programme has produced graduates for at least two consecutive years. This means that if you are considering a programme that has been recently launched, the school may have not yet been able to apply for accreditation. In these situations, if the school already delivers other accredited programmes, you can feel confident that the institution has experience in applying the standards required by the AACSB.

AACSB International's strategy and implementation guidelines of the accreditation process also consider the cultural differences around the world. The quality standards are therefore not rigid parameters, but they are adapted to different situations to support high quality in management education.

AACSB accreditation focuses on three key areas: strategic management standards, which takes into account the school's mission and the way it directs its efforts and resources to achieve its strategic objectives; participant standards, which focus on the quality of faculty and the student body; and assurance of learning, which looks at how the school meets the learning needs and goals of graduates.

Once a school has received accreditation, it must commit to maintaining the accreditation through an annual report and a review every five years. Schools can lose accreditation if they do not demonstrate ability to maintain the standards.

AMBA

The Association of MBAs (AMBA) is a professional membership organisation for business schools, MBA students, graduates and employers. It was established in 1967 and it is based in the UK. AMBA focuses on accreditation of postgraduate business programmes – primarily MBAs and also doctorate degrees (DBA) and Master in Business and Management (MBM). An institution can qualify for accreditation after three batches of MBA students have graduated; that is after a minimum of three years.

AMBA's assessment considers different criteria regarding both the school and the programme provision. Some of these criteria (purpose and outcomes) define what the objectives and learning outcomes of an MBA should be to ensure that it has a practical and professional orientation. Other measures (curriculum and assessment; mode and duration) establish the curriculum content in terms of core knowledge; the minimum length (one year of full-time or two years of part-time studies) and amount of contact and learning hours (500 and 1,800, respectively); and the necessity to use a variety of learning and teaching methods. AMBA insists on the value of networking and learning from your peers on an MBA programme, and therefore requires that distance-learning MBAs include elements of face-to-face learning. This explains why it is not possible to find accredited MBAs which are entirely delivered through distance learning.

Other accreditation criteria which may be of particular interest to you are in regard to faculty, programme management and students. Schools must ensure that the faculty size and the support provided by the administrative staff can meet the learning needs of the students. They are also expected to seek and implement students' feedback on course delivery and content. The majority of the MBA teaching staff must be involved in management research, scholarship and consultancy and be appropriately qualified: at least 75% of the teaching faculty should hold a postgraduate degree and the majority of faculty should have a doctorate. Research needs to show some evidence of international standard. Schools must also provide effective pastoral care and career service provision and encourage an active alumni association. AMBA sets specific criteria also for the admissions requirements and process. All students admitted to the MBA must have at least three years of professional work experience when they start the programme; the average experience of the class should be at least five years. The admissions process must demonstrate rigour in the application of academic and non-academic entry standards and aim to produce a diverse and balanced class. In addition, the cohort must consist of at least 20 students to ensure a good quality of the learning experience.

To date, AMBA accredits around 700 programmes at 187 business schools around the world.

EQUIS

The European Quality Improvement System (EQUIS) is an accreditation process for business schools. EQUIS was established in 1988 by the European Foundation for Management Development, a Brussels-based international membership organisation. This accreditation system focuses on the academic institution as a whole and covers all programmes – from undergraduate degrees to PhD – delivered by those schools. The assessment regards not only the degree programmes but also other activities such as research and development, executive education, community outreach projects and corporate connections. EQUIS standard framework covers a lot of areas.

Schools need to demonstrate a clear mission and strategy and effective governance systems. Strategic objectives must inform faculty recruitment and development, and schools must have a minimum number of faculty (25) to cover the core areas of business and management. Other programme criteria emphasise the need to balance knowledge and skills acquisition and to monitor the quality of students' work through robust assessment processes. Programmes should also be adequately resourced in terms of staff. The teaching methods must reflect current practices and the curriculum must be regularly reviewed through the feedback from students and other relevant stakeholders. Other quality criteria regard the students and aim to ensure that they are selected through rigorous admissions processes. These processes are required to produce representation of a number of diverse nationalities and backgrounds in the student body. Schools must ensure provision of well-resourced student and careers services and actively promote students' personal and professional development beyond academic activities. EQUIS is particularly concerned with the international dimension, which business schools must demonstrate in all their activities.

At the time of writing 130 institutions in 38 countries have become EQUIS accredited.

Career services

One of the key criteria which should drive your programme choice is the ability of the school to connect you with prospective employers in the areas of interest. Career services play an essential role in building and maintaining contacts with prospective MBA employers and facilitating networking opportunities with alumni and faculty. In fact, corporate contacts are sometimes managed by academic staff rather than career services, but it is important that the information is recorded and circulated to the students.

Rankings and accreditation have positively affected careers service provision in business schools, as now most of them invest resources to ensure that careers services teams are appropriately staffed and able to provide effective services to their students. Career services deliver one-to-one coaching sessions and a portfolio of workshops on various themes: from job search, CV and cover letter preparation to mock interviews, networking and negotiating your salary. They also organise on-campus recruitment fairs or companies' presentations and manage databases and web portals on which companies post opportunities for students and the alumni community.

Here are a few tips on how you can evaluate the careers services function of a business school.

- Read through the statistics regarding post-graduation jobs and starting salaries. Many business schools publish data on employment and salaries on their website and in the programme literature. In addition, most rankings contain data on post-graduation salaries and career development. Healthy data will give you an indication of the effectiveness of the school and careers services team in placing graduates.
- Ensure that the careers services team has links with the recruiters in which you are interested. Schools have a tendency to specialise in one or more sectors, which are usually aligned with the key strengths of their faculty. You can enquire about corporates which recruit directly from the school through on-campus fairs or presentations. If you already know which companies you may be targeting at the end of your MBA, it may be worth looking on the career pages of their website for a list of business schools they normally select students from.
- Evaluate how well the career services team is resourced by checking the ratio of staff to students. Enquire about the availability of workshops and one-to-one sessions throughout the year.
- If you are an experienced professional looking to take a PT MBA or an EMBA, ensure that the school has dedicated members of career services staff who focus on PT MBA or EMBA students. It is also important to confirm that the career services provision has been designed to enable you to benefit from an adequate number of networking opportunities.
- Investigate how long after graduation you will be able to use the career services resources. Having the opportunity to access them as an alumnus will be an important benefit.

IE (Instituto de Empresa) Business School

Founded in 1973, IE Business School has been offering outstanding business programmes for more than 30 years, in both Spanish and English, and is recognised as one of the world's top business schools, consistently highly ranked in the international press. In addition, it is fully recognised by the world's three leading accreditation agencies, AACSB, EQUIS and AMBA.

Its mission is to educate business leaders through programmes based on the core values of global focus, entrepreneurial spirit, social responsibility and a humanistic approach.

Recognised as one of the most international schools in the world, IE Business School has an urban campus in Madrid, Spain, and a faculty of more than 400 professors who teach students from over 90 countries on its master's, PhD and executive education programmes.

IE Business School's main campus consists of 17 buildings and is situated in the heart of Madrid's financial district, a strategic location that is very easily accessed via public transport.

IE Business School shapes leaders who promote innovation and change in organisations, equipping directors with an entrepreneurial mindset that generates employment, wealth and social wellbeing. IE students use innovative online and presential learning formats, including the IE Communities platform, where they exchange knowledge and experiences with 40,000 IE graduates who currently hold management positions in some 100 countries.

Catering to the needs of both the future and the recent graduate through to the seasoned executive, and covering a range of formats to suit their students' personal and professional commitments, IE offers a variety of programmes which prepare professionals for whatever challenges the future may bring, regardless of their time constraints or professional background. For more information, candidates can contact one of the 20 IE offices worldwide.

5

Estimating the costs and funding your MBA

In Chapter 2 we discussed the financial and personal rewards gained from undertaking an MBA. It is not a mystery that, in addition to the benefits, MBA programmes involve costs that must be accurately quantified when you are preparing yourself for the big financial and emotional investment associated with it. It is important for you to consider your finances carefully, to ensure that undertaking an MBA is the best decision for you.

It may be an unpleasant surprise for you to hear that the number of scholarships is small. Or, to be more precise, there are several grants offered by business schools and external organisations, but this figure is far lower than the number of students competing for scholarships. In addition, if you are taking a part-time or executive programme, the funding available through scholarships is minimal.

The good news is that most people are able to afford MBAs through alternative means, such as competitive loans combined with personal savings and remuneration from MBA internships or in-company projects (see p.14). If you are thinking of studying a PT MBA while working, obtaining financial support from your employer may also be an option. Most schools offer flexible payment plans that allow students to spread the payment over a longer period. It is worth enquiring about payment plans as the information may not always be clearly published on the school's website and sometimes it may enable you to pay for the tuition fees without taking out a loan.

Regardless of your choice of a full-time or part-time programme, putting together a realistic plan or budget, researching funding sources and meeting financial aid application deadlines are all crucial steps in the preparation process.

Visa considerations

If you plan to study for your MBA overseas and require a student visa, you also need to consider that in some countries visa regulations require students to demonstrate that they have sufficient funds for tuition fees and maintenance for themselves and any dependants.

Financial awareness and planning are also one of the areas that schools may test at application or interview stage: schools are always happy to provide you with information and advice on funding avenues; however, they also expect students to be prepared and committed to pay their tuition fees, or provide a strong and well-documented case for needs-based scholarships.

Quantify the costs

Where you study obviously affects the tuition costs you will pay for your course. Here are a few aspects to consider when you are planning your budget or deciding which MBA to take.

- Generally top schools have the highest tuition fees because they need to offer competitive rates of pay to retain their first-class faculty.
- Tuition fees for FT MBAs in the US are higher than in Europe and Asia.
- PT MBA and distance-learning programmes are normally cheaper than FT MBAs. EMBAs at top schools are usually priced at a similar level to FT MBAs.
- A global EMBA may involve a particularly heavy financial commitment, but some costs (such as books, reading materials, some meals and accommodation) may be included in the programme fee.

Tuition fees are just one of the costs you need to account for. Other items to add to your budget include:

- accommodation
- food
- transport
- utility bills
- books and academic materials
- photocopying and printing
- medical and health insurance and related expenses
- social activities
- relocation costs for you and eventually your family
- flights and other costs for international trips
- student visas.

The cost of social activities should not be underestimated especially if you are planning to study for an MBA in a major global city. Being involved in the student community and taking up any networking opportunities is a very important part of the MBA experience, but this means that you need to appropriately plan for the additional burden on your budget.

Moreover, if you are assessing cost-benefits of different FT MBA programmes, you may consider your foregone salary in the return on investment evaluation. For example, if you are earning $35,000 per year and you expect a pay rise of 5% in the coming year, your forgone salary will be $36,750 if you take a one-year FT MBA or $71,750 if you enrol on a two-year FT MBA. This amount needs to be added to the tuition fees and the other expenses. Obviously a two-year programme has a more significant impact on your budget than shorter MBAs both for the higher costs and for the forgone earnings.

Financial information and an estimate of the main costs are available on the websites of most business schools. Here we give some examples of tuition fees and living expenses as published by some popular business schools in the US and Europe.

Harvard FT MBA class of 2013: tuition fees and average estimated expenses (24-month programme)

Year 1	Single	Married/DP (domestic partnership)	Married/DP with one child	Married/DP with two children
Tuition	$51,200	$51,200	$51,200	$51,200
University Health Services Fee*	$1,186	$3,004	$3,806	$4,210
Blue Cross/Blue Shield (12 months)**	$1,834	$4,518	$6,068	$6,846
Program Support Fee***	$6,390	$6,390	$6,390	$6,390
Room & Utilities (9 months)	$10,800	$16,362	$21,114	$21,114
Board, Personal, Other (9 months)****	$12,590	$16,326	$20,822	$27,040
Total (for Year 1 only)	$84,000	$97,800	$109,400	$116,800

*The University Health Services Fee is obligatory regardless of your health insurance status.
**The BC/BS expense may be waived upon proof of health insurance coverage.
***Fee includes expenses for books, cases, (web-based) course materials, and other materials you receive in your courses. This fee also remains constant, unless you leave for more than one term.
****This number is an estimate based on the experiences of most MBA students. Your actual personal expenses may be higher or lower.
Please note that eligibility for federal student aid is based on the single student budget.
Source: www.hbs.edu/mba/admissions/costsummary.html.

INSEAD FT MBA class of September 2011 and January 2012: tuition fees and average estimated expenses

	Singapore	Fontainebleau
Tuition	€56,000	€56,000
Other academic expenditures (books, etc.)	€800	€800
Student Council fees	€100	€100
Business Foundations Programme (optional)	€1,500	€1,500
Language course fees per period (if applicable)	€500	€500
Laptop (optional)	€1,500	€1,500
Accommodation (includes utilities, charges, insurance)	€8,500	€9,000
Meals	€4,700	€5,300
Local transport (Singapore) or car leasing (Fontainebleau)	€530	€1,800–€6,000
Telephone	€750	€820
Personal insurance for the year	€580	€560
Miscellaneous (excludes leisure)	€1,500	€1,500
Hardware, software (optional)	€500	€550
Travel for exchange and job search (optional)	€2,000	€1,900
Total	€79,460	€81,830

London Business School FT MBA class of 2012: tuition fees and average estimated expenses

Estimated expenses for 18 months	Single
Tuition	£53,900
Accommodation	£26,316
Food (excluding restaurants)	£6,588
Utilities and council tax	£4,446
Phone and internet	£666
Leisure (cinemas, restaurants, pubs, etc.)	£6,588
Total (for Year 1 only)	£98,504

Please note that the figures are correct and up-to-date as based on information published on the schools' website as of September 2011.

You may have noticed that the expense items included in each table vary from school to school. We have developed a checklist which will help you account for most of the expenses you may incur and budget accordingly for the programmes or schools that you are planning to attend (see p.91).

ESCP Europe Business School

ESCP Europe Business School, located in Paris, London, Berlin, Madrid and Turin, offers a wide range of graduate business education programmes. Our European EMBA has been ranked number 7 worldwide for career progression by the *Financial Times*, and number 4 for international experience.

The European EMBA is a modular programme designed to meet the schedule of busy executives. Business success and career progression are the key goals of our EMBA.

Participants achieve these goals through a rich transformational experience, including:

- soft skill development such as leadership and people management
- creating strong relationships with a diverse international group of fellow class members
- building a network from among our 35,000 alumni worldwide.

The programme curriculum is made up of four distinct parts:

- nine core courses: master the fundamentals of effective management
- 12 electives: choose from a portfolio of over 30 topics, including both soft and hard skills such as leadership and people management
- five international seminars: experience the business context specific to Europe, Asia and the Americas
- International Consulting Project: design a real-case executive analysis in a multicultural team.

With 125 permanent faculty members, presence throughout Europe and close ties with partner schools around the world, a highly international student body and programmes in which the focus is on the participant, ESCP Europe is the choice for people looking for a unique EMBA experience.

ESCP Europe's EMBA gives participants the opportunity to study with 100 executives from 25 different countries.

Data and contacts

Class of 2012 overview: Class Size 110; **Percentage international:** 100%; **Number of nationalities:** 25; **Average years work experience:** 10

Start Date: January; **Programme duration:** 18 months; **Tuition fee:** €51,000

Entry requirements: min. years of work experience 5; significant international exposure; university degree; min. TOEFL computer based score 250; Min. TOEFL paper based score 600; Min. IELTS Band 7

www.escpeurope.eu/mba

Paris campus: Jeanne Weckler – jweckler@escpeurope.eu; **London campus:** Linda Brunello – ukexeced@escpeurope.eu; **Madrid campus:** Natalia Andia – solicitudes@escpeurope.eu; **Berlin campus:** Anne Ulbricht – mba@escpeurope.eu; **Torino campus:** Giorgia Bava – infomba@escpeurope.eu

Case study

AN EMBA gives back to the community

In December 2009, Lindsey Nefesh-Clarke graduated with her executive MBA from ESCP Europe. In the same year, she was awarded the prestigious Student of the Year Award by the Association of MBAs (AMBA), which recognises the broad scope, international attitude and leadership of today's most outstanding MBA scholars. "It was an intense, incredibly fast-paced and challenging 18-month course," she recalls, but the impact was immediate. "No sooner had I started the EMBA than I was putting into practice the business and managerial insights from my classes and seeing tangible results in my work," Lindsey says.

Entrepreneurial ideas

Lindsey's "workplace" is her own entrepreneurial project, the Women's Worldwide Web (www.womensworldwideweb.org). It's an online philanthropy platform dedicated to women's empowerment through microfinance, education, mentoring and networking. "I worked on the business plan of the Women's Worldwide Web during my EMBA. It was developed within the frame of the 'International Consulting Project', a 12-month team project which is a milestone in the ESCP Europe programme," Lindsey explains. "In my case, it was an ideal opportunity to work on the business plan for the Women's Worldwide Web."

The platform's diverse range of programmes focus on education, microfinance, entrepreneurialism, and women's human rights. Both monetary and non-monetary support and exchange is possible through the Women's Worldwide Web. Visitors are invited to support home-grown development initiatives across the globe, as donators or lenders.

The return on investment of the EMBA

"I committed to the executive MBA at ESCP Europe because I wanted to apply business, management and leadership skills to strengthen my work in the humanitarian field. I also wanted to explore the possible synergies between corporate social responsibility and humanitarian work, and to move into the field of microfinance," Lindsey says.

Lindsey is conscious of the impact her time at ESCP Europe, studying for her EMBA, has had on her abilities. "I think one of the greatest advantages to having an EMBA degree is the sense of opportunity it affords – it radically opens up one's professional horizons – and the skills and confidence that it provides to embrace those opportunities."

ESCP
EUROPE
PARIS LONDON BERLIN MADRID TORINO
BUSINESS SCHOOL
EXPAND YOUR WORLD
escpeurope.eu/mba
European Executive M
Programme
Take your international career to
next level
The European Executive MBA Prograr
provides a transformational experienc
high-potential, ambitious executives
international career aspirations.
• course tracks available on 5 European campuses
• 5 international seminars
• participants from 25 countries
• peer learning and networking
Register to meet us at an information session on escpeurope.eu/mba.
Contact: Jeanne Weckler
jweckler@escpeurope.eu / + 33 (0) 1 49 23 27
ESCP Europe on the social networks:
http://www.escpeurope.eu/news/social-me
You Tube
Chambre de commerce
et d'industrie de Paris
EFMD
EQUIS
ACCREDITED
Accredited by
Association
of MBAs
AACSB

Tuition fees and living expenses checklist

	Amount
Tuition fees	
Accommodation	
Utility bills	
Local transport	
Flights and accommodation for overseas assignments	
Meals	
Books and reading materials	
Photocopying and printing	
Computer, laptop and software	
Medical, health and personal insurance	
Visa	
Relocation costs	
Leisure/social activities	
Forgone salary (FT MBA)	
TOTAL	

Funding your MBA

Loan schemes

Loans are a popular way to fund MBA programmes as students and lenders look at the post-MBA salary increment as the repayment vehicle. After the credit crunch the number of loan schemes available for postgraduate education has obviously decreased and students worldwide have had problems in obtaining loans or the exact amount they had asked for. Recently the situation has improved and there are again more products available on the market.

Loans as well as scholarships usually have strict eligibility requirements in terms of nationality, residence and type of programme (full or part time). You can start gathering information by checking or discussing loan schemes with the relevant schools' representatives or financial aid office; they can point out a few products for which you would be eligible. Many major banks work with top business schools in their country, offering well-established loan schemes to their students. You can also check with your own bank if it can offer you any deals.

Some business schools have also come up with innovative solutions to solve the issues faced by international students in accessing loans for an MBA outside their home country. For example, in 2006 INSEAD started Prodigy Finance, a scheme based on community funding in which individual alumni fund MBA students and the loan does not require a co-signer. A couple of years ago in the US, Harvard created a private student loan scheme

An example of funding options

Lamar Richardson, Director of Financial Aid at Duke's Fuqua School of Business tells us about the school's MBA funding options:

> *"Many loans require students to have co-signers based in the US, which may pose a challenge to many students residing outside of the US. Our commitment includes assisting all international students with competitive financial aid arrangements. We have worked hard to find no-cosigner loan options for their entire studies and committed substantial school resources to guarantee favourable terms for the international student loan programme.*
>
> *"US-based no-cosigner loan programmes for international students began in 2000. As there has been little history with which banks can judge the credit-worthiness of such programmes, lenders have always required us to substantively guarantee defaults on these loans. Currently, we are partnered with Coastal Federal Credit Union, and we were able to negotiate a very favourable loan rate for our students. As a way to make this possible, Fuqua is required to guarantee 100% of the loan defaults. Therefore, as students invest in their education through loans, so too does Fuqua.*
>
> *"On the scholarship side of our financial assistance opportunities, every admitted applicant is eligible for the Merit Scholarship. Recipients are selected by an Admissions Merit Scholarship Committee. The criteria for selection are prior academic achievement, demonstrated qualities of leadership, involvement in the community, extra-curricular activities and professional accomplishments. These awards are for the two-year duration of the MBA programme and range from partial to full tuition. Generally, Fuqua's merit scholarships*

are awarded on a two-year basis to enable applicants to plan for the entire cost of a Fuqua education. The merit scholarship awards are made independent of determining a student's eligibility for student loans.

"The Center for the Advancement of Social Entrepreneurship (CASE) also provides several assistance programmes to reduce financial burden and attract the most talented students dedicated to making a positive difference in the world."

through the Harvard University Employees' Credit Union, a local, member-based not-for-profit organisation. Most top schools in Europe and the US have partnered with local or international banks to offer accessible loans regardless of the students' nationality. Most of these loan programmes require a co-signer who is a citizen of the country of study. However, schools such as Chicago and Wharton offer schemes which do not require a US co-signer; specific information regarding these programmes is made available after admission.

US citizens

US citizens studying in their country or in most top European business schools can access a number of loan schemes to fund a significant amount of the costs of full-time or part-time programmes. For example, the Direct Loan Program, in which students borrow directly from the US Department of Education through the school; and Sallie Mae Smart Option Student Loan, which enables students to borrow 100% of the amount required to cover school-certified costs of education.

UK and European citizens

UK and European Union (EU) citizens resident in the UK can access the Professional Career Development Loan scheme for full-time and part-time programmes in the UK. In addition to being ordinarily resident in the UK and having unlimited right to remain in the UK, students are required to work in the EU countries, Iceland, and Norway after completing their MBA. This loan does not provide a huge amount (currently between £300 and £10,000) and therefore would need to be used in combination with other sources. Interests is not charged during the study period and later it is charged at a fixed rate depending on the bank administering it. The repayment period starts one month after graduation and you have up to five years to repay the loan.

As you would normally do when comparing loans, ensure that you make an informed decision and you are fully aware of interest rates, lender or administration fees, repayment periods and early repayment charges. In addition, availability, eligibility and terms and conditions of loan schemes frequently change, and we strongly recommend that you check the latest available information with the lenders or the business schools.

Scholarships

All institutions offer a number of scholarships to their MBA students. Some are designed to support students with high potential but in financial need (for example, students from developing countries). Others aim to increase the number of graduates from under-represented categories (for example, ethnic minority students; women; representatives from non-traditional MBA sectors such as the not-for-profit). There are also merit-based scholarships which are awarded to students with an exceptional leadership potential and an outstanding record at academic and professional level. Very rarely these grants finance the costs of the programme in full; in most cases they cover a certain percentage of the tuition fees and maintenance. Usually admitted students are automatically considered for the available scholarships, but sometimes schools may require a separate application and an additional essay or other piece of work.

The majority of the scholarship schemes are designed for FT MBA students only. There is little financial aid for PT MBA or EMBA students; the general assumption is that full-time students have greater financial need than part-timers, who do not lose their source of income. The limited grants offered by schools for their part-time students target primarily under-represented participants, such as women and professionals working in the public or no-profit sector. They are usually partial scholarships that cover part of the tuition fees for the programme.

The level of funding is higher in US schools, which can rely on generous donations from students, alumni and supporters. According to the *Financial Times*, at Harvard almost 50% of the class receives need-based scholarships. European schools have worked very hard to catch up with their US counterparts on endowment and scholarship funding, but there is still a big gap in terms of resources.

In addition to the business schools' own scholarships, there are grants offered by external bodies. Some of these organisations are international and award scholarships to students from different nationalities who can study their MBA at leading schools in a wide range of countries (for example, the Rotary Foundation and the Richard Metzler and Roland Berger AMCF Scholarships); others have a more regional focus and target specific nationalities. If you are a national from a country outside the UK, you could also investigate forms of financial support which may be offered by your government.

New legislation to be introduced by the UK government will put an end to nationality-based scholarships.

Working while studying

If you are not willing to take up the big financial burden of an FT MBA, part-time, EMBA or distance-learning programmes are good options to fulfil your graduate management education needs and keep your income. However, you need to be aware that taking an MBA qualification while working requires a strong focus, commitment and the ability to juggle work, study and private life. In addition, the workload and the pressure may not enable you to take full advantage of the social and networking opportunities offered by the school (see p.38 for the key advantages and disadvantages of the different types of programme).

For FT MBA students, working part time while studying may not be feasible. One-year programmes are usually too intensive to allow any part-time jobs; two-year programmes may be more flexible during the second year. Most schools would discourage you from taking up any part-time jobs by saying that it could have a negative impact on your academic performance; or that you could prevent yourself from fully participating in the networking opportunities offered by the school community. If you decide to work part time during your FT MBA, ensure that the quality of your academic work does not suffer, be prepared to prioritise it and take the extra pressure off if you are unable to cope.

Students can also earn while on their MBA through the internship or consulting project that they undertake as part of the curriculum and which is often remunerated by the hosting organisation.

Employer support

Most organisations have training and development policies in place and may sponsor work-related continuing education for employees. Employer support can include financial sponsorship for tuition fees and/or other costs, study or sabbatical leave and access to company resources and career opportunities. Students taking PT MBA, EMBA or distance-learning programmes are more likely to look for support from their companies. Before the global economic downturn a significant percentage of these students were sponsored; some companies used their training and development budgets to attract and retain their best talent. Unfortunately, company sponsorship has become very tight recently.

Securing employer sponsorship is certainly not easy and you will need to be prepared to face a lot of resistance; it is not uncommon to receive negative answers when the perspective of an MBA is outlined. In most situations, obtaining employer support requires research, time, perseverance and a good grasp of the internal decision mechanisms for sponsorship approval. Given the huge investment that supporting an MBA involves, your employer will thoroughly question and assess your motivations and the value that the MBA would bring to the organisation. Especially at a time of tight financial and staff resources, you need to clearly justify why they should give you funding and/or time off for business school.

Students who have been successful in winning the case for sponsorship have normally started the process by information gathering and fact finding from different sources.

- First of all, it is important that you develop in-depth knowledge of the key features and benefits of the particular programme(s) and school(s) that you want to attend; programme curriculum and structure, starting dates, attendance, faculty, networking opportunities and other tangible benefits for employers. Schools are usually very helpful in providing unique selling points which you can use for your case.
- In addition, it is useful to speak to students or alumni who have prepared business cases for company support; you can meet them at MBA events and information sessions or sometimes the admissions staff may be able to put you in touch with students or alumni who have approached their employers for funding.

- You should also investigate if there have been previous cases of support for MBAs or other postgraduate degree programmes, or if there are already existing relationships with business schools for leadership training and development or other projects. Your networking skills and organisational knowledge will help you obtain data, which perhaps is fragmented and spread within several departments.
- Your background research will also focus on the mechanisms and stakeholders involved in the decision making on corporate sponsorship. The internal knowledge will enable you to devise an effective strategy to approach your employer targeting the right people. Based on your individual circumstances and the way sponsorship operates in your company, you must decide on whether it is convenient to approach your employer before or after securing admission to the MBA.

If you have built solid relationships with your seniors and the relevant decision makers in your organisation, sometimes it may work to make your case and obtain buy-in through informal channels before requesting the official seal of approval for sponsorship. In other instances, you may need to go through a staged process and present a persuasive case to different people within the organisation (your line manager, human resources, senior management, etc.).

When you prepare your case for employer support, you must analyse and include the following points:

- your own needs and your organisation's needs
- the benefits for you and your team or department and the organisation as a whole
- the return on investment for your employer
- why a particular programme and school
- the type and level of support required from your employer
- your plan to ensure that work deadlines and commitments will be met.

Need analysis

You can start from the analysis of the objectives of your team or department and the challenges in achieving them. You should be able to demonstrate a solid knowledge of current trends or issues in your sector and area of work. It is important to show how your role fits within the department and contributes to achieve the overall objectives of the organisation. You can certainly refer to development needs that may have been identified through formal performance appraisals. It is helpful to give an indication of where you see yourself within the organisation in the medium and long term. However, be aware of your audience if you are speaking to direct managers who may be intimidated by your MBA ambitions.

Benefits

It is crucial that you think of the benefits for you as functional to improving your performance and effectiveness in achieving business goals. Referring to the programme features and content that address your employer's needs and developmental objectives will be very effective; for example, you could find links to specific modules and faculty areas of expertise.

Return on investment for your employer

You must prove that the MBA can bring back a tangible return on investment for the organisation. If you are aware of specific projects that your company is undertaking to improve business performance and productivity, you can give examples of how particular elements of the programme will add value; for instance, refer to assignments or projects which would help you investigate solutions to business issues and obtain feedback from faculty and experienced peers. You could also highlight how the networking opportunities may assist your company in winning new clients or expanding into new markets.

Why a particular programme and school

You may have already decided on a particular programme or school, or have a few names in mind. In any case, you will clearly outline the unique advantages of your target institution(s) and programme(s) for you and the organisation. It is important that you have all the correct information about programme timetable, curriculum, etc. Also, be prepared to answer to some of the objections that they make and present your counter-arguments against other options which they may suggest.

Required employer support

You should outline very clearly the type of support that you are seeking in terms of time, funding or access to company resources. For example, you may need additional time off to attend weekly classes and study leave to prepare for exams. Financial sponsorship could be requested for tuition fees, accommodation, travel costs and books and reading materials. However, you should consider that full funding is rare; most students taking part-time programmes receive partial sponsorship for the tuition fees and sometimes a refund of some of the programme costs. Moreover, the programme may require that you have access to the company's information and resources for project work and assignments. This can be presented as one of the ways in which you can give back to your employer by using some of your time on the programme to tackle issues of particular relevance to your organisation. At the same time, obtaining this type of support could give you exposure to areas of the organisation in which you are not normally involved.

Work deadlines and commitments

One of the objections from your employer could be the risk that key tasks or projects fall behind due to conflicting academic deadlines. It is critical that you have a clear plan on how you will manage your time and team to ensure that there will be minimum impact on key deliverables.

Finally, be prepared to negotiate and accept that your employer may set different conditions for the corporate sponsorship; for example, performance targets or lock-in clauses, which require you to reimburse the funding if you leave the company before a certain stipulated period. Ensure that you are able to commit to what is expected of you.

Salary sacrifice

Salary sacrifice could be a funding vehicle for UK tax payers, and salary sacrifice agreements are usually set up with the help of a tax consultant. There might be other countries in which there are equivalent systems and if you are a non-UK tax payer it could be worth exploring this with the tax office in your country.

The "salary sacrifice" is a contractual arrangement between the employee and the company which changes the terms and conditions regarding pay (www.hmrc.gov.uk/specialist/salary_sacrifice.htm). Based on this arrangement, the employee sacrifices part of the future salary over a period of time in return for the employer's agreement to pay the tuition fees in full or in part. The mutual benefit consists of the fact that neither you nor your employer pays National Insurance contributions on the amount which is sacrificed.

However, when entering a salary sacrifice agreement it is essential to understand carefully what it actually means in practical terms. As an employee this scheme may have an impact on future rights to higher earnings, pension schemes, entitlement to Working Tax Credits or Child Tax Credits, state pension or other benefits such as statutory maternity pay.

Most students fund their MBA with personal savings and a combination of the above sources, which are matched in accordance with individual circumstances. Having a clear picture of all the costs involved will help you budget and hopefully avoid the situation of finding yourself short of funding at times of strong academic pressure. Some graduates have also been successful in obtaining partial refunds from their post-MBA employer. In most situations, the salary increase that students experience after completing the MBA enables them to repay the costs of their studies and schools do their best to support their students in obtaining good jobs.

Athens University of Economics and Business

ATHENS UNIVERSITY *of* ECONOMICS & BUSINESS
mbainternational

MBA International at a glance

MBA International is a world-class programme particularly suited in the global, dynamically changing, and technology-driven business environment. The programme, located in Athens, Greece, and offered exclusively in English, is accredited by AMBA, the Association of MBAs, and attracts students from more than 20 countries. Participants of the programme can select, besides the general business administration track, one of the five majors offered, thus gaining additional knowledge in an area of interest, or facilitating a career switch.

Two of the outstanding features of the programme are the Personal Skills Development Program (PSDP) and the Immersion/Field Study Project. The PSDP is a year-long programme that runs in parallel with the other courses, and allows students to improve their "soft skills", such as stress management, time management, leadership, team-building, and emotional intelligence, through a variety of pedagogic activities.

The Immersion Project, that can involve a field study consulting project, and international internship, a business plan for a student initiated venture or another relevant team or individual project, is a much sought-after component of our programme.

Besides the very broad curriculum, students participate in a number of extra-curricular activities that aim to develop further their personal or professional interests, as well as their networking, such as company days, career days, business games and competitions, athletic events, etc.

... anywhere in the world

We are pursuing our strategy of going global by expanding the career opportunities of our students and alumni beyond the Mediterranean rim and the Balkans, since many of our current students and alumni come from outside the region and a large number of our Greek and local students are interested in building global careers.

The MBA International Career Office offers a comprehensive range of services including on-campus events, career fairs, online job and internship postings, and interviews and workshops with representatives from multinational companies. Our main target is to enhance the opportunities for international careers and internships by building a network of companies and organisations interested in our top-quality graduates.

Additional information about the programme, curriculum, scholarships, etc., can be found at www.imba.aueb.gr.

Build your own MBA

Most of the leading business schools worldwide have now personalised their MBAs and tailored them to meet the specific needs and goals of each individual student. Focusing on the individual client rather than on what can be taught means that students are not only satisfied but get much more mileage from the time and money spent at business school. They also face better career prospects since they can stand out better in the global job market amongst the sea of undistinguishable MBA graduates. But how has AUEB managed to successfully personalise its MBA International Program to its diverse pool of students?

Simply, in five main ways:

- flexible study (full or part time)
- numerous major and electives
- supple capstone requirement (field study project, personal business project, CSR project, academic dissertation, internship or simply additional electives)
- personal skills development
- one-to-one coaching in the career office and personalised career targeting through the business advisory council, industrial training programmes and company days with global corporate leaders.

However, the most important aspect that enables personalisation at AUEB is a philosophy and tradition that can be traced back to the teachings of Socrates, Plato, and Aristotle in as Ancient Greece. This philosophy transcends to modern business and life and blends the West with the East in producing a unique culture, ethos and wisdom which is characterised by openness, rationality, reason on the basis of evidence, fairness and the promotion of leadership coupled with excellence. This characteristic of the programme can be with international conferences, such as the recent "Management in a Changing World: Lessons from Ancient East and West Philosophy". This event attracted leading authorities from ivy league schools to discuss developments and innovative approaches to management and leadership inspired by or in any other way enlightened by ancient Eastern and Western philosophies. The India-funded Chair of International Entrepreneurship and the Confucius Institute, both recently established at AUEB, ensure the continuation of a tradition lasting 3,000 years, which wants Athens to be the often unsettled hub of creation, innovation and cross-fertilisation between the West and the East.

6

Understanding the admissions process and planning your strategy

The number of applications to MBA programmes increase year on year and inevitably this will result in more competition. As more and more candidates are vying for the number of same places, many will unfortunately be unsuccessful in securing a place on their first choice of school. In this chapter we will explore the admissions process and explain how to plan your strategy and how you can use this guide to help you tailor your approach to the schools of your choice.

Understanding the admissions process and decisions

Choosing a programme or a school is not the only time-consuming task in the journey which will take you to the right MBA. Applying to a top business school is also a lengthy and laborious process which requires submission of several documents and, if you are successful at application stage, at least one interview. Business schools have devised competitive admissions procedures to select their students. They aim to recruit candidates who are a good fit with the school's culture and ethos, who can contribute to the student and alumni community, and who have the strongest chances of securing a good position after graduation.

It is crucial that you are aware of what schools are looking for in prospective students and what they assess throughout the different stages of the admissions process. This will help develop your admissions strategy and present your case for the MBA more effectively.

No matter which school or programme you are applying to, admissions processes are designed to test and assess the candidates' abilities in several areas and to benchmark them against each other. Obviously in top schools you will compete with a wider and stronger pool of applicants.

Generally, any admissions process aims to evaluate candidates in four main areas.

- Core knowledge and skills: these includes academic and intellectual abilities; professional background and achievements; management experience and industry knowledge; international exposure.
- Soft skills and leadership potential: a strong emphasis is always placed on team skills, which are today considered one of the key attributes of successful leaders.
- Career objectives and motivations for taking the programme.
- Contribution to the class and the wider school community: schools are interested in candidates who can add value to the learning experience of their peers and to the student and alumni network.

The above skills and areas are assessed through the following requirements and elements of the application:

- application form
- academic transcripts
- GMAT® score (see Chapter 8 p.152 for more information)
- English ability (through a test if English is not your first language)
- essays
- references
- CV/résumé.

We will look at these elements of the application form in greater detail in Chapter 7.

> *"IE Business School looks for people who are change agents and willing to be future leaders in their areas of interest. We look for students who bring a diverse background and unique outlook into the classroom, different academic backgrounds, experiences, industry sectors and job functions."*
> *Lisa Bevill, Associate Director of Admissions, IE Business School*

The academic qualifications and grades combined with the GMAT® give the school an indication of the candidate's intellectual power and ability to perform academically. Professional experience and industry knowledge provide the basis to contribute to class discussions. A successful career track also demonstrates leadership potential and ensures that the candidate can attract prospective MBA recruiters.

Schools would normally adopt a holistic approach and consider all the different parts of the application before making a decision on whether to invite you to interview. However, sometimes there are minimum thresholds (for example, GMAT® score or years of work experience) which must be met to be considered for the programme. FT MBAs typically require at least three years of postgraduate work experience, while most EMBA programmes expect at least five, including some management experience. Regarding the GMAT®, schools do not always set a minimum score required for admission, but the GMAT® average of the class will give you a good indication of how competitive a particular school is.

Clearly schools do not weight the different elements of the application in the same way; for example, some place a strong emphasis on the GMAT® score and academic qualifications, while others score candidates with managerial responsibilities higher. What schools consider management experience may not be consistent and therefore leads to different assessments; while some of them accept a wide definition which includes the management of people, budgets, projects and clients, others focus on people and budget management only.

When selecting MBA students, admissions teams always aim to recruit a diverse group of people who are able to learn from each other. Class diversity is expressed in terms of nationalities and industry sectors represented as well as participation of women and minority groups. On the one hand, coming from an under-represented category will give you a competitive edge towards other candidates, on the other hand, if you belong to a group or sector which is traditionally well represented among MBA students (for example, financial services, consulting and IT/telecommunications) you will need to work harder to bring out your differentiating factor.

Do business schools have quotas?

Many students believe that schools use informal quota systems in MBA recruitment. Regardless of all the myths surrounding the existence of quotas, it is clear that it would neither be beneficial for the school nor the students if the class did not express a balanced representation of different groups. Students want to learn with peers from different backgrounds and a diverse class positively impacts on their learning experience, in addition to programme rankings. Although quotas may not correctly describe the mechanisms to ensure that the class is as diverse as possible, it is understandable that admissions teams carefully monitor the overall class profile and raise the bar for groups from whom they may have received a huge number of applications. Later on in this chapter, we will explore in detail how to highlight your unique profile in order to differentiate yourself from other candidates.

The application review stage

In terms of the admissions process, applications are usually reviewed separately by at least two people who are normally members of the admissions team. In the US, some schools have started involving current students in the evaluation of application files, while in Europe current students and alumni are involved in the interview stage only. When screening the applications the reviewers have three options:

1. shortlist the candidate for interview
2. reject the candidate
3. state that they are undecided.

When both reviewers agree on shortlist or reject, the outcome of the review is very clear and the candidate receives an interview notification or a reject letter. If the reviewers have a different view on the application, there are further discussions and sometimes the application file is forwarded to a senior member of the admissions team, faculty or careers services, depending on the nature of the doubts expressed by the reviewers. Schools which are particularly competitive may decide to keep those applicants whose review decisions are not straightforward on a waiting list until they have a better idea of the candidate pool. In these circumstances, the final review decision may be delayed until the very last available dates.

If shortlisted, candidates are invited to attend interviews at the school or in locations close to their country. Depending on the institutions and the programme, interviews can be with a member of the admissions team, alumni, students and members of faculty. We will discuss interviews in Chapter 9.

Final decision on the application

After the interview, schools make their final decision on the candidate. Sometimes this is based exclusively on the interviewers' recommendations, which are analysed and confirmed by the admissions staff. In some schools there are admissions committees that meet regularly for the final evaluation of candidates who have been interviewed. Admissions committees can have different compositions; normally representatives from admissions, careers services, faculty and programme management are invited to participate. Members of the admissions committee are briefed by the admissions staff on the recommendations from the review and interview stages.

At this point, candidates who received strong positive feedback from both reviewers and interviewers are normally admitted. Candidates who went through the process on weaker grounds may be rejected straight away, or discussed again at a later stage of the admissions cycle, once the school has a full picture of the candidate pool and the acceptance rate of offers which it had previously made. In these circumstances schools may issue waitlist offers or letters explaining that the decision is still pending.

Sometimes schools make offers subject to specific conditions, which include retaking the GMAT® or TOEFL (Test of English as a Foreign Language) test, or submitting additional documents and evidence. We look at possible outcomes of the application process in detail in Chapter 10.

In most business schools your application and profile will be evaluated by different people playing various roles in the admissions process. If not decision makers, the admissions directors are always key influencers in the offer decisions.

Here are some guidelines on how to prepare for the toughest admissions process, identify your "X factor" and market yourself to the schools.

Timing your application

Business schools start recruiting their MBA students well in advance of the programme start date. For FT MBA, schools usually organise application deadlines according to three or four application rounds or stages, with the earliest usually in October and the latest in March or April if the MBA starts in September. Each round or stage has a separate deadline and they make their shortlist and admit decisions after assessing and benchmarking all applications received by that date.

Typically, rolling admissions are used for EMBA, PT MBA and distance-learning programmes. Rolling admissions processes means that the admissions decisions are made as soon as the applications are received, on the basis of first come, first served. There are also hybrid systems where schools establish a set of rounds, but they still process and decide on the applications as soon as they receive them.

Preparing an application for an MBA at a top school is a time-intensive task and you should start by researching programme features and school culture, which also requires time (see p.110). Most candidates start the application process at least six months before the application deadline that they are targeting. The average preparation period before starting the actual MBA application is between nine and 24 months.

The timing must take into account the preparation required for the GMAT® (see p.178) or any English language test. If you are preparing multiple applications, you need to be particularly efficient and accurate in managing all the tasks, possibly avoiding sending to a school, essays containing your motivation to attend an MBA somewhere else!

Once you have developed a good understanding of what is expected of candidates, you can start building the different blocks of the application. It is difficult to estimate with precision how long you will need to get everything prepared. There are some factors to take into account:

- if you are organised, focused and enjoy writing, it could be quite quick
- if you are not a native English speaker or are not familiar with behavioural questions and general management jargon, it may take you longer.

In our experience, it is difficult to prepare a good complete application in less than four weeks. Normally candidates review their essays and application form a few times to obtain the clear and polished product that they will submit to the schools.

Schools always recommend that you apply early in the admissions cycle and seem to indicate that there are more chances to secure a place if you are one of their early applicants. Entry requirements are typically the same throughout the cycle, but many schools decide to make the majority of their offers early for logistics reasons; accepted candidates will have more time to organise their funding, visas and accommodation. In addition, if your background is very common among MBA candidates, an early application will stand a better chance to be shortlisted, while at the end of the cycle the admissions staff may raise the bar after receiving many applications of the same type.

However, it is also important to ensure that your application is ready. If you realise that you need more time to achieve a satisfactory GMAT® score or to write essays at the required standard, you should wait until you are fully prepared rather than apply early and submit a weak application. In addition, there are situations in which a few extra months may make your case for the MBA more compelling: for example, you have slightly less than three years of work experience and you are waiting to take up a more senior role or to complete a major project.

Occasionally, late candidates have better luck than early applicants. This may happen if the school has had a bad cycle and received fewer applications or acceptances than predicted. However, these circumstances are rare and not easy to anticipate, therefore it is strongly recommended that you apply as soon as you are ready.

Once you have submitted your application, for an FT MBA it takes on average four to five weeks to receive a notification on whether you have been invited to attend an interview. After the interview, you may still need to wait a few weeks to receive the notification of the final decision. On average, at most top schools it takes between 10 and 12 weeks to obtain the final admissions decision for an FT MBA application.

For EMBA, PT MBA or other flexible programmes the decision making is usually faster and, depending on the school, it could take between six and eight weeks for the final decision after you have submitted your application. Sometimes you may receive an invitation to attend an interview just a few days after sending your application documents.

Planning your strategy

We cannot emphasise enough the importance of having a clear strategy to obtain admission into the school you see matching best your career, development goals and ambitions. Applicants who are serious about getting into top MBA programmes start their preparation early, building their portfolio of skills and achievements to match the requirements of the school(s) they want to apply to. This is all done in parallel with preparing for the GMAT® and making yourself a desirable and attractive candidate (see p.111 for more on your unique selling points).

By "strategy" we mean a complete and well thought-out plan of step-by-step actions focused on building a relationship with the school(s) of your choice. From the initial contact with the school for information until the moment you accept an offer for a place on their programme, you need to be conscious and consistent in terms of the messages you convey.

Your strategic planning should be in the following three distinct stages.

Stage 1: Factual and information gathering

This entails building your portfolio of data researching and using all available sources such as websites, forums and discussions with the schools' admissions teams, current students, alumni, other applicants and faculty.

- Remember first impressions are the most important ones. Although schools admissions teams deal with hundreds of candidates every day, they start to build a profile for each and every candidate from the first point of contact with them, whether it is an online or email request for information or a query about the programme. The rule of thumb is never doing anything casual when it comes to your interaction with business schools you are seriously considering.

- Alumni and current students are another great source of information regarding the schools in which you are most interested. If you can find contacts through your professional network and/or via friends who may know alumni or students of the school(s) you are targeting. Having a conversation with some of these people could prove to be an invaluable source of information about the school's added value effect. Furthermore, a recommendation or letter/email of reference above and beyond your referees could work wonders towards you standing out from the crowd and getting accepted into these highly competitive courses.

Stage 2: Understanding the school's unique culture or "way of doing things"

It is important for you as a candidate to try to establish the clear as well as more intuitive sets of criteria the school is using to evaluate your application. It is equally important to understand the application process from beginning to end, ensuring you are gradually building a "portfolio" of yourself in the way the school wants to see it.

At this crucial stage you also need to be thinking about the GMAT® (see Chapter 8, p.178). Most schools do not appear to be asking for a minimum GMAT® score, and only present prospective applicants with a class average or class range. However, especially for degrees such as the FT MBA where competition for admission is really strong, top business schools use the GMAT® as one of the key benchmarking tools and sometimes you may need to achieve a score of around 700 to be a competitive candidate.

- The second stage is all about the "feel and touch" of the school(s) of your choice and your relationship building with them. Once you have spoken to students and alumni, thoroughly researched the programme, you then need to think about meeting the school and its representatives through any means available or offered. The usual way of engaging with a school directly is via information evenings, open/experience days. Different schools have different names for these events; however, their purpose is the same: inviting prospective candidates to visit the school and discover the unique benefits it offers to its students and alumni. As a prospective candidate you will be given the opportunity to speak to students, alumni staff and faculty. This will help you decide whether the school "feels" right for you and for your objectives and career vision.
- Schools attend a number of education fairs and other student recruitment events in the main cities around the world so you can find an event in a region near you. These interactions with the school are of critical importance, since they offer a great chance to get to know the school and get in touch with its culture. Your objective should be to talk to as many interested people as possible – across functions and roles – and build relationships with them to ascertain you are at the right place for your career, as well as have the right information to proceed with your application.

Stage 3: Starting the application process and carrying it out in the most thorough and professional way

Consult admissions teams in a non-intrusive and non-irritating way; tap into the wealth of information available from alumni and professional admissions experts as and when necessary. Remember that the school's people are there to help you with any information you may need in this long and time-consuming process; however, they are not there to be harassed, absorb your anxiety about your admission into the course of your choice, and manage your application completion process. This is your responsibility; they can only offer pointers from their perspective, as, when and if deemed necessary.

Here is a summary of our top tips when approaching the admissions process for competitive business schools.

- Start your application early, since it is a time-consuming process.
- Investigate the admissions criteria thoroughly and get an understanding of what the business school(s) of your choice is looking for when assessing candidates.
- Talk to people and get as much information as possible. Ensure that you speak to people with a formal role in the process; students and/or alumni with the experience of having successfully been through the application process; and the right advisers who will tell you what you need to know, as opposed what you want to hear. Ideally, you will have gained insights and information from all three different types of sources to maximise your chances of getting accepted into one of the top schools you apply for.

Understanding your unique selling points and competitive advantage

Now we come to the crux of it: do you have what it takes to be accepted to business school? Do you have the ability to communicate this through your application, convincing the school of your choice that you are one of the candidates they should be actively pursuing since you have a lot to add and contribute as well gain from the school's experience? Do you want to apply for a life and career changing experience?

Understanding what makes you special

The questions you need to ask yourself honestly and to which you also need to give equally honest answers are: What makes me special? What are the elements of my career and achievements so far that will make my profile unique in the eyes of admissions teams and help me secure a place at the best and most competitive schools? There is various criteria that you can use to assess yourself in order to answer these questions:

- demographics
- career profile

- achievement, motivation and track record of success
- personal vision and a realistic sense of achieving it
- contributions to community, society, extra curriculum activities/engagements and projects
- validation from others. Other individuals' belief in you is fundamental. This makes the tables turn to your advantage pretty quickly. References therefore are of critical importance towards landing a place at the top business school you are looking to apply.

Ideally you should see your references before they are submitted. If this is not possible we strongly suggest you work closely with your referees to ensure the references are constructive and portray you in the best possible light. Not having strong and supportive references will definitely undermine your chances of success.

The references, as well any supplementary recommendation of a potential alumnus or current student, add an invaluable edge to your application. In a nutshell, business schools are looking for competency, skills, diversity, ability and great vision. They are looking for a diverse background. It will help you if you have lived and worked in a number of different countries, or if you have been exposed to a variety of sectors and business environments. They need to see that you have the ability to move, make critical transitions and achieve in a number of different settings, and proactively change your orientation in line with your vision of yourself and the objectives you want to achieve.

At the same time, the career path you have chosen needs to reflect your aspirations, and the vision you have carved out for yourself in line with the exciting things you want to do, the actions you have already put in place to achieve them as well as your plan for the future. Your personal vision of the future needs to be reflected accurately not only in your career up to this point, but also in your future career aspirations. Keep this in mind well before you even start thinking about applying for business school.

Sean Rickard, Admissions Director, Cranfield School of Management

Cranfield looks for three key attributes when assessing applicants. The first is a track record of success in their chosen career and this dictates that they must have several years' work experience and international experience is ideal. The second is evidence that they have the academic ability to gain the MBA, and finally we seek diversity be it in business experience, nationality or voluntary work.

Applicants who meet these criteria will be invited for interview. As we believe students learn much from their fellow students we are particularly interested at interview in learning how they might contribute in the classroom to the benefit of their fellow students. To this end we require all applicants to make a three-minute presentation on a subject we give them.

Throughout the application process you need to convey your personal unique selling point, i.e. your profile, as accurately as possible to ensure that your application package is truly competitive. Furthermore, it is very important that your CV reflects not only a solid track record in terms of your work achievements but also displays a commitment to being involved in a range of activities at different levels, such as charity work, social enterprise, entrepreneurial activity, etc. (see Chapter 7).

School culture: universal process or different for each school?

In Chapter 4 we discussed that school culture is one of the key aspects to consider when selecting the school of choice. Every business school has a completely different way of existing and adding value to the missions of their prospective students. Depending on their individual legacy, their "parent" institution, years in operation, location and levels of funding, each school is offering a different value proposition which is reflected in their "feel and touch", which you can sense from the first time you start interacting with the school staff.

Some schools have massive campuses and form part of larger institutions where you have the chance to mix and mingle with a variety of people studying different subjects. These schools are generally more traditional in their approach compared with the more "independent" schools and campuses totally dedicated to just business and management education. Business schools stepped in tradition such as Harvard, Stanford, Yale and Wharton offer a very different experience to places such as London Business School or INSEAD; besides the obvious difference that the former are in the US while the latter in Europe. The MBA legacy in Europe is a quite young business in comparison with the US, where MBA programmes were introduced much earlier (see Chapter 1).

You can get a "feel" of each school at a glance when you attend informational events and speak to members of staff, faculty and alumni as well as current students. You will notice observable and significant differences among schools in terms of the feel and the look, the way you are approached and welcomed, the information presented as well as the taster classes. The differences come in all sorts of shapes and forms but the main ones to look out for include the following.

- **Intelligence and educational achievement levels**. Business schools are looking for candidates with very good levels of educational achievement so that they pull together classes of similarly minded people that can be a challenge as well as a help to each other.
- **Intellectual curiosity and openness to change**. These are two of the critical dimensions of the personality tests that students are asked to take after they have been selected and are in their first week of the course. A typical MBA student will tend to score quite highly on either or both, since these are two of the founding elements of change and exposing oneself to new learning experiences.
- **Ambition and drive (realistic)**. Aspirations and big vision, as opposed to mediocre plans and tunnel vision, are very important for business

schools. It is important, however, to remember that your goals need to be realistic at the same time. For example, if you are a project manager in a telecommunications company and your goal is to ultimately become the chief executive officer, this is certainly achievable as long as you do not convey the message that you would like that to happen immediately after graduation. Thinking that an MBA degree and the two years it takes to complete is the fast route to jumping a significant number of levels in corporate hierarchy is quite unrealistic. Indicating in your plan that you would start working towards this goal in a step-by-step manner and take positive and constructive steps towards realising it in the next 15 years of your career would be much more of a realistic aspiration and vision.

- **Self-awareness and ability to collaborate as well as compete**. Building on the last point, realism and planning are two important ingredients of success in getting accepted on the programme of your choice. Business schools are looking for people who have the ability to see themselves clearly and pursue their goals while recognising their strengths as well as their weaknesses. Schools also want to see students build support networks and feedback mechanisms around them to ensure they are healthily competing in line with their big aspirations and dreams but at the same time shaping and creating environments and are able to respond to change fast and efficiently. This can only be achieved through collaboration and team spirit where students working together are helping each other to be at their best.

Summary

The decision to take time out to pursue a business education is not to be taken lightly. Finding the right school that allows you to successfully achieve your objectives is a difficult task in itself. However, it becomes more complex when you are trying to find an environment which will not only test and stretch you and also balance that with an environment where you feel you belong. The culture of a school, its feel and touch is largely intangible. There is no one place or document where this information is available; therefore, you really have to rely on your interactions with staff, students and alumni to understand what it feels like to be part of that particular school's environment.

Think about how comfortable they make you feel when they deal with your questions and when you speak with faculty and the programme team running the administration side of the programme. Find out how engaged alumni are once they have graduated, this is a strong indicator to see how proactively involved they are with the school. If they had a good experience while on the programme they are likely to want to still be involved and help their school stay a success.

Once you have a better understanding of the values and ethos of the school(s) that you are interested in, it is vital that you highlight this knowledge and understanding in your application. The reviewer(s) will pick up on this and be impressed with your research and knowledge of the school.

Nottingham Business School

Enhance your management knowledge, your leadership capabilities, your global perspective and your professional career. The MBA is the education for managers, and it has become the most popular postgraduate course in the world due to its international recognition and transferable skills.

Nottingham Business School is proud to offer an intensive, relevant, high-quality international MBA educational experience. Managing in the second decade of the 21st century, following the dramatic global economic crisis of the last few years, requires highly educated managers, and our MBA focuses on developing managers through strategic leadership to succeed in this increasingly complex global business environment.

Through a range of modules and live consultancy projects, our MBA develops understanding and provides experience of global issues. It has been designed to prepare you to handle a wide range of challenges inherent in managing organisations, so that you are able to see the interconnectedness of your actions.

Our MBA curriculum blends theory with application and experiential learning, while at the same time enhancing professional and personal skills through personal and professional development workshops. These workshops may include, among others, leaderships skills, communications skills, influencing skills and negotiations skills.

The two consultancy projects – a team consultancy and an international business consultancy – provide you with the chance to apply the knowledge and skills learned on the core programme to real companies' problems. The first of which is carried out within the UK, and the second of which is carried out across international borders, in different business environments and varying cultures, providing another layer of complexity for managers. Examples of previous companies and locations include: Golden Charter, Toronto; Coats Viyella, Mauritius; Red Cross, Cayman Islands; and, Daimler Chrysler, Detroit.

As part of the international consultancy project, £800 is refunded from the course fee in order to travel abroad as a team of consultants to work on the identified live business issue.

Nottingham Business School offers a full-time, 12-month programme beginning in September and a part-time, 24-month EMBA beginning in January. Contact us now to start seeing things from different perspectives.

Durham Business School

Professor Susan Miller, MBA Programme Director, Durham Business School

The MBA is, by anyone's measure, a challenge, and the reasons for undertaking this world-recognised qualification vary from individual to individual. Perhaps therefore the first thing one should consider is: is the MBA right for you?

Begin by thinking about what it is that you seek to achieve; to further your current career, change careers, or gain specific knowledge and skills? Perhaps it's a mixture of these things. An MBA will introduce you to a wide range of theories, ideas, concepts and debates, some perhaps controversial and contested. Few master's degrees require a learner to have quite such a wide-ranging command of so many, often fairly disparate, areas of enquiry.

Assuming you are now decided on this course of study, making the decision of where to study is the next critical step. There are obvious but essential elements to consider. These will vary and be highly personal to you, but may include practical considerations such as what mode of delivery suits your needs, and do you have a budgetary constraint?

When it comes to choosing a business school, quality and reputation are key. The multitude of freely available rankings information offers insight into a wide variety of criteria. Also important to consider are: the academic faculty's research and specialisms; the depth and breadth of its alumni network; the diversity of the cohort; its corporate connections, and where graduates go on to gain employment.

At Durham Business School we also ask prospective students to consider what they will be contributing to the programme. Through teamwork and a generosity of spirit you should expect to learn from your fellow students, especially if the cohort is extremely diverse. This is why we focus on the building and development of essential management, teamwork and interpersonal skills, and also the provision of a learning environment that attracts an experienced and diverse mix of students from different professional backgrounds and nationalities.

The relevance of an MBA programme to today's challenging business environment is of great importance and, in response to these challenges, we have designed and developed a bespoke continual professional development programme – Leading Edge – around the needs and demands of global MBA recruiters.

Once you've drawn up a shortlist of potential schools, try to visit in person. Getting a feel for the place, whether attending an organised "preview event", or a one-to-one visit, will help immeasurably in deciding whether you have the right "fit" with each other.

I wish you well in your decision making!

Professor Susan Miller recently compiled *The Essential MBA*, published by Sage (ISBN: 978-1-84787-061-2).

7

Completing the MBA application form

The MBA application form

The application form is designed to gather and present structured information regarding your career, academic qualifications and extra-curricular activities. Essays, references and CV are an integral part of the application. You may come across similar or duplicate questions in the form and some questions appear to collect marketing data. These questions are used by the admissions staff for different purposes including helping them to:

- obtain standardised information which can be easily assessed
- evaluate how well you have researched the school and the programme
- assess your objectives, motivations and understanding of the commitment the programme requires
- check consistency (or incongruence) between form, essays, references and CV.

Nowadays all application forms are available online and can be accessed and completed over a number of sessions. You will normally complete the following sections:

- employment history
- academic and professional qualifications, including the GMAT® and English language test scores
- extra-curricular activities and interests
- researching the MBA and the school
- motivations and objectives.

Understanding the admissions requirements

Postgraduate or relevant work experience

Schools are interested in assessing the length and quality of your professional experience for two key reasons:

- your previous career track is one of the best indicators of your leadership potential and ability to achieve your objectives
- your experience determines the level of contribution to class discussions and shared learning.

For most FT MBA programmes you are required to have at least three years of professional experience by the time the programme starts. Canadian schools consider younger applicants with less work experience (they require a minimum of two years). The work experience required for EMBAs is less consistent across business schools, however; typically EMBA programmes require seven or eight years of relevant work experience, including around four years at management level (see Chapter 3).

Normally there are no upper limits in terms of work experience entry requirements; however, business schools will look at this aspect together with the post MBA goals, ensuring that they are realistic and achievable. Some careers have a rigid structure and people can move up or transfer from other sectors only at specific points in their professional life.

How do I calculate the relevant work experience if I do not hold a degree or I graduated as a mature student?

If you do not hold an undergraduate degree and you are still considered eligible for the programme, relevant work experience will normally be regarded as that in which you had some management responsibilities. This also applies if you completed a degree as a mature student after being in employment for a while.

Completing the application form

Employment history section

Often the application form will ask you to indicate the number of years of postgraduate work experience, which refers to full-time employment periods since the completion of your undergraduate degree and by the programme start date. For example, if you graduated in March 2008, have been working full-time since and you are applying for an MBA starting in September 2013, your experience will be quantified as four to five years of postgraduate work experience.

You will need to provide details of your employment periods in chronological order, starting from your current or most recent job. For each employment it is normally required to provide a short description of:

- the sector in which your organisation operates
- the function which better describes your role (accountant, human resources, finance, general management, consulting, etc.)
- your responsibilities and achievements
- number of people you manage and report to you
- title or position of your line manager
- reasons for taking and leaving the job.

Here are some tips on how to present your professional experience.

- Plan this section carefully to illustrate how your career has evolved and when you have been promoted, or taken increasing responsibilities, or made successful transitions.
- Ensure that what you show on the form is consistent with the information provided in your résumé and essays.
- Think of your employment history as a function of the post-MBA career objectives that you want to achieve and highlight relevant or transferable experiences or skills.
- If you do not work for a well-known organisation or your role spans different functions (this is very common in small companies), take extra care to ensure that the admissions directors will be able to easily understand your profile and area of expertise.
- Focus on the core skills that have enabled you to perform in different areas.
- Emphasise your accomplishments for your employers, clients or business partners. It is helpful to express them in terms of figures where possible. Data in which schools are interested include the size of the team, budgets or projects you have managed; the percentage by which revenues or profits have grown during your tenure at the organisation; number of successful contracts that you have won from your clients.
- If you have direct reports or budget responsibilities, ensure that you clearly outline them in the application.
- Highlight any exposure to international business practices such as experience of working outside your own country, liaising with international clients or managing remote teams.
- As teamwork is one of the key aspects of the business school experience, consider situations in which you have collaborated with other departments or colleagues to achieve results.

Some examples are given below:

- If you are a project manager your role will require that you liaise with clients and suppliers; therefore, you could highlight your responsibilities in stakeholder communication and management and your achievements in terms of building relationships, negotiating transactions or successfully influencing clients.
- If you are a strategic influencer you will show how the policies or plans that you formulate impact on decision making at senior level; you may also want to indicate the title and position of the person you report to, if this is a member of the senior management team.

Pitfalls to avoid

- Copying and pasting information from the company's website or literature.
- Confusing industry sector and job function: for example, if you are a system engineer and you work for a bank, your industry sector will be banking or financial services and not IT, which will be your job function.
- Purely listing the tasks included in your job description.
- Using technical jargon that makes the information uninteresting for the admissions directors.
- Complaining or expressing dissatisfaction about a particular role or employer.
- Leaving unexplained gaps in your employment history.
- Providing dates which do not match those in the résumé.
- Making spelling and grammatical mistakes – if the online form does not have a spelling and grammar checker, you should copy and paste the text into a word document for checking before submitting your application.

Academic and professional qualifications, including GMAT® and English language tests

An undergraduate degree from a recognised institution is typically a mandatory requirement for entry into MBA programmes. However, if you do not hold a degree but have extensive professional experience you will still be able to be considered by some schools, especially in Europe. In this case, you should show that you have a solid career track and aim to achieve a strong GMAT® score (if you have not already taken it), at least around the class average. In the US usually, it is not possible to obtain admission to an MBA without an undergraduate degree.

Business schools measure your academic ability looking at your university track record together with any professional qualifications which you may have completed (accounting, project management, marketing, finance, etc.) and your GMAT® score.

GMAT®

The GMAT® is a computer-adaptive standardised test to assess your quantitative and English language skills and measures your aptitude to succeed academically in graduate business studies. For further information about the GMAT®, see Chapter 8.

Business schools consider candidates from a variety of educational backgrounds and are experienced in assessing a wide range of qualifications awarded by overseas institutions. As part of the application process, you are required to submit the official transcripts, which show a record of the subjects that you studied and the achieved grades. Admissions teams will look not only at your grades, but also at the following.

- The reputation of the awarding institution – a degree from a leading university will certainly be considered favourably.
- The subject of your degree – whether you have taken a more quantitative, analytical or vocational programme.
- The number and type of modules you took – did you select a wide range of modules which gave you a solid knowledge in the subject, or did you choose an easy workload?
- The consistency and progression of your results throughout your academic career – does your record show continuous commitment or erratic grades?

Good grades in quantitative or analytical modules will be more impressive than similar or higher marks in vocational courses. Below-average grades in your early academic career followed by significantly improved results will not impact negatively on the evaluation of your intellectual ability.

Professional qualifications will also be considered to measure your intellectual skills and academic potential.

What if I do not have a strong academic background?

The lack of an outstanding academic record will not prevent you from obtaining admission to business school if you can demonstrate that you have excelled at professional level and in extra-curricular interests, and taken up additional training and development opportunities at a later stage of your life.

Be proactive

If you do not have a first-rate academic record, well before starting your MBA application you should try to take courses that can add to your academic background. This could also give you opportunity to build a foundation of knowledge that will be helpful for your MBA; short evening or weekend programmes in quantitative-based subjects such as finance, accounting and economics are available at many institutions. You could check with your human resources (HR) department if there are any training opportunities available through your employer.

Usually business schools ask you to comment on your academic performance, whether it fully reflects your academic skills and potential. This can be either a short question in the application or a theme for an application essay. An example of such questions follows overleaf.

- Do you think that your undergraduate performance so far gives an accurate indication of your potential for success? If so, why? If not, why not? (London Business School)

In all cases, business schools expect that your response fully demonstrates self-awareness and ability to take responsibility for your own behaviour. Criticising your university or expressing pure lack of interest in your undergraduate studies is not a good tactic. A good answer needs to do the following.

- Acknowledge that the academic performance at undergraduate level does not reflect your current abilities.
- Present the facts which may have impacted on your academic record in an objective and positive light. For example, there may have been serious health issues affecting yourself or a close family member; you were working full-time to finance your studies or support your family; or perhaps your focus was on excelling in other activities (sports, music, community involvement, etc.) rather than on your academic performance.
- Reflect on what you learnt from these experiences, which has made you a well-rounded individual and leader.
- Briefly discuss your successes in extra-curricular activities.
- Refer to other postgraduate or professional qualifications that you have achieved since graduation, or career achievements which show your intellectual power.

If you believe that, despite what could be perceived as a low undergraduate degree classification or grade point average (GPA), your academic performance was solid, you need to give evidence that backs up your statement. For example, if you are an international student and you have graduated from an institution which is particularly selective at admission or at exam stage, you need to explain the context and provide facts and figures which show that you were one of the most successful students: percentage of students admitted each year out of submitted application; number of students passing exams and completing the degree out of enrolment, etc.

What GMAT® score do I need to get a place?

In Chapter 8, we will look at the GMAT® in detail, discussing the format and different sections in addition to more practical areas such as deciding when to take or retake the exam, how to book and prepare for the exam. In this section we will look at how the GMAT® score is taken into consideration along with the remaining components of the application.

Most business schools do not set a minimum requirement in terms of GMAT®; however, the statistics regarding the class average score and the GMAT® score range will give you a benchmark. Nowadays, the average GMAT® score of FT MBA classes in top schools is above 700 and the bottom of the score range is often around 600.

If your score is not aligned with the class average, it is usually a good idea to retake the test even after submitting your application. Some schools do not look favourably on candidates with numerous retakes. If you have retaken the test numerous times and still not achieved the satisfactory score you think you need for top-ranked programmes, we suggest you still apply. However, think about applying not only to the top-tier schools, but also to a few mid-tier schools so that you have a fallback plan.

As business schools take a holistic approach in assessing your profile and look at the GMAT® score together with the other elements of the application, a high score will not guarantee admission; in the same way, a score in the bottom range will not necessarily prevent you from reaching the interview stage or obtaining an offer. Sometimes you may be given a conditional offer in which you are asked to improve the GMAT® score.

There are situations in which you need to achieve a strong GMAT® score (in the top half of the school's score range), for example:

- when you have a poor academic history: a solid GMAT® score will give the admissions committee the confidence that you have the academic power and calibre required for their programme
- if you belong to a group which produces lots of MBA candidates (for example, consulting, finance and IT): the GMAT® score can be one of the differentiating factors
- if you are in the early stages of your career and you are unable to contribute a lot of experience to the class: a good academic record supported by a sound GMAT® score, good essays and references will play to your advantage.

GMAT® scores are usually valid for five years from the date when the test was taken.

Can the GMAT® be waived?

Top schools never waive the GMAT® for their FT MBA programmes, while some mid-tier ones offer alternative internal tests. EMBA programmes both at top and mid-tier schools seem to have more flexible requirements in terms of GMAT®; some schools waive it for candidates with professional experience at senior management level or those with a strong quantitative background (for example, postgraduate degree in quantitative subjects or professional experience in areas which require the use of strong numerical skills).

If your profile or background is of particular interest to a school, it might be open to offering a waiver. Waivers are granted on a case-by-case basis and you will need to submit a formal request to the admissions committee or obtain written approval from the admissions director.

Alternative admissions tests

Recently a number of business schools, including top-ranked ones, have started accepting the Graduate Record Examination (GRE®) as an alternative to the GMAT®. The GRE® was initially designed for candidates applying to graduate school and has been revised to match the needs of business schools more closely. Like the GMAT®, the GRE® exam measures verbal reasoning, quantitative reasoning and analytical writing skills. Top ranked schools accepting the GRE® as well as the GMAT® include Harvard, INSEAD, MIT Sloan, NYU Stern and Stanford.

However, the GMAT® is most widely accepted by business schools and by taking the GMAT® exam you will have more choice.

English language tests

If you are not a native English speaker, you will also be required to submit an English language test result. The most widely accepted tests are the Test of English as a Foreign Language (TOEFL) and the International English Language Testing System (IELTS). The TOEFL is still most widely used in the US and some schools such as Wharton will not accept other tests. Both TOEFL and IELTS assess four areas: listening, reading, speaking and writing.

Regarding the TOEFL, there two different formats: the computer-based test (TOEFL iBT) and the paper-based test (TOEFL PBT). The TOEFL PBT is administered in test centres which do not have the availability of the TOEFL iBT. The cost of the TOEFL varies from US$160 to US$250 depending on the type of test and the country in which you take it.

The IELTS is available in two formats that are linked to the purpose for which you need the test: academic or general training. For an MBA, you will obviously take the academic test which has been designed for university studies.

English language test results are usually valid for two or three years. Most business schools accept the following scores:

- IELTS 7.0 or 7.5
- TOEFL iBT 100 or 105
- TOEFL PBT 600 or 620.

English language test waiver

Business schools will waive the English language test if you have studied, lived or worked in an English-speaking environment for a sufficiently long period of time (two or three years). The application form will usually give you the opportunity to explain how you have gained your English language competence, which is also assessed at interview stage.

Answering questions assessing your understanding of and commitment to the programme

Admissions teams will carefully review all your responses to the questions in the application form. Be sure to answer all of them thoughtfully. Your responses should not only answer the question but also demonstrate your level of research and understanding of the programme and school.

Which events did you attend/resources did you consult?

Rather than marketing information, this type of question measures how well you have researched and thought about the programme. Normally schools want to see that you have visited the campus, attended at least one event (it is not unusual for candidates to attend more than one) or spoken to admissions staff and representatives of the student and alumni community. Although you are not expected to have consulted all the available sources, usually applying for a school after researching its programme on the internet only is not a common successful strategy; you need much more than a web search to identify which community and culture you fit better with.

Which other schools and programmes have you applied for and why?

Most schools will ask you which other programmes you are applying for and why. If you are really committed to undertaking an MBA, you should apply to a wide range of schools to ensure that you obtain some offers. However, you should avoid being absolutely candid; do not provide too many details of all schools you are applying to or considering. In fact the question is designed to assess you in a number of areas:

- your decision making in choosing particular programmes and schools and how your choice fits with your objectives.
- whether you are really committed to do an MBA
- whether their school may be your first or second choice compared with the other names that you have indicated.

To answer the question strategically you should think about your objectives and needs and identify schools that are strong in those areas. In Chapter 4 we discussed how to choose the right school for you beyond rankings (see p.55).

Pitfalls to avoid

- Mixing top-tier and mid-tier schools or programmes which do not have any similarities. This usually gives top schools the impression that you are not really confident in your ability to become a member of their student community; however, if you choose your top choices and second bests, sometimes this could prove to your preferred school that you are focused on a particular area or speciality and committed to doing an MBA: for example, if you are pursuing a career in financial services in a specific country you may choose schools whose faculty and alumni community are strong in that area. Equally, the top schools will not look positively at your candidacy if you simply pick up a list of top-ranked institutions which are very different in terms of MBA offering and school culture. When the application form asks you to explain the reasons for your choices, use that opportunity wisely. Mid-tier schools are unlikely to be impressed in seeing their name next to those of Harvard, Stanford, Wharton or Chicago and will not feel excited by your candidacy.
- Refer to data on salary progression or rankings as the only reason to choose particular schools.
- Indicate that your choices are driven by the link between a school and a specific recruiter.

How do you plan to fund your MBA?

This question is designed to assess your awareness of the financial commitment required to undertake an MBA. Schools need to ensure that your financial plan is sound and realistic: in addition to paying the required fee to the institution, planning your finances carefully will avoid stress due to funding shortcomings while you are studying. As discussed in Chapter 5 (p.84) you are likely to look at different sources, including loan schemes and savings.

Stating that you are relying exclusively on the school's scholarships or external scholarships to fund your MBA is an unlikely winning strategy.

Have you discussed your MBA plan with your family/whom have you have discussed your MBA plan with and why?

Schools want ensure that you have discussed the time and financial commitments required for the MBA at least with your spouse or family. It is critical that those around you are aware of the demands of the MBA schedule and coursework and are prepared to provide you with the support that you need. If you are applying for a PT MBA or EMBA programme it is also expected that you have discussed your MBA plans with your line managers, colleagues and direct reports, and put in place appropriate arrangements to cover your areas of responsibility while you attend the MBA lectures.

Essays

Application essays

Each application for business school includes at least four or five essays on different topics, usually with a word limit. Business schools can be very creative with their essay questions; however, regardless of the titles, essays are designed to assess you in four main areas:

- career goals and motivations for taking the MBA
- core skills, professional experience, career or industry knowledge, soft skills
- core skills and leadership potential
- contribution to the class and wider school community (usually posed as open questions).

Some candidates consider essay writing one of the trickiest parts of the admissions process. On the contrary, you should look at them as your opportunity to market yourself to the admissions committee, describing who you are as a person and what motivates and interests you. While a CV is no more than a summary of your skills, educational background and professional experience, the MBA application essays enable you to portray a wider image of you and to tell the school not only what you have achieved, but also how you did things, and what values and aspirations shape your behaviour. In the essays you can choose which aspects or situations to discuss and can take time to plan and prepare your answers, checking and changing what you have written, until you are fully satisfied with the results.

Top essay writing tips

Planning your essays

- Start planning your essays well before the application deadline and give yourself plenty of time to write, edit, expand and change them.
- Think about your core skills and experiences and unique selling points (see p.111) and identify the essay questions that can bring them out.
- Make note of the ideas, topics or stories which you would like to develop in each essay.
- When choosing the situations to discuss in the essays, focus primarily on your work experience but also ensure that you include some examples from your personal life and extra-curricular activities
- Bounce your ideas off your family, friends or colleagues – it would be more helpful to speak to somebody who has either done an MBA or comes from an organisational behaviour background.
- If you are preparing multiple applications you should treat each school as a separate entity rather than copying and pasting the same text for all the schools you are applying to.

Choose which essay or application to start with

- Start with the essay that focuses on your career goals and your motivations for taking an MBA as this will enable you to prepare the building blocks for the whole admissions process
- When you prepare multiple applications, start with the set of essays that you find the most demanding and challenging or the school which has the earliest deadline; it is also helpful to complete all the essays for one school before moving to the next one.

Writing your first draft

- When you are writing your first draft, let your thoughts run free on the sheet at this stage – don't worry about grammar or structure.
- You can start with any part of the essay that will help the words and relation between ideas flow – it does not matter if it is the introduction or the conclusion, or if you simply write down sentences or paragraphs in a random order.
- You could also write down three to five different sub-questions that you think must be addressed by your essay and start writing paragraphs which answer those questions: as an example, check our guidelines for the essay regarding career objectives and motivations (p.127).
- Be consistent with the information that you have provided in your application form and CV.

Revising and editing

If you are an expert writer, each essay will normally require at least two or three revisions; however, don't be afraid of revising even four or five times before being completely happy with the result. Being critical with your work will enable you to prepare a strong application.

If you feel you are getting stuck with your essay, just take a break after each review. Reading it with fresh eyes will also help you spot weak points or inconsistencies which you may not have even noticed before.

- Before carrying out any reviews, make sure that you are happy with the ideas, topics or stories that you have used in the essay. The content should address the essay question and provide all the information which you need to support your points.
- Once you are happy with the content, check how you have organised the information.
- Your ideas should be arranged in a rational sequence and link to each other.
- You can use different paragraphs to outline the major points of your essay. Ideas expressed in separate paragraphs can be linked up by using appropriate transitions, which could be one or two words, or a sentence. Sometimes you will compare and contrast ideas (in spite of; on the contrary; nevertheless; however; etc.); or express similarity (similarly; in the same way). You may also need to add or expand information (moreover; besides this; in addition; furthermore; etc.); to link cause and effect (consequently; as a result; following that; etc.); to conclude or summarise (to conclude; in the end; to sum up; to summarise; etc.).
- Check the balance between paragraphs: the introduction and conclusion should be shorter than the main paragraph. Avoid long paragraphs which divert the attention of the reader.
- Review your introduction and conclusion. The introduction should present the topic or story that you are going to develop in your essay; it could be a statement which you use to answer the main essay question. Your aim is to capture the interest of the reader and make the essay easier to follow. In the conclusion, which should flow naturally from the previous paragraphs, normally you summarise the main ideas expressed in the essay or key learning from the experience that you have described.
- Avoid the use of jargon when describing work-related experience; you need to demonstrate that you are able to communicate with others who are not specialists in your area or field of work.
- Look at the word count and stick to the word limits.
- Check spelling, grammar and punctuation.
- Ask for constructive feedback from your friends and ask them to read through the text. It would be ideal if you could get anyone who has done an MBA to read your essay.

Essay questions on career goals and motivations for taking the MBA

The essay on career objectives and motivations is probably the most crucial one in the whole application: your candidacy for an MBA is unlikely to be taken forward if you are unable to show clear goals and understanding of where an MBA could take you.

However, it is rare to start the application process with the full awareness of why you want to do an MBA and what specific career perspectives it can open up for you. Most people looking at an MBA for the first time have anything but a clear idea of their future plans. Therefore, if you have just started thinking of an MBA and all you know is that you are unsatisfied with your current job, salary or career and you want a change, don't worry: this is a common situation for candidates in the very early stages of their journey towards an MBA. On the other hand, ensuring that you do your research which will help you clarify your objectives and personal motivations to yourself; you cannot risk being confused and vague when you submit your application.

Answering this question is not about what the admissions committee wants to hear; it is about developing the understanding of who you are as a person; what you have achieved in your career; what interests and motivates you; and what else or more you can aspire to given who you are and what you have already done.

There are a number of things which you can do to learn more about career options which could be available to you with an MBA.

- Discuss your interests and possible MBA options with trusted friends or colleagues or with your mentor, if you have one. If there are any MBA students and alumni in your network, seek their input.
- Read the different student and alumni profiles and case studies available through the schools' website and programme literature, paying particular attention to pre-MBA profiles similar to yours.
- Gather information on the careers and/or sectors in which you are interested by consulting relevant publications and websites.
- Speak to a career coach specialised in working with experienced professionals.
- Whether you are planning or not to disclose your MBA plan to your employer, you could still diplomatically discuss career plans with your line manager or HR to evaluate options in your area of work and gather feedback on how your company sees you developing and evolving in the future.

There are several reasons why you may want an MBA and we have explored the most common in Chapter 2 (see p.21). You can check which ones are most relevant to you.

When answering essay questions of this type you need to address the following themes.

- **How your career has evolved so far**. You could start the essay by providing a short overview of your background and professional achievements to date. This will help you set the scene for your future goals and highlight your unique selling points to the readers.

- **What your goals are in the short, medium and long term**. Remember to discuss what you are hoping to achieve while you study (for example, developing knowledge of specific business functions) and immediately after completing your MBA; what kind of post-MBA roles you will be seeking and what you are hoping to be and achieve in the longer term. The admissions committee will not expect that you have planned with absolute certainty what you will do with the MBA, but you need to show that you are exploring a few realistic options.
- **How an MBA fits in with your plans**. In particular, you need to show why the MBA is indispensable to attain your goals and why the same objectives cannot be achieved through other qualifications or experience. There are careers in which the MBA is a "must" to achieve senior positions (for example, financial services and management consulting); however, you still need to come up with other good reasons to avoid that the MBA is seen by the admissions committee as a pure "box ticking" exercise: you could refer to the leadership skills which you are hoping to develop or the areas of business you want to know more about. In other cases, experience could eventually lead to the same results, but an MBA will enable you to get there faster and open new avenues (such as entrepreneurial ventures) for the later stage of your career.
- **Why an MBA now**. This is about explaining why the MBA makes sense at a particular stage of your career and life. For those who have less experience, it is critical to make a strong case for their place in the class now rather than in a few years. You may have progressed very quickly in your career and want an MBA to go even further. In this case, you need to remember that in addition to how you will benefit, you need to show how you will contribute to the class and school community. Or you may have an entrepreneurial venture which has achieved a critical stage and you need the knowledge and pledge of an MBA to expand it. You want to make a specific transition to a different job sector or industry function and waiting any longer will make the shift more difficult. If you are a more experienced candidate who could have taken the MBA a while ago, it is about explaining what you accomplished without the MBA and how the investment will be worthwhile in your career span: you may have taken up senior roles very early in your career and at that time have thought better of interrupting the career momentum; or perhaps after a successful track record in your area you are planning to start up your own company.
- **Why an MBA from that particular school you are applying to and not from others**. You could answer this by listing the strengths of the school in specific areas or your post-MBA objectives.

What admissions committees assess through essay questions on career goals and motivations for taking the MBA

The admissions teams will check that:

- you have thought carefully about your possibilities based on your past experiences, skills set and personal preferences

- your goals are realistic and achievable within the timeline that you have set for yourself
- you have researched the school and gained a good understanding of the culture and the unique features of the programme
- their school can deliver against your expectations.

Examples of questions on career goals and motivations for taking the MBA

- Why do you want an MBA? (Harvard FT MBA)
- Discuss your short- and long-term career goals.
- How will studying at INSEAD help you achieve your vision? (INSEAD FT MBA)
- Give us a brief assessment of your career progress to date. In what role do you see yourself working in immediately after graduation and what is your longer-term career vision?
- How will your past and present experiences help you to achieve this?
- How will the London Business School MBA Programme contribute to this goal?
- Why is this the right time for you to pursue an MBA? (London Business School FT MBA)

Essay questions on your professional experience, career or industry knowledge

Another type of essay question which is quite common in MBA applications asks you to describe or assess your professional experience or comment on business trends in your area. Your essay should aim to provide an overview of the core knowledge and abilities which you have developed in your area.

If you are discussing your experience, career or current job, you will find it helpful to look at the tips which we have provided in this chapter for the employment section of the application. Here the key difference is that your essay has a narrative style.

- You will write about where you have come from, what you have achieved and learnt at each stage and how you have developed yourself through the different challenges that you have faced along your career path.
- You will describe how in your career or current job you have taken up greater responsibilities to broaden your scope.
- You must highlight both the expertise and the soft skills that you have gained.

If you are writing about business trends in your sector:

- choose topics that possibly have a connection with what you do as part of your job: for example, if you are an in-house solicitor working in financial services you may look at the impact of new government regulation on future developments on specific areas of the business
- rather than trying to talk about everything and running the risk of being too vague and generic, decide on one or two themes and develop them in detail
- avoid the use of technical jargon, which will make your essay difficult to read or understand

It may be difficult for you to write about business trends in your industry sector if you simply work within one of the supporting functions: for example, you have an HR or IT job and you work within consumer goods. In these cases you have two options:

- the easiest: you focus on trends impacting on your job function
- the most challenging: you take time to research and understand the wider picture, looking at issues and developments in the sector in which your employer operates as an organisation.

Normally the second approach will impress the admissions committee as you will demonstrate that you have strong business awareness.

Here are a few tips on how you can gather the industry knowledge that you need for your application and, later on, for the interview:

- read the company's strategy documents or plans regarding future developments and projects: today a lot of information is published on the website for consumers, investors or employees
- match the trends you learn about with articles in the *Financial Times*, *BusinessWeek* and *The Economist*
- use your network: speak to colleagues or friends who are more closely involved with the core business: for example, those working within the marketing or strategy department.

What admissions committees assess through essays on career and business trends

- The level of professional experience or seniority that you have achieved.
- How fast you have progressed along your career path.
- How motivated, ambitious or driven you are.
- The knowledge which you have built in your business sector.
- What motivates you.
- How you respond to challenges or setbacks.

Examples of essay questions on industry knowledge

- The EMBA will expose you to broader networks from outside your sector. Describe the current trends in your sector and how your organisation's strategy is addressing them, ensuring that this non-specialist audience will be able to understand and learn from your perspectives. (London Business School EMBA)
- What are the key issues facing organisations in your sector over the next three years? What course of action would you recommend to such organisations? (Judge Business School FT MBA)
- Cite the most difficult situation you have faced in your professional life and how your input helped to resolve it. (IE Business School International MBA and Global EMBA)

Essays on contribution to the class and the wider school community

The admissions committee will assess your potential to add something different to the student mix by evaluating you in a number of areas such as business knowledge, extra-curricular activities and personal skills. Typically the admissions committee gains a picture of you through the information provided in the application form, CV, references and essays.

While the essays on professional experience and industry trends give you the opportunity to discuss your business experience and understanding, other essay topics will enable you to highlight other areas in which you would bring something valuable to the school.

An essay question on what or how you think you can contribute to the school gives you a fantastic opportunity to tell the admissions committee what you would like them to know about you. The following are some examples of topics which could be developed in this essay.

- **Industry knowledge**. If you work in a sector that is not strongly represented among MBA students and you have built a solid knowledge in your area of work, this could be one aspect of your contribution to the class. Telecommunication, IT and finance are widely represented in MBA classes; sectors such as not-for-profit, public, cultural, media and entertainment, hospitality or consumer goods are less common.
- **Understanding of emerging economies**. You may have lived or worked in emerging countries, or have gained exposure working with clients or business partners in these areas.
- **International exposure**. You may have spent your life in several countries around the world or fluently speak different languages and can share insights into business practices in different countries.
- **Extra-curricular activities**. You may have obtained substantial achievements in outside interests such as sports, music, arts and charity or community work. You

can come up with specific ways in which you can support existing student clubs or initiate something entirely new for the school.

- **Exceptional personal qualities**. Usually schools look favourably at candidates that are able to create positive dynamics within the class, so if you have evidence of outstanding ability to build relationships, negotiate, mediate, resolve conflict, etc. ensure that you use it in this essay. The evidence could be in the form of consistent feedback received by line managers, colleagues or friends.

What admissions committees assess through this type of essay

- That you have something interesting to add or say.
- That you are aware of what you would bring and ready to share it.
- That you fit with the school's culture.

Other "contribution-based" questions are those which ask you to discuss which student clubs you are interested in and why; or what your extra-curricular interests are. These types of essays aim more directly to assess how you are at social level and what contribution you will make from this point of view.

An example of questions on contribution

Please qualify the content and scope of your management experience and/or exposure to decision making. How would this help you contribute effectively to the learning of your EMBA classmates? (London Business School EMBA)

Essay questions assessing soft skills

Another common type of essay questions which you will find in the application are those focusing on soft skills which are thought to be crucial to your leadership development or simply functional to a positive MBA experience.

Examples of the soft skills most widely assessed are:

- self-awareness
- team skills
- intercultural awareness
- communication
- leadership.

Self-awareness

Self-awareness is your ability to recognise both your strengths and weaknesses and how these impact on other people. It also refers to taking responsibility for your own actions and behaviour, including accomplishments and mistakes.

Strengths and weaknesses

If you are directly asked to discuss your strengths and weaknesses, you are certainly faced with a dilemma as you are wary of what the school may think about you.

Here are some tips to develop a good answer for this type of essay question.

- Think about your strengths and weaknesses as highlighted in informal or formal feedback you may have received from your line manager or peers. You can also refer to the feedback in the essay.
- Have a chat with your referees and find out, if possible, what kind of evaluation they are giving in the references. Ideally your essay should be consistent with the image of you that the referees will portray.
- Map your strengths against the key skills and attributes which define the school culture and choose the most relevant.
- When you discuss strengths, give examples of situations in which you have shown or used that particular ability.
- You could identify your weaknesses by looking up words that are the antonyms of your strengths: very often a particular quality also carries a flaw. For example, perseverance and persistence in achieving objectives may lead to stubbornness or difficulty in adapting or changing course of action when required.
- After discussing your weaknesses, remember to explain what you have done to address them.

Pitfalls to avoid in answering essay questions focused on strengths and weaknesses include the following.

- Don't provide a long list of strengths and just one meaningless weakness.
- Simply referring to lack of knowledge in finance, marketing or any other functional area is not a good way of answering this question: schools are interested in your personal skills rather than the knowledge gaps that you want to fill.
- Although an honest self-assessment will be appreciated by the admissions committee, avoid mentioning weaknesses which could be considered detrimental for your admission: for example, admitting that you are not a team person will definitely not take you far. If you think your referees may highlight some flaws in such a key area, you can use your strengths and discuss how sometimes the other side of the coin can impact on other people. For instance, your drive and focus on achieving results may be perceived as pushiness by your team members.

Examples of questions on self-awareness

- Please describe a situation either work or personal where you faced a particular challenge. What was the outcome and what did you learn from the experience about your own strengths and personal development needs? (Columbia Business School and London Business School EMBA Global Asia)
- If we asked your closest associates to describe you, what would they say? Which adjectives would they use and why? What would they say are your strengths and weaknesses? (Oxford Saïd FT MBA)

Setback, failure or mistake

Essay questions asking you about your greatest setback or failure are quite common in MBA applications. Schools are not interested in a detailed description of what happened; the focus of your answer should be on:

- acknowledging your weaknesses or mistakes
- discussing what you have learnt from the experience
- demonstrating that you have developed and improved yourself.

Examples of questions on setbacks

- Tell us three setbacks you have faced. (Harvard FT MBA)
- Describe a situation taken from your personal or professional life where you failed. Discuss what you learned. (INSEAD FT MBA)
- What did you learn from your most spectacular failure? (Judge Business School FT MBA)

Achievements

Talking about your accomplishments will give you the opportunity to expand some of your unique selling points. When you write an essay on your greatest achievements, remember that schools are not simply interested in what you have done; they will look at what you have learnt and how you have overcome any issues or obstacles along the way.

There are always doubts on whether it is better to choose examples based on your professional or personal life. Here are some tips which will help you address this type of question.

- If you are asked to discuss your most significant achievements, you could mix professional accomplishments with those regarding extra-curricular interests or your personal life.
- If the question is about the greatest accomplishment in your life, you cannot discuss a series of different successes. Sometimes you may have an achievement you really feel strong about; in other cases there might be a few examples that you could use but you are not sure which one would work better.
  - Seek feedback from family and friends on the achievement that can be seen as the most substantial.
  - Look at this essay in the context of your application and use it to add or enhance areas which you may not have developed earlier: for example, if you feel that your essays and application are full of work-related evidence, you could choose an accomplishment regarding your outside interests or personal life as this will show skills and abilities which may not have come up in the other parts of the application. If you are in your early career and need to prove that you have solid experience, you may wish to focus on work-related achievement which shows that you are able to make a meaningful contribution to the class.
- Use examples based on recent experience rather than what you did a long time ago as the reader may think that you have done nothing noticeable since then.
- Explain why that particular achievement is the most important one for you.
- Talk about the difficulties that you faced and the skills that you used to achieve your goals.
- Discuss what you have learnt about yourself, your company, your community, people's motivations, etc.
- Describe the impact that your accomplishment had not only on you, but also on your employer or community.

Examples of questions on achievements

- Tell us about three of your accomplishments. (Harvard FT MBA)
- Describe what you believe to be your two most substantial accomplishments to date (if possible specify one personal and one professional), explaining why you view them as such. (INSEAD FT MBA)

Team skills

A major part of the MBA experience is about team learning and therefore you may find essay questions which aim to assess your ability to work within teams.

It is easy to choose situations in which you led the team; however, the admissions committee is not assessing your leadership style here. You can give an effective answer by focusing on a situation in which you were a team member and contributed effectively to the task without being in charge. The admissions committee is interested in the range of skills that you can bring to the table to affect positively team dynamics: for example, influencing skills and negotiation; ability to mitigate conflict or to deal with people with different agendas; creativity and innovation; ability to build consensus; problem solving; ability to support others and ask for help, etc. It is important to describe what and how you contributed to the team.

Examples of questions on team skills

- At Chicago Booth, teamwork and collaboration are applied inside and outside of the classroom. Identify what you believe is the greatest asset you will bring to a team here at Chicago Booth. (Chicago Booth PT MBA)
- In one of your Wharton MBA courses, you are given a case assignment to be completed in a study group comprised of six students. What is the most significant strength you would bring to the group process? (Wharton EMBA)

Intercultural awareness

As an MBA student who aims to become a global leader, you will be exposed to people from different cultures and backgrounds. A number of schools have designed essay questions that draw on your attention to the diversity of their student community and assess your intercultural awareness and ability to engage with diverse countries, people or business practices. In this essay it is usually helpful to bring practical examples based on your experience of living in another country; or doing business with overseas companies; or working within multicultural teams. You will usually discuss the following:

- what you have learnt about key cultural differences and similarities
- main issues, difficulties or obstacles arising from cross-cultural management and communication
- what you have done to overcome cultural barriers or misunderstandings
- how you have adapted yourself or changed your approach to be effective in a different context
- how you have developed an understanding and appreciation of other points of view.

Examples of questions on intercultural awareness

- Please choose one of the following two essay topics: a) Have you ever experienced culture shock? What insights did you gain? or b) Describe the ways in which a foreigner in your country might experience culture shock. (INSEAD FT MBA)
- Describe any significant experiences outside of your home country or culture. What did you gain and how will your experience contribute to London Business School? (London Business School FT MBA)

Open essay questions

Many MBA applications contain an open question asking whether you want to add any additional information that you want the school to know. This question gives you the opportunity to present aspects which you may not have been able to discuss elsewhere. You don't need to write an additional essay if you feel that you have extensively covered everything you wanted to talk about in the other parts of the application.

There are different ways in which you can benefit from this essay. For example, if you do not have an outstanding academic record and there isn't any other part of the application that enables you to discuss your undergraduate performance, you can use this question to explain what affected your marks (see p.118).

Some candidates use this essay to talk about outside interests or accomplishments which have not come up in the application: for example, raising funds for a charitable organisation; setting up and running a business in the spare time; coming up with an invention or new product and obtaining a patent to commercialise it.

Examples of open essay questions

- Answer a question you wish we had asked. (Harvard FT MBA)
- Considering what you've already included in the application, what else should we know about you? In a maximum of four slides, tell us about yourself. (Chicago Booth FT MBA)
- Is there anything else you would like to add that would help us in evaluating your candidacy? (Wharton EMBA)

European Business School London

The European Business School London (EBS London) is the oldest private business school in the UK and one of seven specialist schools at Regent's College London – the largest college of private higher education in the UK. Established in 1979, we provide rigorous, academically challenging business programmes with excellent employment prospects.

MBA International Business

This programme has been developed to provide students with the skills and experience to undertake the challenges of senior-level management. The programme provokes theoretical understanding and a critical awareness of the major strategic challenges facing contemporary global business. The MBA has a truly international focus throughout, underpinned by an integral study period abroad. Students can choose to learn additional languages on the MBA programme, and are encouraged to undertake an internship.

Career support and development

Our aim is to develop tomorrow's global leaders and the careers and business relations department is responsible for providing a comprehensive service to all MBA students and alumni.

Budding entrepreneurs

We will support your ambition by providing tailored business and start-up advice and aid you in your search to make the right connections to establish a successful enterprise.

Mentoring scheme

The EBS London MBA programme has a unique mentoring scheme. Each student on the programme is paired with an experienced professional for the duration of the course. Each mentoring relationship is unique and allows the student to draw on the professional and life experiences of their mentor to develop their own skills, ideas and self-reliance. Mentors are recruited from our extensive network of Regent's College alumni and business relations contacts.

London advantage

What better place to study business than the financial capital of Europe? Our single campus is situated in the heart of Regent's Park, Central London. We are only minutes away from the financial centre of London and the West End.

Visit us

Come and visit our beautiful central London campus. Information sessions are held every Friday, 15.00–16.00 or contact us for a personal consultation.

Tel: +44 (0)20 7487 7505
Email: ebsl@regents.ac.uk
Web: www.regents.ac.uk/EBSL

Case study

What do EBS London's alumni say?

Jerome Ahye (UK) MBA International Business tells us.

Why EBS London and why the MBA International Business?

I chose the MBA because I wanted to widen my career options. I had been working in marketing for a few years and I wanted to understand how the rest of the business worked. I looked exclusively in London but very few were committed to entrepreneurship, were truly international and affordable. The European Business School London had a good reputation and offered the personal touch with small class sizes. Plus Regent's College has a great location in Central London.

How has the course aided your career?

It's given me the options I craved. The course is general but the dissertation is your chance to specialise and make contact with industry in your designated field. The three main things I took away were the following:

1. Broad range of skills such as working from briefs, data analysis, communicating and presenting, teamwork and leadership; all under pressure and time constraints.
2. Logical and methodical thought process which I can complement with creativity.
3. The contacts. I formed strong relationships with great people from across the world and was exposed to some valuable contacts, whom I never would have met otherwise.

What did you do after you finished your MBA and what are you doing now?

After graduation, two fellow students and I set up a company based on an idea we worked on in the entrepreneurship module. I now work for Isobar Social as a member of a specialist team in the digital advertising agency Glue Isobar. We are a fairly new team whose mission is to become a centre of excellence for social in the network.

How has the network at EBS London and Regent's College helped your career?

The careers and business relations team at Regent's College were excellent. They supported me with career direction and strategy, CV writing, interview preparation, networking and introductions. Being part of the EBS London consulting and entrepreneurship student-run clubs gave me valuable experience, mentors and networking opportunities. Plus the alumni team were very supportive of our business ventures.

What does the future hold?

A few years where I am – learning from great people and achieving big things for leading clients – then, who knows? In this space things change rapidly so something special can always be round the corner if you look hard enough.

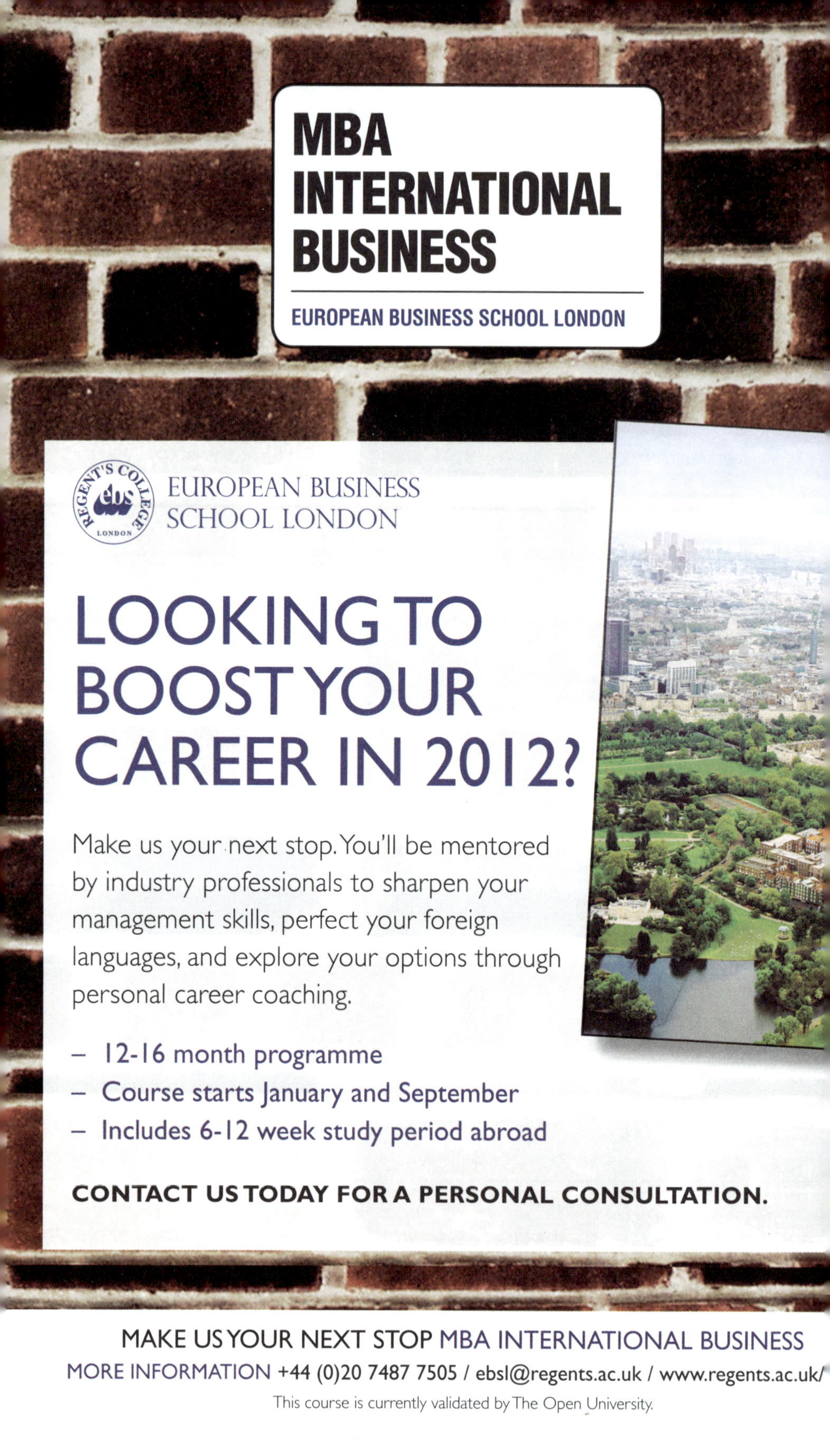
MBA
INTERNATIONAL
BUSINESS
EUROPEAN BUSINESS SCHOOL LONDON
REGENT'S COLLEGE
ebs
LONDON
EUROPEAN BUSINESS
SCHOOL LONDON
LOOKING TO
BOOST YOUR
CAREER IN 2012?
Make us your next stop. You'll be mentored by industry professionals to sharpen your management skills, perfect your foreign languages, and explore your options through personal career coaching.
– 12-16 month programme
– Course starts January and September
– Includes 6-12 week study period abroad
CONTACT US TODAY FOR A PERSONAL CONSULTATION.
MAKE US YOUR NEXT STOP MBA INTERNATIONAL BUSINESS
MORE INFORMATION +44 (0)20 7487 7505 / ebsl@regents.ac.uk / www.regents.ac.uk/
This course is currently validated by The Open University.

CV

Your CV

Your CV is also a very important element of the application. You need to pay extra attention to your CV to ensure that it is:

- current and accurate in order to reflect all the transitions, achievements and qualifications that you have accumulated throughout your career
- succinct, compact and straight to the point
- powerful in terms of conveying your differentiation.

Depending on which programme you are targeting – FT MBA or EMBA – your CV needs to have a different focus and differentiation points. If you are in your early career and you are applying for an FT MBA, what counts more towards your differentiation is your academic track and educational achievement, and the outside interests that show your leadership skills.

A very good CV will describe roles and situations where you faced big challenges and excelled in both your professional life and extra-curricular activities. Were you president of your sports club, did you win competitions as a young pianist, did you exhibit your artwork at important exhibitions, did you engage in theatre or live performance, did you help charities raise substantial funding for important purposes that represent your core values and which you believe in?

Remember: this is not a CV to get a promotion or another job, and hence its point is not only to highlight how good you are at doing your job. The objective of this CV is to present your appetite for achievement and your leadership potential so that you are considered a great "catch" for top business schools around the globe.

It is also important to showcase that you have lived and worked in different places around the world, an experience that is valued highly on CV evaluations. If you are an EMBA candidate your key focus should be more on your work achievements and what you have done to build a career that supports the way you see yourself in the next five to 10 years and the plans you have put in place to achieve your ambitious goals.

Aspects and elements in which top business schools are particularly interested include the following.

- A proactive approach to initiating and implementing projects and programmes of large scale and significant impact. You need to describe them in your CV using key facts and figures, as well as words and phrases such as "I achieved"; "I proposed and designed"; "I pursued and achieved"; "I initiated"; "I designed and implemented".
- Your management and leadership experience – top business schools are attracted to candidates who have had significant experiences in managing and leading people in different settings, especially real or virtual multicultural teams.
- Your willingness to achieve excellence and to take more responsibility in your company, role or function.
- Evidence of extra-curricular activities and interests that show your leadership potential and motivation to achieve great things.

An admissions manager's perspective

Jenny Eriksson, Admissions Manager, Executive MBA Program – Europe, The University of Chicago Booth School of Business

"Applicants should demonstrate a strong career progression on their CV. This is a combination of a growing and more advanced skill set, as well as accomplishments that show impact and leadership within their organisations. The messaging for the CV should be clear, focusing on these accomplishments, and not reading like a list of responsibilities. We recommend a simple yet effective approach – for each position you've held, use strong lead-in action verbs for your work experience bullets and state the quantifiable (or qualitative) impact of your action(s). If possible, keep each bullet to ideally two lines. If you are capturing what you did, how you did it and what the positive impact for your organisation, client, etc. is in two lines, you likely have a message that is effective yet not too long with extraneous detail."

Format guidelines

- Use a profile summary of no more than three lines at the top after your name and contact details.
- Write a thorough educational history and a comprehensive and robust career/ work experience section, which highlights clearly your trajectory from job to job.
- Avoid leaving gaps in time periods and observe religiously CV continuity from beginning to end.
- List your work experience first rather than your education experience if you have been in substantial career roles for more than three years.
- Use bullet points for clarity.
- Keep just one to two lines for each bullet point.
- Use active verbs to highlight achievements and initiative.

- Use facts and figures to signpost significant contributions.
- Separate responsibilities from achievements – especially if you are a more experienced candidate.
- Clearly outline the different sections of your CV, i.e. internships, professional training, voluntary work, hobbies.
- If you have worked for the same organisation for a number of years but in different jobs, put a main heading with the organisation's name and the total number of years and then break down into the different roles with the dates.
- Proofread relentlessly to ensure everything is correct and makes sense, and ask someone else to proofread too.
- Limit your CV to one or two pages maximum.

References/recommendations

References or recommendations, as they are known in the US, are helpful to schools when assessing you as a potential candidate for their programmes. Recommendations are the only tool admissions committees have in evaluating how you as an applicant perform in a professional environment. Business schools place an equal amount of importance on every aspect of an application they receive; however, a candidate typically tends to place more emphasis on the essays or the GMAT® and overlooks the importance of the recommendations.

If references are well thought out and written, it shows the admissions team that you really made a strong impression on your referee and they are therefore willing to support your candidacy.

What constitutes as a good recommendation

The main aim of the reference form or letter is to ensure that the qualities you have highlighted in your application are consistent with your experiences and your claims are corroborated. Business schools want to ensure that you have the right type of experience, exposure, track record as well as the attitude and mentality of a leader in the making. Admissions teams need real-life narratives from people who have worked with you for significant lengths of time in a work setting to ascertain that you have the right profile for the programme, and that you can contribute to as well as benefit from an MBA learning experience. It is imperative that the reference form or letter reflects all those elements of your personality and skills set that make you distinct when compared with a global pool of applicants with very similar backgrounds, aspirations and abilities. The testimony of the referee is critical, since it is the ultimate validation of your skills and ability to perform in different roles and/or situations.

If your current role is in a technical area, it is particularly important that the reference form or letter reflects your skills in a holistic manner.

Checklist for referees

The areas admissions teams are particularly looking for reassurance on the following.

- Strong intellectual and analytical capacity; ability to grasp complex issues, break them down into their elements and provide grounded, complete and tangible solutions.
- Consistent strong performance and commitment to excellence.
- Strong work ethos and conscientiousness.
- Ability to listen and take on critical feedback.
- International exposure and experience of working across countries/cultures.
- Global outlook, cross-cultural awareness and understanding.
- Ability to take initiative and act as a leader of a group when necessary.
- Leadership qualities, ability to manage, motivate people and develop the potential of the team.
- Ability to work efficiently as a member of a team towards common objectives.
- Self-awareness and understanding of personal limitations at work.
- Openness to change and eagerness to learn and develop.
- Creativity and ability to seek new solutions to existing challenges.
- Clear business potential and attributes to develop into a global leader.
- Excellent oral and written communication skills.
- Self-confidence and belief.
- A strong character or personality.

It is up to the referees to choose which areas they can most appropriately comment on, given their extent and nature of involvement with you. You could give them a checklist including the points listed in the box above to ensure that they are covering relevant points in the reference. It is critical that the person completing the reference keeps the following two important points in their mind when completing the letter.

1. It works really well if the area of development reported in the reference letters is aligned to the one quoted by you in your essays. We strongly recommend that you discuss this with your referees beforehand if you have yet to finalise the essays. This will ensure consistency across all parts of your application.
2. Quoting real examples of instances when and how you exhibited the skills and abilities indicated would strengthen the recommendation significantly.

How long should a recommendation be?

Each school will have their own template for a reference that includes specific questions. Usually there is no word limit; however, what you want to avoid is having a recommendation submitted with minimal responses to the questions. To prevent this from happening, it is better to select referees who are able to speak candidly and in detail about you, your professional experiences and your motivations for pursuing an MBA.

Selecting the ideal referee

Think carefully about who you want to approach to write your references. You may think choosing referees is a simple task, but it is not just about selecting the right person; they will need to spend time on the reference and know you well enough to comment upon your strengths and weaknesses. Instead of asking for a reference from someone who will go into raptures over your experience, a recommendation from someone who is honest and offers a candid description about your capabilities and your achievements will be more effective, especially if they highlight areas for development. The difference between a good and bad reference can be the difference between getting accepted and getting rejected.

It is imperative that you share with your recommenders your plans for business school as well as your post-MBA plans. Give them a copy of your CV along with your essays and discuss your short-term and long-term aspirations with them. As mentioned earlier, if your referee is specific about areas for development, the recommendation will be realistic and influential.

Usually business schools have a bias towards or require you to submit two letters of recommendation; however, a few schools ask for three. At least one of the recommendations should ideally be from your current line or reporting manager but sometimes this is not possible. For instance, if you are applying for a PT or an EMBA programme, you may not yet have discussed your MBA plans with them. In such instances you should approach someone who is able to comment upon your career and can evaluate your performance. The majority of schools will accept recommendations that are not written by your line manager; however, if you are offered a place, they may request a reference from them as a condition of your acceptance. In other instances, some schools specifically require a recommendation from your immediate boss. Other options for a suitable referee could include a client you have worked with, a previous line manager or a colleague.

Unless a school specifically asks for an academic reference, we suggest you refrain from submitting a letter of recommendation from a professor. All MBA programmes require some level of work experience, usually a minimum of two to three years; a reference from a line manager, client or colleague who knows you in a work context will make your candidacy stronger. References from friends or from family connections are also not suitable unless they are an alumnus of the school you are applying to.

When choosing a referee, it is also important to consider the following points.

- You should choose someone who knows you very well and will take time to write a detailed recommendation, someone who is able to provide specific examples of your experiences and is able to reinforce with anecdotal facts.
- A previous or current manager is usually a good choice but it is imperative to choose someone who knows you in both a professional and non-professional context.
- If you have not been in touch with your previous manager, you should take some time out to reconnect with them. If you have not spoken to them for a while, it will appear a little strange that you are now getting in touch with them. Contact them some time before you require the reference and keep the relationship warm. It will be much easier for them to write about you at length and in detail while focusing on your leadership potential and personal qualities. This will make the recommendation all the more impactful.
- Select someone who is able to submit a recommendation on time. It is great to have a reference from a successful business professional; however, time may be an issue for them.
- Most schools will allow you to submit your application without the references but they will not read your application until it is complete; without your letters of reference your application will not be considered. To avoid this situation, give your referees plenty of time and notice to write the reference but also alert them of the deadline. We recommend that you give them an earlier deadline to the one you are working towards, avoiding any last-minute issues.
- A referee who is either a current student or an alumnus of the business school you are applying to or better still a student or alumnus who has undertaken the same MBA that you are applying to will most definitely help your candidacy.
- Try to select someone who has a good command of English. A well-written recommendation will of course be more helpful than a badly written reference from someone who is unable to express their views on you in a clear manner.
- Approach someone who is higher up the corporate ladder or more senior than you. This is more ideal than a peer recommendation, although some schools require a peer recommendation. If it is not a requirement, then we strongly recommend choosing referees who are more senior than you and also know you well in a professional capacity. However, do not make the mistake of asking someone just because they have a senior title such as CEO, chief financial officer (CFO) as admissions departments are rarely impressed with references from these big titles unless they know you well. You are better off asking someone who actually knows you well in a professional capacity.
- Choose a referee who is helpful and generous, is willing to give you feedback on your candidacy and can spot weaknesses in your application or essays. This should help to prevent any unpredictable references from being submitted.

Writing you own references

On occasion, if recommenders are too busy to write the reference they will ask you to write it on their behalf and will sign off on the finished reference. If you approach your referee and they suggest you write your recommendation ensure that you speak to them beforehand to get a good understanding of what they see as your areas for improvement. Explain the need for the reference to be critical and subjective rather than just an opportunity to state how good you are.

Referees from particular industries such as finance, investment banking or consulting are adept at writing references as these industries have a very MBA-driven culture; consequently they understand the MBA admissions process and, more importantly, are more willing to support you to get into a good school. Referees from other industries such as not-for-profit or government may need to be briefed about the MBA, the recommendations and how to approach them.

Reference letters are powerful in influencing the decision making of the admissions committee at business schools. It is critical that the referee understands the nature of the programme, the ethos of the business school you are applying for and its criteria in selecting their students.

How to strengthen your profile

You have spent a copious amount of time writing and re-writing your essays to perfection; worried for hours on end about what your referees are going to write about you while spending weeks if not months preparing for the GMAT®. What else can you do to help you get accepted? Actually, there is a whole host of other things that you can do to enhance your application. You want to show the admissions committee that you are a diversified, well-rounded individual capable of much more than your academic qualifications or professional experience.

Your personal achievements will help to differentiate yourself from the hundreds of other MBA applicants who are also applying to the same schools as you.

A word of warning

Do not seek to take on any new personal achievements in the months before submitting an application. More often than not the admissions committee will see through your unconvincing efforts and perceive this as a way of you ticking a box to help with your candidacy. They may not be convinced that last-minute volunteer work is a genuine interest to better yourself as an individual while helping others.

Demonstrate your leadership potential

Fundamentally, an MBA will give you an overview of general management while enhancing your leadership skills. However, what will help your application further is previous leadership exposure; experience of working with an organisation or part of a committee where you led will be beneficial. The nature of the organisation is not really important; what admissions teams want to see is that you can clearly articulate in your essays how your leadership made a difference to the organisation.

Take up a sport or hobby

Sports such as sailing and cricket can display your leadership ability, motivating individuals to get the best out of them, or other sports such as basketball, football, rugby, rowing and other team-based sports will demonstrate your ability to work effectively in a team environment. This can help admission teams to assess you in a different aspect. Unusual hobbies are always interesting, which can highlight your creativity; try to demonstrate how your hobby might contribute to the learning environment at business school.

Join a professional organisation

The majority of professions have some kind of industry membership or organisation. For instance, lawyers have the Bar; finance-related professions have the CFA (Chartered Financial Analyst) Institute and IT professionals have the Chartered Institute for IT. Find an organisation that is related to your profession or industry. This will show you as someone who is knowledgeable and demonstrate your keenness to progress within the industry.

Become a volunteer

Being a volunteer will not make or break your application to business school but it will prove you to be a substantive individual who has more to offer than a typical MBA candidate. You should choose an organisation depending upon where your passion lies. Like anything else, if you enjoy spending your free time working on this, you will be more committed and talk about your experiences passionately and enhance your candidacy.

As mentioned above, do not volunteer just because you think it will look good on your CV. When you are invited to an interview, the interviewer will no doubt ask you about your reasons for joining and what difference you have made. You will have to speak convincingly of your reasons.

Take a quantitative course

If you have a poor undergraduate academic record you can reinforce it in two ways: achieve an excellent score in the quantitative section in the GMAT® or failing this, take a further maths course. Admissions teams will of course question a poor GPA or academic problems; however, they will be more forgiving if they see that your academic performance improved considerably at postgraduate level or you are able to give a solid reason for the poor academic performance while showing that you learnt from past failures. In situations like this, admissions teams will be worried that you will not be able to cope with the quantitative part of the course.

If your poor academic performance was due to issues around maths, we strongly recommend you enrol in a statistics or calculus course. An MBA will have a significant quantitative workload. By enrolling on a maths course you are demonstrating to the admissions teams that you have identified that there is a potential problem and you are being proactive by putting measures in place that will allow you to cope with the heavy quantitative workload.

Take an English course

If English is not your native language you might think it is at the right level for you to participate on an MBA; however, the admissions committee may have other ideas. Most business schools have a prerequisite when it concerns English. They usually require a minimum number of years working or studying in an English-speaking environment before they consider waiving the English requirement. The admissions teams will look specifically at the verbal and analytical writing scores to assess your ability. Furthermore, they will also look at your application and essays as a measure of your written English ability and will assess your verbal ability especially at interview stage.

If you are a non-native speaker you should bolster your candidacy by either taking one of the English language tests mentioned earlier in this chapter or take an intensive English course. Another way to work on your English and to familiarise yourself with regional English accents and speeds is to listen to English radio stations or read English newspapers on a daily basis.

Lancaster Business School

Make your difference in the real world with the Lancaster MBA

The triple-accredited and top-ranked Lancaster MBA serves leaders who make a difference in the real world – a world typified by uncertainty, ambiguity and complexity.

To increase performance in this dynamic environment, we offer three programmes: the full-time MBA; the EMBA; and the global MBA. All three programmes employ "learning through action" to develop "senior strategic leaders".

Introducing "learning through action"

"Learning through action" is our process. Throughout your MBA, you will engage real business issues in meaningful and challenging ways. Each programme employs:

- Real organisation-based projects or assignments – *to apply your learning*
- Real engagement in your reflective practice – *to challenge your learning*
- Real interaction with senior strategic leaders – *to extend your learning*

For instance, you will tackle a live client issue during the consultancy challenge. And on the international business in context experience, you will make a short, intensive study visit to a rapidly developing economy.

Senior strategic leadership

Senior strategic leadership is our purpose. Each programme emphasises:

- Advanced knowledge – *in change, strategy, and leadership*
- Supported opportunities – *to hone your key leadership skills*
- Capacity building experiences – *ensuring you have the resourcefulness, resilience, and sense of purpose senior strategic leaders require*

Triple accredited and top-ranked

The Lancaster MBA is taught at the world-renowned Lancaster University Management School (LUMS), part of Lancaster University. Fully accredited by the Association of MBAs, The Lancaster MBA shares LUMS' AACSB and EQUIS accreditation.

The FT MBA is ranked:

- top 5 in the UK (*Forbes* 2011)
- top 10 in the UK (*FT* 2011)
- top 50 in the world (*FT* 2011)
- top 100 in the world (*The Economist* 2011)

What does Lancaster offer MBA students?

Lancaster faculty are among the best management consultants, educators, and research scholars in the world. *This gives you access to some of the world's best minds during your MBA and beyond.*

LUMS enjoys new state-of-the-art facilities and international accolades for excellence. *This gives you confidence that our MBAs are high quality, and valued by employers worldwide.*

Join an international community of excellence

Lancaster students study alongside experienced managers from many different countries, and engage with a truly international curriculum, and a faculty with extensive worldwide experience. *This will enhance your international outlook.*

Lancaster alumni hold positions of responsibility across the full spectrum of industries and organisations worldwide. *You will get access to this global network of employers and collaborators.*

The right MBA programme for you

Lancaster offers one MBA in three programmes. All three emphasise learning through action to develop senior strategic leaders, but with differences that enable you to study either full-time or part-time or in or outside the UK.

The FT MBA programme suits leaders with proven potential to take on more strategic roles. The intensive one-year format allows a fast career return, with the full benefit of a world-class MBA that is fantastic value for money.

Throughout your FT MBA, you will undertake a comprehensive, challenging and progressive set of "learning through action" activities including:

- The New Venture Challenge: working in teams, you'll help develop a business plan for a new commercial or social enterprise
- The Consultancy Challenge: working in teams, you'll help a client organisation manage a live business issue
- The Corporate Challenge: working in teams, you'll tackle a substantial strategic project for an international corporation, and you'll do this alongside a major individual assignment.

The Lancaster executive MBA (EMBA) and global MBA are designed for experienced and aspiring senior managers. These two-year, part-time modular programmes meet your career and personal development needs, while allowing you to maintain your work/life balance. Teaching is delivered in block residential modules by Lancaster faculty. Taught by the same core faculty from Lancaster, the EMBA programme is based in the UK while the global MBA runs in Jordan, Zambia, and Singapore.

"Learning through action" activities for the EMBA and global MBA include work-based assessments, where your MBA knowledge is applied directly to your organisation. *This free consultancy and hands-on experience adds value to you and your employer.*

Contact

We invite you to learn more about The Lancaster MBA. Visit: www.lums.lancs.ac.uk/mba. Email: mba@lancaster.ac.uk. Lancaster University Management School Bailrigg, Lancaster, LA1 4YX, UK.

8

The GMAT®
Michael Birdsall, partner at www.gmatix.com

MBA programmes typically have a strong element of statistical and quantitative content, and unless the undergraduate degree you undertook had elements of these in the curriculum, you may find that you will struggle on the MBA. Although business schools highlight the need for softer skills such as leadership and interpersonal skills, they are essentially looking for candidates who can demonstrate solid numerical skills through their background and other means such as the GMAT®. The quantitative content of the MBA is the reason why the GMAT® plays an important part in your application.

If you want an MBA from a top business school, you will need to take the GMAT®, in fact the majority of business schools require it.

What is the GMAT®?

The GMAT® is a computer-adaptive psychometric test designed to assess your ability to succeed in a graduate business programme. Over the past 50 years the exam has been undergoing constant development. There is research showing that the test you take today is a very reliable predictor of a candidate's success.

At this point there may be a number of thoughts running through your head.

- What does "psychometric" mean?
- What topics does the GMAT® test cover?
- How should I prepare for the test?

- How much emphasis do admissions committees put on a candidate's GMAT® score?

Psychometrics is the field of study concerned with both educational and psychological assessments. The GMAT® is similar to those tests you might take when applying for a job. Although the GMAT® does not claim to measure any psychological construct, it is generally true that those people who are more focused, calm and conscientious tend to do better than others on such tests.

In other words, while there are different topics tested on the GMAT®, it is important to recognise that the test is a measure of your ability to perform under time pressure.

The GMAT® is computer-adaptive: the questions on the exam are determined by your performance on previous questions. If you get a question correct, the next question will be more difficult. If you get a question incorrect, the next question will be easier. The difficulty of a question is determined by the number of previous test-takers who answered the question incorrectly. If many test-takers answer a question incorrectly, the question is considered difficult. If many test-takers answer a question correctly, the question is considered is easy.

There is a lot of speculation concerning whether or not computer-adaptive tests are easy to outsmart by, for example, spending more time on the first 10 questions. The quick answer is no. If by answering the first 10 questions correctly at the expense of later questions you could obtain a great score, would the GMAT® be a valid indicator of those skills necessary to perform in business school? Top schools such as Harvard, Wharton or London Business School would not be likely to use a test that can be gamed by answering the first 10 questions correctly and ignoring the final ones.

> *"The GMAT® exam was designed by business schools to measure the skills that are needed for students to succeed in the challenging academic curriculum of graduate management programmes. It gives admissions staff a consistent and objective measure by which to evaluate candidates no matter where in the world they come from, their academic background or levels of work experience. The GMAT® is given under standard conditions around the world, with the highest level of security, to ensure scores are comparable across all applicants. In addition, the commitment, focus and discipline needed to prepare for the GMAT® exam and do well are valuable skills which business schools evaluate throughout the admissions process."*
> *Deborah Somers, Director Client Services EMEA, Graduate Management Admission Council*

GMAT® format and score

The topics tested on the GMAT® are quantitative and verbal reasoning skills.

- **Quantitative skills** are tested on a 75-minute multiple-choice questions section and, from June 2012, also tested in a 30-minute integrated reasoning section.
- **Verbal reasoning skills** are tested in two 30-minute essays and a 75-minute multiple-choice questions section. From June 2012, verbal reasoning skills will include a 30-minute integrated reasoning section instead of one of the essay questions.

The current format of the exam is as follows:

Analytical writing assessment (AWA):

Analysis of an argument	30 minutes
Break	1 minute 30 seconds
Analysis of an issue	30 minutes
Break	8* minutes
Quantitative reasoning	75 minutes
Break	8* minutes
Verbal reasoning	75 minutes

From June 2012, the exam will have the following format:

Analysis of an argument	30 minutes
Break	1 minute 30 seconds
Integrated reasoning	30 minutes
Break	8* minutes
Quantitative reasoning	75 minutes
Break	8* minutes
Verbal reasoning	75 minutes

*The break times have in the past been five and 10 minutes and can change without notice. You should check the length of the break times when you arrive at the testing centre.

For more information on the GMAT®, look at *The Official Guide for GMAT Review*, 12th or 13th edition (John Wiley & Sons). You should also download and take a free practice test from www.mba.com. The following advice will likely make more sense if you familiarise yourself with the exam.

The total GMAT® score varies between 200 and 800. Usually around 67% of test-takers score between 400 and 600. The scores on the quantitative and verbal reasoning sections range from 6 to 51. The AWA is given an overall score that is the average of the ratings of the two sections and ranges from 0 to 6.

Most business schools do not set an explicit minimum requirement, but provide an indication of the average GMAT® or range of GMAT® scores of their class. For further information regarding the GMAT® as an entry requirement and its use in the admissions process for various programmes, see Chapter 7.

The analytical writing assessment

The AWA section is the only open-ended response question on the GMAT®. You are expected to write two essays in response to two separate questions. All of the possible questions that could be presented in these areas can be downloaded and studied in advance from the official GMAT® website (www.mba.com).

Analysis of an argument

The first section is analysis of an argument. You need to analyse the quality of the author's reasoning. The author typically will have made reasoning mistakes that are very similar to those made when interpreting data. For example, the author could have assumed that the past is a predictor of the future; that because two events happened together one has caused the other; or that a supported statement is true.

Analysis of an issue

The second section is analysis of an issue. You will be asked to take a position in response to a written statement. The topics are pretty wide in scope and can range from how power is perceived to the extent censorship should be used in society. It is more important to construct a well-reasoned argument than it is to write how you really feel about the topic.

Both of these sections are very similar to what an MBA candidate would be expected to do in a classroom that uses the case study method. The case study method is widely used in MBA programmes and involves students being given real-world business problems and coming up with solutions to these problems. Students are expected to give the reasons for their proposed course of action and defend those reasons from the criticism of the professor or other students.

The analysis of an argument section is similar to you being in an MBA programme evaluating your peers' arguments, while the analysis of an issue section is similar to you being in an MBA programme making your recommendations to the class.

The most important element of these responses is your use of evidence to support your argument. When refuting a point, a good strategy is to consider an extreme example. For instance, if you find that the text in the analysis of an argument section assumes that the past is an indicator of the future, an extreme example could be to use, for instance, "Making this assumption is the same as assuming that because Dutch tulip bulbs were a great investment during the 17th century, investors should allocate a large portion of their portfolio in tulip bulbs today." Obviously, this is not sound reasoning for an investment strategy unless you want to own a nursery.

On the analysis of an issue section, when making a point you need to anticipate weaknesses in your position and address those weaknesses. Think of these as being similar to a question about your weaknesses that you may be asked during a job interview. You will not want to talk about something that would prevent you being offered the job; you will bring up some topics to show the interviewer that you have considered your weaknesses and have room for improvement.

Remember: if you plan on taking the GMAT® after June 2012, the analysis of an issue section will not be part of the exam anymore.

Finally, there is a lot of discussion as to whether the AWA section is even worth doing. The short answer is: in most cases, it is. Although admissions committees may not weigh this section very heavily when evaluating applications, the essays are used to compare a sample of your writing style to the style on your application essays. We have only known one case where a school explicitly told a candidate not to worry about the writing section. (In that case, the student graduated with a first from Oxford in Modern Languages and spoke five languages fluently). In addition, the student in question was retaking the GMAT® for a conditional offer rather than taking the test for the first time.

Quantitative section

The quantitative section consists of two types of question: problem solving and data sufficiency.

Problem solving

Questions in the problem-solving section are in multiple-choice format: you are given a maths-based problem to solve and expected to select the correct answer from five given answers.

The topics tested are arithmetic, algebra, Euclidian geometry, coordinate geometry and word problems. In general, the level of difficulty in the topics tested does not exceed what a high school student in the US would be expected to know before graduation. This does not mean that the questions are easy. Consider the following question.

Given that $a^2 + b^2 = c^2$, how many integers a, b and c are there that satisfy the equation $a^n + b^n = c^n$, when n is an integer greater than 2.

(A) None

(B) 7

(C) 43

(D) 97

(E) An infinite number

The correct answer is A. Do not attempt to solve it.

The ability to understand this question is not beyond what is expected of a high school student in the US. However, this is a particularly well-known problem and is called Fermat's Last Theorem. It took the world's best mathematicians more than 360 years to solve it. This question would not be beyond the scope of the GMAT®. Although the level of knowledge required to understand a problem on the GMAT® may be relatively low, the ability to solve the problem may range from very low to extraordinarily high.

Common strategies and techniques to answer problem-solving questions

In terms of strategy, there are many ways to answer the question other than solving the problem. These include back-solving, plugging in numbers, solving a similar easier problem to establish a pattern, drawing a picture, estimation, and identifying a property of the correct answer choice.

Back-solving

Back-solving involves trying out the answer choices in the question by substituting them into the variable in the question. Whichever one of the answer choices results in the equation being true, must be the correct answer choice. The key to back-solving is that most often you only need to substitute in two of the answer choices, the second and fourth answer choice. The reason for this is because unless a question asks you to determine which of the answer choices is largest or smallest, the answer choices will be arranged from either the smallest value to the largest value or the largest value to the smallest value. As a result you can determine whether the answer should be smaller or larger than the value you have substituted. Consider the following question.

The equation for converting degrees Fahrenheit to degrees Celsius is $F = \frac{9}{5}C + 32$. The equation for converting degrees Celsius to Fahrenheit is $C = (F - 32)\left(\frac{5}{9}\right)$. At which of the following temperatures is Fahrenheit equal to Celsius?

A. 40

B. 20

C. 0

D. –20

E. –40

To use back-solving, you would start with answer choice B and substitute it onto one of the two equations above. It does not matter whether you substitute 20 for degrees in the Fahrenheit or Celsius equation, since we are looking for the temperature at which they are equal. Using the first equation:

$$F = \frac{9}{5}C + 32$$

$$F = \frac{9}{5}(20) + 32$$

$$F = \frac{180}{5} + 32$$

$$F = 36 + 32$$

$$F = 68$$

Since the temperature we get is larger than 20, what we should have got if this was the correct answer, we know that we need a temperature less than 20. If our answer choice had been below 20, we would know that A, 40, was the correct answer choice.

Now we try substituting in answer choice D.

$$F = \frac{9}{5}C + 32$$

$$F = \frac{9}{5}(-20) + 32$$

$$F = \frac{-180}{5} + 32$$

$$F = -36 + 32$$

$$F = -4$$

Since the temperature we get is larger than −20, the correct answer must be less than −20. Since there is only one answer choice that is less than −20, answer choice E, −40 degrees, must be the correct answer. If the temperature we solved for was less than −20, we would know that the correct answer choice would have to both be greater than −20 and less than 20, in which case the correct answer would be C, 0.

Plugging in

Plugging in numbers is generally a good option on algebra questions that have variables in the answer choice. On certain arithmetic problems, i.e. number theory questions, plugging in numbers often does not produce a conclusive result.

To plug in, you simply assign a number value for each of the variables in the question. Do the arithmetic on the equation in the problem and the answer choices and see if they match.

If $x^2 + y^2 = a$, and $x + y = b$, then $6xy$ equals which of the following?

(A) $3(b^2 - a^2)$

(B) $3(b^2 - a)$

(C) $3(b - a)$

(D) $3(b + a)$

(E) $3(b^2 + a^2)$

Rather than solve this algebraically we can assign values for x and y to solve the equation. In general, you should avoid plugging in the numbers 0, 1 or 2. So we will use 3 for x and 4 for y.

$$3^2 + 4^2 = 25 = a$$

$$3 + 4 = 7 = b$$

$$6xy = 72$$

The answer choice that equals 72 is the correct answer.

(A) (72 – 252) = 2(49 – 625), which will equal a negative number, so it cannot be the correct answer.

(B) 3(72 – 25) = 3(24) = 72, which is the value of 6xy so this is the correct answer. Since there is only one correct answer we need not evaluate choices C through E. They are listed here in case you chose to solve this starting from choice E and working your way to choice A.

(C) 3(7 – 25), this answer will also be negative so cannot be the correct answer.

(D) 3(7 + 25) = 96.

(E) 3(72 + 252) = 3(49 + 625) = 3(674) = 2,022.

Determining a pattern

Sometimes determining a pattern can help you answer a harder question. This is helpful with questions that ask about sequences, but can also be helpful on other types of questions. For example, consider the following.

How many diagonals can be drawn in a 19 sided regular polygon?

There is a formula for working out this type of problem. However, if you do not know the formula you could start by drawing diagonals on polygons with very few sides to determine the formula. Since the only information we are given is that the polygon has 19 sides, than we know that the number of diagonals must be a function of the number of sides.

A triangle is a 3-sided polygon that has zero diagonals, i.e. 3 => 0, so we must multiply 3 by zero or subtract 3 from it. Since multiplying by zero will not produce a useful equation, we must subtract 3.

A square is a 4-sided polygon that has 2 diagonals, i.e. 4 => 2, so we must divide by 2 or subtract 2, but we cannot subtract 2 since that wouldn't work for the triangle. So we must divide by 2. Combining this with what we know above, we know we must subtract three, and divide by two. Trying to get a formula that is based on the number of sides (n) we get:

$$\text{Diagonals} = (n-3)/2$$

Since this gives us ½ and not 2 it cannot be correct. If we made the formula n(n−3)/2, we would get 2 when n equals 4.

A pentagon is a 5-sided polygon that has 5 diagonals, i.e. 5 => 5. Checking our formula from above:

$$n(n-3)/2 = 5(5-3)/2 = 5(2)/2 = 5$$

Our formula works. Using it for the 19-sided polygon gives us:

$$19(16)/2 = 19(8) = 152$$

which is the correct answer.

Admittedly this technique has a bit of a trial and error element to it. As long as you are aware why it succeeds and why it fails, it can help you get closer to the correct answer. Use this technique primarily when trying to work out untimed practice problems. With practise, you will get better at it.

Drawing a picture or diagram

Drawing a picture or diagram can help you see relationships that you might not have otherwise noticed. The best example of this is a Venn diagram. Consider the example below.

75% of the students in a certain class study French. 60% of the students in the same class study Spanish. If 12% of the students in the class do not study any language, what percentage of the students study only French?

The given information could be represented as:

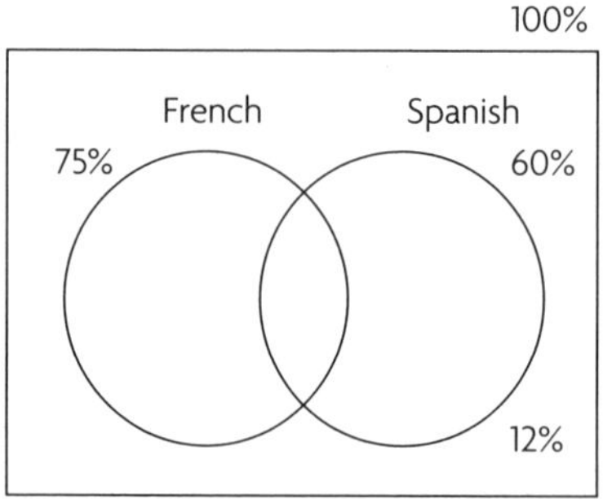

Since you cannot have a number greater than 100%, we know that there must be some students who take both French and Spanish. We can represent the overlap with x.

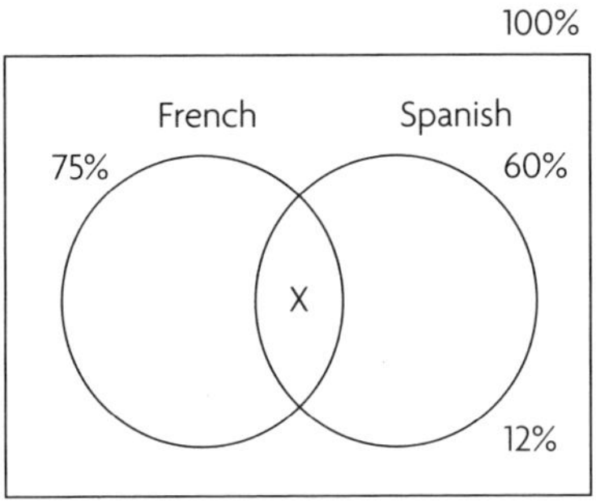

We also know that the total number of students studying languages must be 88% since 12% don't study any language. So we know that 75% + 60% –x = 88%, which gives us that x = 47.

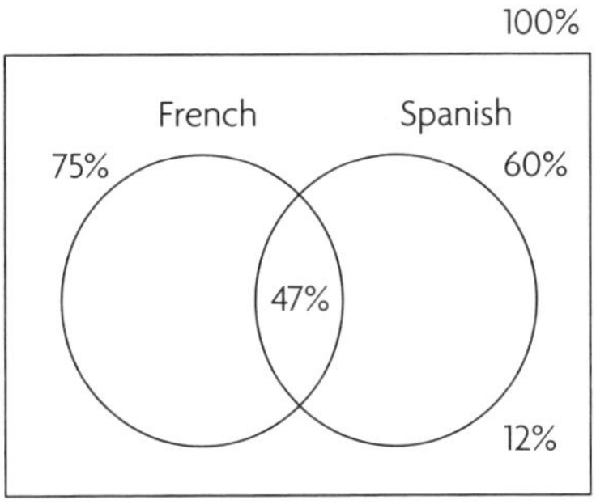

Since the percentages we have above for those students studying French and Spanish are inclusive of that 47%, we can solve for those students who study only French and only Spanish by subtracting 47% from the percentage representing all students studying French and all students studying Spanish.

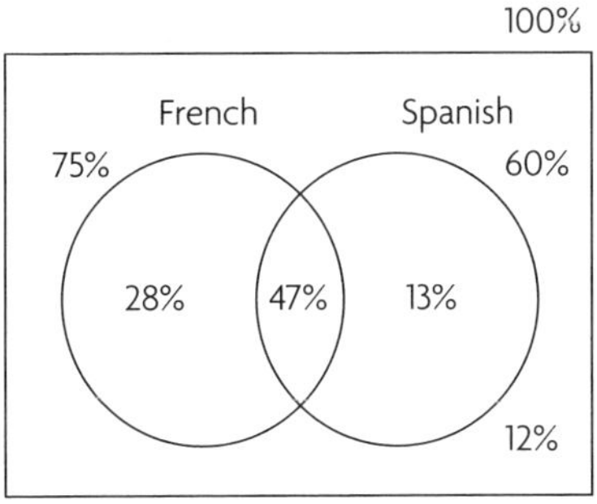

With the completed diagram, it is straightforward to answer the question that was asked: What percentage of the students study only French? The answer is 28%.

Estimation

Although estimation is a useful technique, it should only be applied to problems that ask for an estimation and that have answer choices that are significantly different from each other. Of course, the natural question is how significant? The answer is that if a number would affect the final digit of an answer when rounding it is significant. For example, the two numbers 64.5 and 66.8 may be significant only if you are working with values that are less than or equal to one tenth, i.e. 0.1.

Of the following, the closest approximation of $\sqrt{\frac{3600}{16}}$ is:

- 5
- 10
- 15
- 20
- 25

Since the question asks for an approximation and you are given values in tenths in the answer choices, the answer choices are significantly different from each other.

This question can be turned into:

$$\sqrt{\frac{6 \times 600}{16}} = \sqrt{\frac{6 \times 6 \times 100}{4 \times 4}}$$

$$= \sqrt{\frac{4 \times 9 \times 4 \times 25}{4 \times 4}}$$

$$= \sqrt{\frac{\not{4} \times 9 \times \not{4} \times 25}{\not{4} \times \not{4}}}$$

$$= \sqrt{9 \times 25}$$

$$= \sqrt{9} \times \sqrt{25}$$

$$= 3 \times 5$$

$$= 15$$

Determining the property of an answer

The final strategy is to determine a property of the answer. If there is only one answer choice with such a property, it must be the correct answer choice. This could be any number of properties; however, the properties that come up most often are that the answer choice must be a multiple of a number or the unit's digit of the answer choice must be a certain number. Consider the following example.

When the integer n is divided by d the result is 75.15. Which of the following could be the remainder when n is divided by d?

(A) 63

(B) 64

(C) 65

(D) 67

(E) 70

The remainder equation, n = Qd + r, can be stated as n/d=Q + r/d. Since the remainder over d must equal 0.15, we can state that r/d = 15/100. The fraction 15/100 reduces to 3/20. This tells us that the ratio of r/d is 3/20. Since that is the case, r must be a multiple of 3 and d must be a multiple of 20. The only answer choice that is a multiple of 3 is answer choice A, 63.

Despite all these techniques, if you are trying to get a very high score, you should probably focus on actually just solving the problem. These techniques will help you with difficult problems, but you should try to understand the straightforward maths approach to solving the problems.

Data sufficiency

Data sufficiency questions are unique to the GMAT®. These are questions that ask you to determine if there is enough information given to answer a question. The trick is that you do not actually have to solve it for an answer. Because of that, these questions test logical reasoning skills more than they test quantitative skills. However, quantitative skills are occasionally necessary to understand the logic.

Is the integer x positive?

$x/y > 0$

$y^3 < 0$

(A) Statement 1 ALONE is sufficient, but statement 2 alone is not sufficient to answer the question.

(B) Statement 2 ALONE is sufficient, but statement 1 alone is not sufficient to answer the question.

(C) BOTH statements 1 and 2 taken TOGETHER are sufficient to answer the question, but NEITHER statement ALONE is sufficient to answer the question.

(D) EACH statement ALONE is sufficient to answer the question.

(E) Statements 1 and 2 taken TOGETHER are NOT sufficient to answer the question.

Statement 1 tells us that x and y must both either be positive or negative. Because it could be either positive or negative, statement 1 is not sufficient.

Statement 2 tells us that y^3 is negative. For that to be true y must be negative. Because statement 2 tells us nothing about x, statement 2 is not sufficient to answer the question.

Combining the two statements, y is negative and x must have the same sign as y. Since y is negative x must also be negative. Although x is not positive, we needed only to determine whether we could answer the question is x positive. Since x is negative, so statements 1 and 2 are sufficient and C is the correct answer choice.

Nothing about this question was quantitatively difficult. Answering it simply required constructing a series of "if/then" statements.

There are two important strategies for data sufficiency. The first is to be disciplined and consider only one statement at a time. Since you will read statement 1 before reading statement 2, it is quite common to still hold statement 1 in your mind when considering statement 2. As a result, you would end up choosing answer choice B when the correct answer would be C.

The other strategy is to simplify the question before considering the two statements. Consider the following question.

Is car x travelling faster than 90 miles per hour? (5,280 feet = 1 mile)

1. Car x is travelling faster than 88 feet per second.

2. Car x is travelling slower than 132 feet per second.

(A) Statement 1 ALONE is sufficient, but statement 2 alone is not sufficient to answer the question.

(B) Statement 2 ALONE is sufficient, but statement 1 alone is not sufficient to answer the question.

(C) BOTH statements 1 and 2 taken TOGETHER are sufficient to answer the question, but NEITHER statement ALONE is sufficient to answer the question.

(D) EACH statement ALONE is sufficient to answer the question.

(E) Statements 1 and 2 taken TOGETHER are NOT sufficient to answer the question.

This question requires you to change miles per hour into feet per second. While you could attempt to change statements 1 and 2 into miles per hour, this would require twice as much work as turning the question into feet per second.

$$90 \text{ miles/hour} \times 1 \text{ hour/3,600 seconds} \times 5{,}280 \text{ feet/1 mile} = 528/4 = 132$$

So the question is asking whether car x is travelling faster than 132 feet per second. Since statement 2 tells us that car x is travelling slower than 132 feet per second, answer choice B is the correct answer.

Verbal reasoning

The verbal section of the GMAT® consists of three sections: reading comprehension; critical reasoning; and sentence correction.

Reading comprehension

The reading comprehension section requires you to read a written passage that is between 300 and 600 words in length and answer questions about the passage. Questions can range from those that ask for what was explicitly stated in the passage to those that ask you to infer something about the structure of the passage or a logical consequence of the ideas presented in the passage.

There are five points to remember when answering reading comprehension questions.

- Be sure to analyse the passage for not only what is being said, but why and how it is being said.
- Pay special attention to the use of commas in the passage. Commas are often used with contrasting terms or with linking phrases. Understanding why a comma was used will often help understand the flow of ideas and the structure of the passage.
- Answer the question that is asked. Sometimes the incorrect answer choices are answers to questions similar to the one that is asked but are slightly different.
- Understand why the incorrect answer choices are wrong. This requires a bit of extra work but is worth the effort. Often these questions are answered by process of elimination. That means the skill you need is not your ability to identify correct answers but your ability to identify incorrect ones.
- Consider the answer choices starting from answer choice E and working your way to answer choice A. That is, the strategy should be to consider the answer choices in any direction other than from A to E. By reading the answer choices in this order, you are less likely to be fooled by tempting but incorrect answer choices.

Critical reasoning

The critical reasoning questions give you short arguments or statements and ask you to consider the quality of the argument or a logical consequence of the statement.

The key points to critical reasoning are as follows.

- Distinguish between facts and opinions. You can never argue with a fact. Even if you do not believe something is true, if it is stated as a fact, it is unassailable.
- Be aware of logical flaws committed when interpreting data. Many of the logical flaws committed in either the arguments or the answer choices are flaws that frequently occur when interpreting statistical data, such as the ones listed below.

- The assumption that correlation is causation. For example, when car windshield wipers are moving, people take out umbrellas, thus windshield wipers cause people to use umbrellas.
- The assumption that the past predicts the future. Dot-com stocks were a great investment if you bought in 1998 and sold in 1999; thus if you want a quick return on money invested for one year, Dot-com stocks are a good bet.
- The assumption that the behaviour of a group is indicative of the behaviour of an individual of that group. For example, most MBAs work in consulting. John is an MBA. So John probably works in consulting. John either works in consulting or he does not.
- The assumption that the behaviour of an individual in a group is indicative of the behaviour of the group. For example, Warren Buffet is one of the world's wealthiest men. He believes the wealthy are under-taxed, so the wealthy believe they are under-taxed.
- The assumption that because a person in a position of authority has an opinion, that opinion is a fact. For example, the Chairman of the Federal Reserve believes that the mortgage market will recover this year, so it is likely the mortgage market is going to recover this year.
- The assumption that those individuals who answer a poll are representative of the population. For example, a poll of recent MBA graduates indicates that the salary of recent graduates is higher than ever. Such a statement fails to account for the possibility that those MBA graduates earning higher salaries are more likely to report those salaries than those graduates who are earning low salaries.
- The assumption that what exists today is representative of what existed in the past. For example, if you bought every stock on the New York Stock Exchange (NYSE) at its initial public offering (IPO) you would have a net worth in excess of a trillion dollars, so it is a good investment strategy to invest in every new IPO. This strategy does not acknowledge that those companies listed on the NYSE today are only those companies that have survived. In other words, it does not consider those companies that had an IPO and failed.

This is not the entirety of the logical problems that arises in critical reasoning questions, but it does cover many of them.

Be argumentative. We find many students simply accept what is given in every critical reasoning question. You will improve your critical reasoning results simply by disagreeing more often. After reading every question, you should try to find any reason to disagree. Even if you are trying to strengthen the argument, you will have a better chance of being able to strengthen an argument if you understand the weaknesses.

Understand the incorrect answer choices. Just as it was a good idea to identify what made incorrect answers wrong in reading comprehension, it is a good idea to identify why incorrect answers are wrong in critical reasoning.

Compare answer choices two at a time. Since you will be answering the question by a process of elimination, only try comparing two answer choices at a time and eliminating one. For example:

- Which is better answer choice E or D? E.
- Which is better answer choice E or C? E.
- Which is better answer choice E or B? B.
- Which is better answer choice B or A? B.

The correct answer is B.

While this might seem like common sense, it is very easy to get your thoughts muddled by trying to compare three or four different options at the same time.

If English is not your native language, we recommend you start off studying with a dictionary. Although, you will not be able to use a dictionary on your GMAT®, you will improve both your language and reasoning skills by using a dictionary for the first few study sessions.

Sentence correction

The sentence correction section tests your knowledge of English grammar in the context of a sentence. You do not need to be familiar with the parts of speech used by grammarians – such as phrasal verbs, predicate and past participles. However, if you are familiar with the concepts these words represent, you have an advantage.

There are two key strategies for sentence correction. The first is that if you cannot understand the meaning of a sentence, it is wrong. Very frequently self-doubt creeps in and we start convincing ourselves using absurd logic. Consider the following reasoning:

I think answer choice A sounds best. However, I am not really good at sentence correction. I do not understand answer choice B, but it sounds more academic. Because I am bad at sentence correction A cannot be the best answer choice. Since I do not understand B, I am probably just missing something and B is the best answer.

If this reasoning style sounds a little familiar, you need to change the way you answer these questions.

The second strategy is to compare answer choices. The differences in answer choices must demonstrate the problem with the answers.

Consider the following statement.

Although he was well respected by those serving with him in North Africa and Europe, General George Patten could not have become the president of the US because he was politically unpopular with Americans living in the US.

(A) General George Patten could not have become the president of the US because he was politically unpopular with Americans living in the US.

(B) Because he was politically unpopular with Americans living in the US, General George Patten could not have become the president of the US.

(C) The president of the US could not have been George Patten because he was politically unpopular with Americans living in the US.

(D) General George Patten, who was politically unpopular with Americans back in the US, could not have become the president of that country.

(E) Because he was politically unpopular with Americans living in the US, the president of the US could not have been General George Patten.

Answer: A.

In the question above, the difference between the answer choices is the word order. However, differences in word order may be because the problem with the sentence has to do with logic and not necessarily with grammar. Below is a list of differences that may occur in answer choices and what those differences indicate.

- A difference in prepositions often indicates a problem with an idiom.
- A difference in verbs indicates either a problem with verb tense or a problem with subject verb agreement.
- A difference in the auxiliary verbs *have*, *had*, and *has* indicates a problem with aspect (i.e. verb tense).
- A difference in the noun that follows a subordinate clause indicates a problem with logic.
- A difference between conjunctions, commas and semicolons indicates either an incomplete clause or a run-on sentence.
- A difference in a list indicates a problem with parallelism.

While this is not a complete list, if you study by asking yourself what the differences between the sentences are, you will make steady progress with sentence correction.

Integrated reasoning

The integrated reasoning section is designed to test a combination of both quantitative and verbal skills. This section is a lot like using Microsoft's Excel or IBM's SPSS to mine data or solve problems. These questions will start appearing on the GMAT® in June 2012.

There are four formats of integrated reasoning questions.

1. **Multi-source reasoning questions.** These are questions where you are expected to answer questions using data contained in multiple sources. For example, you may have to extract data from an email, a chart, and/or a table of figures.
2. **Table analysis questions.** These are questions that test your ability to analyse tables. This is a lot like sorting a table or using a pivot table in Excel.
3. **Graphics interpretation questions.** These are questions that require you to extract data from a chart or graph. You can expect this to be a lot like reading a graph to either find a value or extrapolating to predict a value.
4. **Two-part analysis questions.** No surprise, these questions require you to answer two parts to reach the solution.

In April 2012, the Graduate Management Admission Council (GMAC), the organisation responsible for the GMAT®, released study materials for Integrated Reasoning.

"The GMAT® preparation and test-taking has been one of the most challenging and interesting exercises I have come across in my life. GMAT® is more than a test, it also measures your mental resilience and systemic thinking. Preparing for the test and achieving the required scores are not an easy task for many of us. My first score was 530 resulting in a conditional offer for the EMBA programme at London Business School. I knew I had to obtain 600+ and I started working methodically and diligently towards it. GMAT® became more than a test to crack, it became a goal I had to achieve and on which my future and dreams depended upon. Everything was at stake and I was not prepared to give up. I immediately set my goal as reaching a 700 score and I broke the task down into smaller manageable parts depending on my areas of particular difficulty and importance. I adopted a robust and solid routine of focused preparation. I studied three hours each morning and took mock tests for three hours in the evening for six weeks. GMAT® had basically become my bread and butter and part of my brain's hardware as opposed to a limitation or inconvenience.

The final result? When I retook the test and I saw the score on the screen, I was over the moon! I improved my score by 120 points achieving 650. I am now setting myself the challenge of reaching 800 as the next step challenge developing in the process a method for cracking the GMAT® using the full potential of our amazing brains."
Athina Kafetsiou, Business Psychologist and Executive Coach, London Business School EMBA 2007

Practical considerations

When to take the GMAT®

In an ideal world, candidates should take the GMAT® before they start to work on their application to business schools and most certainly before they submit an application. Realistically, however, candidates usually start their GMAT® preparation while in the process of undertaking their research on schools and programmes or when completing their application. Giving yourself plenty of time to prepare for the exam will hopefully result in you achieving your target score and therefore eliminate the need to retake the test. We would strongly advise against submitting an application for an FT MBA programme without a GMAT® score; your application simply will not be reviewed until it is complete with the GMAT® score. For applications to EMBA programmes, the requirements may be less stringent and schools may review your application for an interview place without a GMAT® score. It's important to check the requirements for each of the schools you are applying to.

Where to take the GMAT®

The GMAT® exam is offered worldwide in most major cities. You can identify your closest test centre through the online search on the GMAT® website. You can take the test at almost any time of the year although you will need to check availability at your nearest test centre. You will need to register to take the exam online at www.mba.com and then search for available dates at the test centre of your choice You can take the GMAT® test up to five times during any 12-month period, but only once during any 31-day period. The test costs US$250 (approximately £160).

Preparing for the GMAT®

It can be a difficult task to prepare for the exam whilst simultaneously putting your application together and continuing your research into schools. Timing may be an issue. There are three ways that you can prepare for the test:

- by yourself using specific preparatory guides
- by taking preparatory courses
- through the help of a GMAT® coach.

There are a multitude of books and materials available to buy or accessible online. If you decide to go down this route it is significantly cheaper than using a coach, you are in control of your own schedule and you tailor it to your own learning style; however, you need to be extremely self-disciplined to succeed. Alternatively, preparatory classes and GMAT® coaches enable you to really pinpoint areas for improvement; you have an expert at hand to prepare a study schedule for you and help you stay focused. In addition, you will be studying with others with whom you can compare your level of ability against. This method is relatively more expensive, although if you are looking for a more focused approach, this may suit you better.

Preparation time

It is difficult to tell you how much time you need to allot for the GMAT® preparation. To start with, we suggest you take a look at the sample test on www.mba.com. Become familiar with the test and questions and from there you will get a sense of what your level is and how much work you need to put in to achieve you target score. We would certainly recommend against taking the test without any preparation whatsoever. Preparation time can vary from one to six months, studying anything up to 10 hours a week. How much time you allocate to GMAT® preparation is a highly individual decision, depending upon your work/personal commitments, attention span and existing knowledge of the subject matter.

Taking the GMAT®

In most countries you will be asked to provide one of the following forms of identification (ID) at the test centre:

- passport
- government-issued driver's licence
- government-issued national/state/province identity card (including European ID card)
- military ID card.

ID requirements can differ from country to country, be sure to check beforehand at www.mba.com.

Furthermore, on the day of the test you will also be required to have your palms scanned by a sensor. This records the pattern formed on your palm veins which means you will have a single GMAT® record. This is to prevent fraudulent activity such as someone else taking the test for you if you decide to retake it.

All tests are audio and video recorded and you are not permitted to bring any food, drink, any personal items or testing aids such as notes or calculators.

Before you start the exam you can select up to five recipients for the results. Every school has their own unique GMAT® code and results are sent within 20 calendar days and are accessible to the schools via an online system. If you do not select five recipients on the day, you can add more at a later date. You can also send your results to more than five recipients at an additional cost. However, you can obtain a copy of the unofficial verbal and quantitative scores immediately after the test is complete. As schools will receive the score only after a few days, if you are planning to take the test very close to the application deadline you should inform the admissions team at the relevant school(s) and fax or email the unofficial score report to them as evidence that you have taken the test by the deadline.

Retaking the GMAT®

In the previous chapter we touched on the average GMAT® scores you should be aiming for (p.119). If you have taken the exam and not achieved your target score, you do have the opportunity to retake after 31 days. However, as mentioned before, you need to be mindful of the number of times you retake the test as some schools do not look favourably on candidates with a GMAT® retake score. The official GMAT® report will list all your scores including retake scores. If you take the GMAT® three times, the score will appear on the report three times although, any new scores will not automatically be sent to previous recipients unless you specify this at the time of retaking the GMAT® exam.

If I obtain a low score, can I choose not to send it to the schools?

Not sending your score report to the schools of your choice will not change the end result of the admissions process. Top schools will ask you to make the score available to them while you go through the various stages of the application. Refusing to give them access to your full GMAT® results will send warning signals to the admissions committee. Before taking the test you should carefully research the scores you need for the schools in which you are interested. If you require more preparation to achieve a target GMAT® score, you can postpone taking the test. After obtaining a low score, you should ask yourself what has not worked out and eventually dedicate extra time for the preparation, or obtain support for tackling your weak spots. If, after a number of attempts you still do not produce the results you were hoping for, you should consider your options and look at other schools whose GMAT® profiles and requirements are a better fit with the level that you have achieved.

Final thoughts

Regarding admissions committees and the emphasis put on the GMAT®, it is best to say that a high GMAT® score does not guarantee admission; however, a low GMAT® score can prevent you getting into top programmes. In addition, many scholarships consider the GMAT® score in their merit criteria.

For those attending university, the GMAT® is nothing like your university exams. In university, it is possible for everyone to get a top score. You can cram for the exam and do very well. Your exams were likely static and did not adapt to your ability level.

GMAT® scores are graded on a bell curve, which means you are in direct competition with all other MBA applicants for a top score. So unlike university exams, on which everyone could get a top score, the GMAT® is designed so that only 1% of the population will get a score in the top 1%. The maximum score you can achieve on the GMAT® is 800. Most candidates are shooting for a score in the top 10%, which means the majority of candidates will be disappointed. It is worth asking yourself:

- Why will you be in the top 10% of exam test-takers?
- What is it that you know that 90% of the other test-takers don't?
- Will you work harder than 90% of the other test-takers?
- Are you just cleverer than 90% of test-takers?

Our advice is not to rely on having done an advanced degree from a top university. You are competing with MBA applicants, not the general population. Much of your competition comes from degree holders from top universities. From our point of view, the answer to this question needs to be 10% more effort.

Let us not confuse effort with time. Countless candidates put in endless hours. But simply sitting and redoing the same work again and again is not effort. Effort comes in the form of constantly challenging yourself to be more confident in your answers, sticking with a question until you legitimately understand the underlying concept, and being disciplined enough to follow a constant study plan day after day, week after week.

If you did not previously study in the US, that is, you studied in Europe or other countries, the GMAT® may be unfamiliar to you for a couple of reasons:

- it is in multiple-choice format
- it is computer-adaptive.

We are sure you have seen multiple-choice questions before, and you expect these question types to be much easier than open ended response questions. On the GMAT® this is not the case. Multiple-choice questions on the GMAT® are just as capable of testing higher order skills as are open ended questions.

Points to consider

The GMAT® is administered on the computer, subsequently some students find it more challenging. While this was a large concern when computer adaptive testing was introduced in the 1990s, it is fair to now expect MBA applicants to be sufficiently familiar with using a computer to take an exam.

Since the GMAT® is computer-adaptive, some test-takers will find it more difficult than paper and pencil exams. Every question after the first five will likely be delivered at or above your ability level. Therefore, it is unlikely that you will feel you did well on the GMAT® when you finish. Regardless of this feeling, be sure you report your score.

The University of Southampton

The Southampton MBA will challenge your thinking. No matter how much experience you already have in business, studying for an MBA with us will expand your world. Our experienced and research-active lecturers will introduce you to the latest management theories and discuss how you can make the most out of them in your organisation. You will learn how to lead and manage in today's ever-changing global market. We will expect a lot from you if you sign up for an MBA. But, if you put in the effort, you may be amazed at the results.

The University of Southampton is one of the UK's top research-led universities, committed to high quality teaching and the advancement of knowledge. Studying for our MBA will challenge you to develop the essential understanding, knowledge and confidence to question conventional thinking and succeed in our fast-moving business world. You need to stand out, not blend in.

Our MBA, accredited by AMBA, is rigorous, engaging and worthwhile, taught in groups of around 50 people. You can study either full time or part time to suit your circumstances.

Throughout and beyond the programme, we will encourage you to explore business issues from different perspectives. Alongside the compulsory modules, you will have the opportunity to choose the equivalent of two options to tailor your MBA to your personal needs, drawing from specialisms in the management school and the wider university.

Our innovative application of management skills element will enable you to engage in integrated, multidisciplinary group work, taking on the role of creator, investigator, decision maker and champion within a business context. These cross-functional roles will provide a broad approach to management challenges and the personal reflections that make up part of the assessment for this section will help you to consolidate and consider your newly acquired knowledge and your future role within an organisation.

You will have the opportunity to network with other future business leaders from around the world in a stimulating, exacting and interactive environment making contacts and friends for life.

Case study

Mary Knoll

Mary Knoll travelled from the US to study for the University of Southampton MBA. She had worked in insurance in her home state of Michigan, leading a team of 12 people, but wanted to add to her qualifications and learn more about the world.

"Business is so globalised and I felt that studying in another country would benefit my career," she explains. "I researched the Southampton Management School, which I found was well respected and part of a leading UK university. I knew the city to be a friendly place as well from my previous travels here. I hadn't been away from home for more than a month before so it was important I made the right choice."

Mary has enjoyed her year in Southampton: "It has been an excellent programme and there have been so many highlights. The placement of the effective leadership module in the year's study was key to developing worthwhile business relationships with my colleagues and I also enjoyed the sessions on strategy in business." She chose to examine a key issue in human resources for her dissertation, analysing the importance of references in recruitment and selection.

Outside her studies, Mary valued the opportunities to spend time with students from all over the world. "I have made so many good friends and learned a great deal about different cultures. I know I will keep in touch with my fellow graduates and, who knows, maybe we can work together one day."

Now that she has completed the MBA, Mary is planning to build on her new qualification. "I'm looking forward to seeing how my career path will develop over the next few years. I know I want to get involved in international business and I'm sure my experiences at Southampton will aid my success."

£50

Westminster Business School

Today's business environment is one of rapid change and diverse challenges. The Westminster Business School MBA develops leaders and innovators who can meet those challenges, driving organisations forward.

Westminster's MBA programme is constantly evolving, offering an integrated perspective on the challenges facing global businesses, equipping students with the leadership skills essential in today's demanding business environment.

The programme's holistic approach combines the fundamentals of key functional business areas with modules which take a multidisciplinary approach to real-world business issues incorporating sustainability issues and corporate social responsibility, and investigating how various areas of business and the business environment work together and influence each other.

Specialist modules include subjects such as HR, strategies for change management, foresight and future studies, project management and financial studies. The programme also includes an international study trip, residential weekend, mentoring scheme and social entrepreneurship module.

The social entrepreneurship module is a unique opportunity for MBA students to relate their entrepreneurial learning to social problems in a global context. Students travel to a developing country, such as Uganda, and work with charities to help address local issues, for example implementing a management information system to help distribute drugs to AIDS victims.

MBA graduate Leanne Shulman, says of her Westminster experience:

> *"Studying at a university that was internationally accredited, multinational and that offered a diverse environment was important to me. I wanted to develop an international network and to learn about and to experience different elements influencing the business world and Westminster Business School offered all this and more. Yes, the course is intense and challenging, but it has been very rewarding, stretching myself beyond what I ever thought would be possible."*

Westminster Business School's MBA is accredited by AMBA, reflecting the high quality of the programme and giving students access to AMBA resources including alumni and career development.

Westminster's MBA programme is delivered in both full-time or part-time formats but whichever option students choose, they receive the same high-level of teaching from dedicated and experienced faculty members.

For more information about the MBA, please see www.westminster.ac.uk/mba.

9

Interviews

Athina Kafetsiou, Business Psychologist and Executive Coach, London Business School EMBA 2007

What's in an interview?

You have landed that much wished for interview with the school of your choice. Congratulations, this is great news indeed! You have made it through a rigorous first level selection process that increases your chances of getting accepted by 25–50% depending on the school and programme of your choice (see p.179 for how we calculate this). However, these figures do not reflect the real weighting the interview makes towards the admissions decision.

Interviews are as important as any other part of the application process and, however good your experience and application package are, if you do not perform well at interview stage you will not stand a strong chance of obtaining an offer for the school of your choice. How could a 45-minute to 1.5-hour meeting determine the admission outcome to that degree? This is the typical dilemma of the interview as a selection tool in any context.

The interview is designed to reveal important clues about your leadership attributes and how you are as a person in your interpersonal interactions with people. The only way to see whether you are fit and ready to take on the MBA challenge to the next level is by seeing you in person and putting your personality, communication and temperament to the test.

Success rate of being offered an interview

FT MBA programmes

Approximate total number of applications per school: Between 7,000 and 8,000

Places available: 380–800

Ratio of probability with no weighting: 1/20 = 5% or 1/10 = 10%

This is your ratio/percentage before the first selection process, which involves the admissions committee reviewing your application before inviting you to an interview. Business schools usually shortlist for interview a number of candidates, which is about twice the number of places to fill, which increases your chances of being accepted (assuming you already have the required qualification in place as well as the GMAT® score required by the school of your choice.

EMBA/PTMBA

Approximate total number of applications per school: 200

Places available: 50

Ratio of probability with no weighting: 1/4 maximum or 25%.

This number varies significantly depending on the school and programme as well as what is happening in the global business and finance cycle, which impacts on the overall number of applications that schools receive. There is a tendency for EMBA or PT MBA application numbers to fall in conditions of economic crisis or turmoil and uncertainty, the exact opposite of the picture for FT MBAs. In the case of EMBA or PT MBAs you would normally expect the school to invite for interview about 50% of the original applicant pool. This is a significant rise in probability of getting accepted.

These calculations are just rough examples of how you could start thinking about your chances of getting accepted into a top school of your choice assuming that you have all the right credentials, qualifications, achievements, vision and exposure that top schools are looking for. One thing is for certain; the more prestigious a school, the greater the chance that once called for an interview you are considered a strong applicant. Equally true, if you lack the fundamentals a top school is considering when assessing their prospective applicants, you need to reassess your options.

Why an interview?

Why do business schools interview candidates who have already been carefully selected?

Business schools attract thousands of applications for their MBA programmes. A well established truth is that the applicant pool is amazingly full of candidates who look "great on paper", with fantastic academic achievements, strong GMAT® scores, experience of working for top firms at a global level, fantastic aspirations and plans for adding value and changing the world. Most candidates look perfectly competent to join a top MBA programme and complete it successfully as well as excel at their careers.

The interview is all about getting to know you as a person; how you interact with people; how you hold yourself in a classroom environment as well as in your study group and interpersonal relations with the whole school community. The questions going through the minds of the interviewers and members of the admissions teams are:

- Does this individual belong here?
- Does he/she have the psychological make up to do great things and achieve as an individual as well as part of the study group and school community?
- Would we like to have this person sitting in our classrooms or next to us?
- And most importantly, can this carry the school's flag proudly, passionately and appropriately after graduation?

This part of the admissions process is all about personality, values, worldviews, communication styles, attitude to learning, responses to stress and challenges. It is the school's key objective to admit to its ranks only those people who are able to cope, adapt and excel under conditions of extreme pressure and within a group of highly talented and motivated people, who are quite demanding of themselves and others.

Through the interview you need to prove that you are an exceptional candidate with the right balance of academic excellence, interpersonal skills and appetite for learning and development that will enable you to move up the leadership ladder.

If you read through the business school's literature to extract their "ideal candidate profile", you will read about the key attributes they look for in terms of vision, aspirations, contribution to business or communities, integrity, influencing, robust decision making, and ability to take responsibility for self and others. This is what business schools expect to see articulated and communicated at the critical stage of the interview. The three main goals that a business school interview aims to achieve are the following:

- have a personal interaction with you and check that what they see on paper corresponds to how you are as a person – that your application and accompanying essays are not the product of anyone else apart from your own
- see "with their own eyes" whether you fit well with the school culture, that you can demonstrate that you have a lot to offer as well as contribute to the school community

- assess whether you would be a good ambassador for the school brand and ensure that you leave the interviewer with a good impression.

One of the key things that will win over your interviewer is a true and authentic interest in the school and everything it offers, rather than just the "brand name". The interviewers assess you on a number of different levels – not just your academic skills, professional experience and ability to move up and fast in your career; they want to know how much you are prepared to invest in being at the school, making the best out of your experience and being able to represent its brand after graduation as an ambassador.

Interview preparation

Identifying and understanding different types of interview and interview tools

One of the first aspects to consider when you prepare for the interview is the type of interview you may have. There are different ones which assess your suitability for a top business school.

Competency interview

The interview style that has become prominent in business schools and workplaces alike is the competency or behavioural interview.

This type of interview measures your skills, competencies and knowledge. The main instrument for quizzing you at a competency interview is the use of examples to quote your experience. Typical questions you would come across at this type of interview start with expressions such as the following.

- "Give us an example of ... "
- "Tell us about a time when ... "
- "What did you do when ... "
- "What would you do if ... "
- "Tell us about a time when ... "

Success at this type of interview relies on thorough reflection of your experience and career from the perspective of your achievements and your impact on the people you have been working with. You will need to be in a position to quote specific examples and situations in which you were faced with these circumstances or challenges and responded in the way you did, explaining why you did so. Your explanation needs to be thorough, succinct and clear, and you will need to express yourself in a brief but engaging manner to win your interviewer over.

The other typical instruments used to make the difficult decision of "who stands out from the crowd and who does not" are case studies and presentations.

Case study method

The case study method is used extensively as a recruitment tool in consulting and in other industries as well as a learning method in the MBA class. Thorough knowledge, experience and understanding of the subject is of vital importance to succeed in this type of interview, which tests not only your knowledge and grasp of the subject but also your ability to think critically, looking at things from a global perspective to offer solutions and conclusions that are relevant, efficient and realistic.

You normally have at least one or two weeks to prepare yourself for this final and utterly critical stage of your admissions process. Depending on the programme and the school you are applying for, the interview process and experience will vary significantly. At the interview itself you may also be asked to analyse a case study and discuss it with your interviewer in length and depth. Top schools go to great length to match the profile of your interviewer with yours so that you have a real and good chance to interact with them and be evaluated properly. They carefully select alumni or students who are able to recruit the right candidates for their programmes.

It is also quite common for FT MBA candidates to be asked to prepare a presentation for their interviewers. In some cases the topic of the presentation is emailed in advance; in others, candidates are invited to choose the subject they are going to present on. Sometimes the subject of the presentation is offered to the candidates at short notice or on the day. Through this task, schools may assess you in a number of areas such as communication, analytical skills and problem solving.

Telephone and videoconference interviews

Some schools may offer you the opportunity of a telephone or, occasionally, a video interview when there are practical circumstances that may prevent you from interviewing in person: for example, the school is unable to find available interviewers in your area and you have not had sufficient notice to organise international flights and/or visa. This type of interview can make you even more anxious than standard ones.

It is important to ensure that you are able to pick up the call in an environment where you are able to hear and be heard properly. If you cannot avoid using a mobile phone, make sure that you are in an area where there is strong signal and no risk of the communication being broken.

Interviews with more than one interviewer

At times, interviews are conducted by a panel of two or three interviewers; or in sequence with different interviewers. Interviewers may be a mix of alumni and members of the admissions staff. The objective is to obtain a more balanced view on the candidate from a number of different people, thus from different perspectives. The best way to deal with this type of interview is to ensure that you have a coherent "story" to present; your unique selling points need to come across consistently while engaging different types of people, using your emotional intelligence skills.

If you are in a panel interview, ensure that you make eye contact with all the panel members; you would normally focus on the member who is asking you the question and then move your eyes around other members while answering the question. A good panel interviewee will also try to refer to aspects highlighted by panel members in the earlier discussion or question.

Interviewer's profile

Your interviewer could be a member of the admissions committee or faculty, an alumnus/alumna who has already been through the MBA experience or more rarely a student. Some interviews by alumni or students; some schools ensure that you are interviewed by alumni with relevant experience in your industry so that you have the chance to be fairly assessed by someone who has expertise in your area. Some schools put you in touch with your interviewer and ask you to liaise with them directly in order to find a mutually convenient time for the interview to take place in. In this case, you do have the "luxury" to know in advance your interviewer, hence look them up and be better prepared for your meeting.

Make sure you research the person in advance and use this unique opportunity to your advantage. There are numerous places to search for information, such as professional networking services and of course search engines. Find out about your interviewer's career trajectory, about their profile, their interests and, more importantly, how the MBA degree fits in their evolution. The interviewers background should give you a good amount of information about what he/she will be quizzing you about, i.e. prepare yourself for a lot of numerically driven questions if the person is coming from a finance background and more of a case study approach if they are coming from a consulting one. Knowing who the interviewer is in advance helps you prepare a good set of tailored questions to ask as well, which is a great opportunity for building rapport.

Students and alumni interviewers are volunteers who offer their time to help out the school with this critical part of the admissions process. Interviewers have their own style, personality, professional expertise, and they will inevitably have different ways of approaching the task. This is not a reason to feel that candidates are not treated fairly at interview and should prepare you to the fact that at business school you will be exposed to inquisitive people with diverse personality, styles, interests and motivations.

The technical interviewer

There are certain interviewers who will dig deep into your experience and technical knowledge, especially if you come from a more specialist background such as finance or technology. Their aim is to measure the depth and breadth of your experience and expertise, and whether it matches the "paper profile" which you have built throughout your application.

The key to winning over this type of interviewer is by keeping a clear focus on the questions asked.

The factual interviewer

This type of interviewer will delve into every single detail of your application, quizzing you around anything and everything and especially information which does not make sense or sounds too good to be true. You would expect this interview to last a bit longer than usual.

The key to winning over this very sceptical interviewer is staying calm, focused and managing your responses not to come across as arrogant or defensive at all. It is also important that you prepare yourself before the interview by reading your application and identifying any potential incongruities or weak spots.

The people interviewer

This interviewer will focus more on your interpersonal and leadership skills and will question you directly and indirectly on areas of your experience which demonstrate these skills. This type of interviewer tends to ask about challenging situations in which you had to make tough choices which show your management and leadership style; how you deal with people and see yourself; and what you have done to learn and change following constructive feedback. The important elements for winning over this interviewer are honesty and willingness to understand yourself and people around you. Even if your leadership style is more authoritative or pace-setting, you will still be able to make a positive impression by demonstrating awareness of your style as well as the "implications" to others and being honest about it.

The easygoing interviewer

If you are extremely lucky, you will come across an interviewer type that can be equated to winning the lottery: the easygoing interviewer, who is the best person to have a great conversation with as well as to feel great about yourself and the whole experience that lies ahead. This is one of the best interview experiences one could have, but is not as easy as it sounds!

This type of interviewer is by nature a warm person who comes across in an extremely polite way; however, they are really instinctive and will make their recommendation not only based on what they see on paper or hear from you but also based on their instinct or gut feeling about you. To win over this type of interviewer, you need to be yourself and allow yourself to shine and get out. If you employ a cautious and reserved attitude out of fear of making the wrong impression, you may risk coming across as manipulative and calculative, and this will not go down too well with this type of interviewer.

All the information you have provided about yourself will be put under the microscope and investigated for validity, reliability and accuracy. Your interviewers have full access to all your application materials prior to your interview and will have analysed it in order to pick up any inconsistencies and unclear points, which they will investigate, putting you on the spot. Ensure that you know your application inside out and refresh your memory promptly before the interview.

The most critical elements of your application are:

- your career track record to date and key achievements within this
- your aspirations and realistic vision for the future
- the personal strengths and assets that have helped you and continue to help you in your path to excellence and global leadership
- your weaknesses and important lessons learnt from "mistakes" or miscalculations.

International Institute of Business

Get your MBA Degree in Kiev!

The International Institute of Business is the leading business school in Ukraine and offers you two choices when you are looking for an MBA degree.

The EMBA programme (www.iib.com.ua/E-MBA) is designed for "people, who are responsible for, and determine the future of their companies". High level of motivation, business experience and participation in decision making at strategic level are important characteristics of people who apply for IIB EMBA. The programme combines local relevance and global perspectives and aims to change the way of thinking.

A part-time programme is completed in 22 months. It comprises intensive monthly five-day sessions from Wednesday to Sunday. There are 20 sessions each of 33 in-class guided learning hours.

To be considered as a potential candidate you should submit (available at website): application form; essay/motivation letter; two recommendation letters; copy of diploma and transcript from all universities attended; copy of passport; three passport-size photos; CV.

Intakes: October; working language: Russian; price: €17,000 including tuition, books and study materials provision, administration and service.

The International MBA programme (www.iib.com.ua/I-MBA) is a double-degree programme delivered by IIB in partnership with the University of New Brunswick, Canada. The International MBA is designed for managers looking to equip themselves with a broad range of management skills, greater knowledge in business management, and enhanced management competence, with the result that they are better able to successfully develop their careers in today's fast-changing, complex global environment.

It is a part-time programme completed in 18 months. The programme comprises intensive monthly five-day sessions from Wednesday to Sunday.

You should submit the following documents: application form; statement of interest; resume; copy of diploma and official transcript(s); two letters of reference; TOEFL (iBT) certificates (min. 92); copy of passport; three passport-size photos.

Intakes – March; working language: English; price: €16,500 including tuition, study materials provision, administration and service.

The IIB International MBA and EMBA programmes are included in the "Top 200 Best Masters and MBA Programs Worldwide in 2011" (www.eduniversal-ranking.com).

IMD International

The IMD MBA

The IMD MBA is an international, one-year leadership and general management programme. Based in Switzerland – a hub of the financial, industrial and luxury industries – the campus is located in the city of Lausanne on the banks of Lake Geneva, renowned for its natural beauty.

Leadership

Intensive personal development and individual coaching create a challenging and transformational year where participants develop their leadership skills every day. An optional 20 sessions with a trained psychoanalyst offers them a further opportunity to increase self-awareness and become more effective leaders.

Learn more. Do more. Become more

The consistently top-ranked programme prepares participants to tackle complex business challenges and lead in a responsible manner. The integration of classes, live business cases and hands-on projects allows participants to apply what they learn in an international context. Working across the globe on real issues, participants live the start up experience through entrepreneurship projects, help develop sustainability through the Discovery Expedition in South Africa, and work with top management on international consulting projects.

Admissions

From the written application to the on-campus assessment day, IMD looks to select the best group of 90 from around the world: a talented group of people from diverse backgrounds who have demonstrated the potential and desire to make a difference. These dynamic individuals represent over 40 nationalities, typically have between four and nine years of full-time work experience and have an international outlook, excellent interpersonal skills and strong leadership potential.

Career enhancing

The IMD MBA is a world-class graduate programme, which is life changing and career enhancing. IMD supports MBAs in their job search by organising career training and facilitating contacts with recruiters from diverse sectors and locations looking to find new talent for their future leadership roles.

Areas explored in most business school interviews

An interview is the last safeguard of the school in terms of recruiting candidates who are a good fit with the school and its objectives. Depending on the course and the school there are going to be varied degrees of probability of how close you are to securing a place having reached the interview stage. In mid-tier schools, where there is a bit less competition for securing a place, you would normally expect that you would be 75% in when offered an interview. The list below details typical areas covered in business school interviews.

- **Clear and ambitious vision about adding value to the world**. Business schools are looking for people with a burning desire to do great things for themselves and the people around them while maintaining and exhibiting a balanced and realistic approach of how they would go about achieving this.
- **Motivation, achievement and drive**. The interview stage is a great opportunity for you to show what you have achieved so far in your career and life, and how your strong drive to achieve, add value and contribute has helped you navigate difficult situations, overcome potential personal obstacles, and get to the place where you are today, standing out from the crowd.
- **Post-MBA career goals and aspirations**. Interviewers will probe your short-, medium- and long-term objectives to ensure that they are realistic, achievable and aligned with what you have also stated at application stage. They will be interested in hearing directly from you how an MBA degree and that specific school will make a difference in enabling you to achieve your objectives.
- **Self-awareness**. It is of utmost importance that you have reached and communicated a view of yourself that contains a healthy self-esteem together with a actively putting yourself under the microscope to learn from every situation you expose yourself to. Your interviewer will be probing you on how important it is for you to improve and develop and how you go about doing this. Do you actively try to obtain feedback from others and reflect and learn from their inputs?
- **Understanding of your leadership style**. This is complementary to the above theme. Schools are looking for the best, whole-rounded business leaders who know how to look at themselves critically and assess realistically how they are doing on their leadership journey. Successful leaders are able to embrace change and adapt to new challenges and circumstances, remaining competitive and efficient in their roles and increasing exposure. The interviewers will be probing clarity of communication and your ability to handle complex concepts and situations managing pressure, anxiety and stress. They will be interested in learning about difficult situations that stretched your comfort zones and produced important developments and learning about yourself and the world. You need to show a good balance of personal and positive disposition, an open mind, flexibility and commitment to leadership and skills development.

- **Interpersonal skills, the ability to deal with other people effectively.** One of the most important parts of the MBA is the exposure to interactions with faculty, seasoned business people, guest speakers, your class and most importantly your study group. Success in an MBA course has a lot to do with how good you are at:
  - interpersonal relationship management
  - working with people on one-to-one, small or large group basis and achieving together
  - verbal and non-verbal communication
  - understanding and managing your and other people's emotions (emotional intelligence) (see also next point)
  - achieving as an individual and empowering people to achieve together
  - engaging in meaningful or difficult conversations and producing winning climates as well as win-win results
  - conflict management and influencing skills.
- **Managing others**. A closely related theme is that of exposure and experience as well as success in managing others. One of the most critical skills of successful contemporary leaders is their ability to mobilise, energise and incentivise people to work together for the challenging and stretching goals and targets set for the unit, department and the organisation. Emotional intelligence is the core skill for every aspiring future leader. Research has proven that all top contemporary leaders share this skill. At your interview you will be asked to provide examples of situations where you were entrusted with the management of others and demonstrate how you managed to deliver on it efficiently. This area of experience is more relevant to EMBA or PT MBA programmes, where the overall level of experience expected is much higher and people management is seen as one of the entry requirements.
- **Experience and knowledge of your sector or area**. It is important to clearly show to your interviewer that you have depth and breadth of knowledge in your subject matter/industry/company that will deem you an expert in what you do. It is also crucial to demonstrate that you understand the past, the present and the future, and are able to analyse complex issues and matters in your area of expertise, providing a clear global picture. Expressing your views in a clear and succinct manner as well as quoting in a balanced way, opinions and views of key opinion leaders and major publications such as the *Financial Times*, *The Economist*, industry publications, and business reviews will go a long way in an interview.
- **International exposure and cross-cultural awareness**. You will need to provide clear examples of working or living in different cultures and settings that have stretched your way of thinking and looking at the world towards a more open and balanced approach. Situations which are of interest to interviewers normally include those in which you communicated, influenced, negotiated

or engaged people across cultural settings, adapting quickly to the different business environments or local contexts.

- **Dedication and commitment to get through the programme**. It is crucial that you show understanding of the nature of the commitment required to successfully complete the programme, and are prepared to go to great lengths to achieve success academically and in your career. Interviewers will assess whether you are aware of the workload that the programme involves; for EMBAs or PT MBAs, how you are going to combine work, study and private life, and whether you have the support of important people around you (such as your family, your employer, your line manager and your team). The interviewer may also ask you how you plan to meet the required financial commitment; you may also be asked about the types of arrangement that you have made in terms of relocation or commuting.

Linden Selby, Senior Admissions Manager, London Business School

"When interviewing candidates I expect strong preparation and a well-researched case for a particular degree, school and even city. The interview helps me understand how you will contribute, how you expect to benefit, and is an opportunity to bring your application to life with examples. You should expect to be questioned on your objectives and your background. If you have gaps or 'problem areas' in your CV, be prepared to talk about them. After all – you have been invited for interview, so don't be defensive.

"Some practical interview tips that might help are: do not launch straight into a pre-prepared pitch; keep an eye on the time; remember to ask if you've answered the question or is there any more information that would help; practise your handshake and eye contact with a friend. Everyone has an occasional 'freeze-up' on a question – so ask if you can move on – you will almost certainly have an answer before the interview ends. Speak generally to start, then offer something specific for each question."

- **Worst-case scenario**. You need to prepare extensively for this theme. The preparation needs to comprise two areas in particular:
  - o your consolidation of experience and honest account of situations that were of difficulty for you without compromising your presentation of your strengths and abilities
  - o your attitude to becoming defensive when people ask difficult questions around areas that you consider "precious" or "challenging". Being as open as possible, acknowledging and discussing that something bad may have happened, but demonstrating your learning and development from it will be key to your interview success.

Questions you can expect to be asked

The types of question you will be asked at interview stage will be many and quite diverse (see themes in the previous section). The rule of thumb you need to follow religiously is "do not try to second guess, just answer to the best of your ability". You need to be savvy and smart in terms of phrasing your responses in an open, honest and straightforward way that does not expose you. When applying for business school you are expected to have developed an understanding of the world and that you are in a position to articulate clear views and opinions about politics, religion, culture and everything that surrounds us nowadays. The most important success factor is not only having an opinion, but being able to present it in a structured, organised and succinct way that supports it, and allows the other party in the conversation to engage into a constructive dialogue.

A good interviewer at a top school will be focusing on the core themes: What makes you unique and special? And why should you be in this school versus any other candidate?

Typical questions to be prepared for

- Why an MBA/EMBA/PT MBA?
- Why now?
- Why at this particular school? What has attracted you?
- What do you know about the programme or the school that prompted you to apply? How do these aspects connect with your vision and mission?
- What can you contribute to your class and the school?
- What makes you special?
- What has your career been so far? Are you a fast-tracker or more slow-burner?
- What is your vision of yourself in the future and your aspirations?
- Where do you see yourself in five years' time?
- What are your key industry trends and how do your plans fit into this?
- What is your experience of managing people?

- What is your leadership/management style?
- What are your key strengths and weaknesses? What are you doing to address the latter and reinforce the former?
- What is your biggest strength?
- What is your biggest weakness? How have you discovered it and what have you been doing to address it?
- Do you believe that leaders are born or made?
- Do you think you have got what it takes to be a global leader? How have you been developing yourself to achieve this?
- What has been the most difficult situation in your experience in managing people? What did you do about it and what have you learnt from it?
- Have you lived/worked in many countries?
- What are your hobbies and spare time activities? Are you at all involved with giving back in any way?
- Do you play sports and if yes, which ones?
- How many cultures have you interacted with and what issues have you faced when working with people from other cultures? How have you overcome them and what have you learnt from this experience?
- Do you have the support of your employer (more relevant for EMBA or PT MBA programmes)?
- Have you discussed your MBA plans with your family? What was their response?
- How are you going to finance the programme?
- Is your employer prepared to give you the necessary time off work to attend the programme (more relevant for EMBA or PT MBA programmes)
- Have you applied to other business schools/programmes and which?

Logistics

When you receive your interview confirmation, our advice is not to panic or get overexcited. Remain composed and make sure you respond within the required timeline, thanking the school for inviting you to the interview and stating in an appropriate manner how much you appreciate the opportunity you are being offered.

If you are asked to indicate your availability or contact an alumnus who is going to be your interviewer, ensure that you are punctual, fast and offer the person at least three possible dates for interview choices: one sooner, one in the middle and the third one towards the end the designated period. If you are offered the option, ask exactly who you will be interviewing with so that you can do your research properly. You should also ensure that you understand fully the process of the interview, the date and time, the duration and what you are expected to prepare. You should make absolutely certain that you know how to get to the interview location and be there five to 10 minutes ahead of time.

If you are not based in the same country in which the school is based, you will usually be offered the opportunity to interview at a location near you, and this will certainly save you the costs of international flights, accommodation, visa, etc. However, choosing to interview "regionally" instead of visiting the school campus will prevent you from making a direct and personal impact on all the relevant stakeholders who are involved in the decision-making process.

Therefore, if possible you should always try to interview at the school campus, especially if you have not had the opportunity to visit the school prior to the interview. Getting a feel of the environment is certainly very important.

Dress code

The only attire acceptable for this crucial interview is business attire – a formal suit for both men and women, well fitted and in a sober colour. First impressions are very important; you need to pay extra attention to coming across as yourself whilst maintaining a professional and pleasant presence. For business school interviews as well as those in areas such as finance and consulting, it is good to avoid trendy hair styles, make-up, jewellery, bright colours and perfumes. This will allow you to minimise the risk of forming an adverse impression before you have even had the chance to express your first word.

At the interview

Interview etiquette

First and foremost, you need to be respectful and present a balanced profile in terms of how you come across in your communication style and what you say.

The best interviewees are very good at picking up their interviewers' style and mirroring it in order to build rapport and engage them better. Building rapport has two distinct parts:

- your words and content of your conversation and you need to be well prepared (see previous sections)
- the way you sit, talk, move and communicate.

Your articulation and body language

- **Answers need to be brief and articulated in an interesting and engaging manner**. Follow a one to one and a half minute rule (depending on the question asked), being consciously aware that you should be conveying your message in no less or more time. This allows time for the other party to chip in constructively and ask their next question; it also ensures that you keep to the point and do not waffle aimlessly. Simple answers that are too general or monosyllabic responses are to be avoided unless the interviewer prompts you to respond in this way; more often than not, this is a sign that you have overdone it and they are giving you a hint to change your approach (grab this lifeline if offered, keep your antennae up for clues and hints aimed at helping you do well).

- **Be confident but not arrogant or self-centred**. It is very important that you come across as smart and attuned to everything that is happening around you and the interviewer. However, you need to avoid looking hyperactive at all costs or being easily distracted, too nervous and insecure, fidgeting and non-focused, or too cautious and withdrawn on the other extreme. You also need to avoid using "I" all the time; ensure you offer views that are holistic and appreciative of the people who have helped you, work/worked with you or are your role models. There is a fine line that separates confidence from arrogance and arrogance, and make sure you do not cross it.
- **Maintain a composed confident body language, avoiding changing your posture too much**. Be as relaxed as you can while staying focused on the conversation and keeping the interest of your interviewer alive without making too much effort to engage him/her. Your voice should be calm and smooth and the way you express yourself should be clear, organised, with good pace and speed, allowing for reflection times and ensuring you fully understand the questions being asked. Rushing into offering the first thing that comes to mind could get you in trouble. You need to be able to continue along the line of thought you have started exploring without contradicting yourself..
- **Do not get defensive**. The interviewer may put pressure on you to test your resilience, patience, temper and self-esteem, do not fall into the trap of defensiveness. Try to investigate a collaborative angle for getting to the requested answer and if unsure, always clarify.
- **Be careful of revealing weakness and areas for development**. The rule is that there is only one allowable weakness that can be revealed and "excused". Follow this rule at your interview, making sure you do not put yourself in tough spots by saying too much, and in a way that does not work to your advantage. Self-awareness means that you know what could impede you and have the courage and ability to work timely and continuously to improve it.
- **Practise active listening**. Make sure you pay full attention to what the interviewer is asking, no matter how nervous you are or anything that is happening around at that moment in time. Make sure you understand the question clearly, take your time to clarify any unclear aspects and answer. Start a new line of thinking only if it is related to the question asked, and it works to your advantage, i.e. takes the interview to areas of conversation that can work to your benefit. Successful interviewing is a fine art, for both the interviewer and the interviewee. In this case you are the latter and you need to ensure you make the best of it.

The end of the interview

It is imperative that you also ask questions when given a chance to, which is typically at the end of the interview.

Questions you should ask the interviewer

It is important at this stage that you ask questions to clarify areas of uncertainty, keeping the fine balance between procedural matters which can be answered via email or a direct question to admissions staff and aspects that have been discussed at the core interview stage – be careful not to repeat areas that have already been covered, and do not ask questions just for the sake of asking instead out of genuine interest.

Ask questions that you are curious in finding the answer to and ensure they are related to the person across the table and their experience. Your questions need to be articulated in a clear and confident way, keeping in mind that you should spend no more than five to 10 minutes on them. Try to read the interviewer's mood in responding, and be diplomatic, gentle and very careful with how you ask and follow-up on answers. Some indicative questions include the following.

- How has your experience of going through the programme been, and how has it affected your personal and professional development?
- I have heard that the programme requires x number of hours per week (depending on the programme). How much time did you devote and how did you manage to juggle everything? (Especially relevant to PT MBA and EMBA programmes).
- Have you faced any particular challenges while taking this programme and what were they? How did you cope?
- How much support does the school provide in terms of career services, finding a job/changing jobs and generally in terms of professional development opportunities?
- What was the best part of your experience and why?
- If you had the chance to do the programme again, what would you have done differently?

Questions you should never ever ask

- Feedback on how you interviewed, asking your interviewer(s) how you did at the interview is a big mistake and a temptation to avoid at all costs.
- A second inappropriate question (more in relation to its tone than its content) is "What does this school have to offer me versus other schools?". You should know that already, hence why you are there; it is not the interviewers' task to persuade you.
- Another line of questioning you should carefully avoid is information-based questions, such as "How much does the programme cost?" and "What exactly are we going to do in the first/second year?". You should have researched this information before attending your interview.

After the interview

The admissions team or your interviewers will usually give you an indication of the timeline for the final decision on your application. This varies, depending on the school and programme you are applying for; sometimes you may hear after a couple of weeks or even after a few days; in other instances you may need to wait much longer. If you have not been given any timeframe before or at the end of your interview, we suggest you ask a question along the lines of "When can I expect to hear from the school?"

Following your interview, there are different types of decision that schools can make. Chapter 10 will give you an overview of the possible outcomes, including positive decisions, how to deal with disappointing news and how to seek feedback from schools.

Final comments

Besides your best intentions to excel at the critical business school interview, there can still be some "unknowns" in relation to your interviewer and their skills in interviewing. This is a factor that you need to take seriously into consideration when getting to that stage of admissions. When coming across a tricky or not that skilful interviewer, the first thing to do is to keep your calm and focus on finding points of connection and proactively shaping the interaction to your advantage. You could also come across people who either have poor interviewing skills or want to intentionally make your life more difficult by interrupting you continually or by asking consecutive questions in one go without allowing you to complete

Our top three tips

- **Preparation, preparation, preparation**. Research the school, the curriculum, faculty, structure, know your application inside out, talk to alumni and admissions staff at open days and other events, find out all the programme logistics, the requirements, the expectations. Prepare your interview in advance and run mock sessions with people you trust or relevant professionals.
- **Professionalism and confidence**. Watch out for arrogance. The way you come across will determine whether you fit or not, so do not send the wrong message. You are trying to engage your interviewers into a meaningful conversation which will persuade them that you are able to do the programme – succeed and become a valued member of the school's community. Use humour only if you are good at using it and be extremely careful of:
    - how you come across when you use it, and
    - not to offend your interviewer(s) with inappropriate and non-politically correct humour.
- **100% presence during the interview**. Be authentic and natural. Listen carefully, look at non-verbal clues, and answer succinctly and clearly. Do not try to second guess, and give yourself time to answer the questions adopting a normal conversation and response pace.

your initial point before moving on to the next. The best way to deal with these types of interviewer is to keep clarifying and specifying, keeping the focus on what you are trying to convey, without losing your nerve or temper. Your key objective here will be to answer the questions one at a time while keeping the pace of your responses to a level that is comfortable for you.

Reaching the interview stage is a very important achievement; it is therefore very important that you devote your full attention to this part of the admissions process. There is no room for mistakes at this point, especially since you are evaluated in real time and there is no way to "skip it" or "twist it". Taking shortcuts will end up in disappointment and failure. The people across the table from you, whether admissions staff or alumni, who kindly give up their time to be there, are passionate about choosing the best of the best and bringing into their community only those people who really fit and can be good ambassadors for the school.

10

Possible outcomes of the application process

In previous chapters we explored the factors you need to consider when carrying out your research for programmes and schools, discussed the application process and its different components, and then looked at the interview stage and how to prepare yourself for the interview. The next stage in the process is probably the most tense and anticipated aspect of the process – receiving a decision on your application. Different schools require different times for making decisions; they will inform you when they expect to get back to you.

There are various types of decision that business schools can make on your application at different stages of the application cycle. In this chapter we discuss the possible outcomes of the admissions process and how to manage multiple offers and deal with disappointing decisions.

The positives

Conditional offers

Business schools can make you an offer subject to specific conditions that you must satisfy to obtain a place on the programme, often by a set date. One of the most common conditions stated in this type of offer is the improvement of your GMAT® or TOEFL score. Sometimes the school may require that you provide additional information or fulfil specific tasks: for example, submitting a third reference; taking a short programme in a relevant area; etc. After implementing the condition, the school will issue a straight offer.

Straight offers

Receiving an offer from your preferred school or one of the top choices will certainly put a big smile on your face after months of hard work and waiting. Straight offers include a deadline for the payment of a deposit, which is required to formally accept your place.

If you have been accepted by one or more schools that are not your first choice and you are waiting to hear from your preferred school, you may be faced with a situation that requires a tactical approach. There are a number of options that you can explore.

- Ask the admissions staff to extend your deadline for acceptance. Obviously the school may realise why you are holding out, but often they will give you a reasonable extension without asking for further details.
- Carefully explore with your preferred school the opportunity to receive a quicker decision, without mentioning the other school(s) you have received an offer from, unless you are directly asked and it is a comparable school.
- Evaluate the school's deferral policy and submit a deferral request, which will give you additional time to hear the decision of your preferred choice or perhaps submit a reapplication to the same school. Your deferral request needs to have appropriate grounds; you cannot say that you are awaiting the outcome of another application. Rather than inventing tragic personal circumstances, refer to outstanding projects or commitments which need to be completed before starting your MBA, which will add benefit to the learning environment or funding reasons which require that you postpone your MBA to be able to raise the finance that you need for yourself or your family. Once your deferral request is accepted, you will normally have to pay a deferral deposit to keep your place.
- Pay the deposit to the school that you would accept as your second choice or plan B while you await your preferred school to complete the decision making on your application. However, be warned that deposits are usually non-refundable.

If you are wait-listed by your top choice (see below), only the last two options will be relevant to you.

Once you have accepted your place

- Celebrate!
- Thank your recommenders for their invaluable input and time.
- Apply for a student visa if you need one. Visa regulations may be complex and it is recommended that you give yourself as much time as possible to apply for a visa. If you are relocating with your family, all family members will need a visa.
- Sort out other logistics such as flights, accommodation, childcare or schooling for your children, etc.
- Resign from your job if you are taking an FT MBA. It will be easier if your line manager is aware of your MBA application and prepared for your departure; however, in most instances you will have applied to business school without letting your boss know about it and you need to manage your resignation considerately. Give as much notice as possible and try to keep a positive

relationship with your employer. Completing any outstanding work, ensuring you have a handover period and offering support to your successor are a good way to leave on good terms.

- Put appropriate arrangements in place if you are starting an EMBA or PT MBA; you may need to arrange time off to attend classes and allocate some of your work responsibilities to your manager, peers or subordinates.
- Familiarise yourself with relevant subjects through short courses or self-study; you may benefit from brushing up on the basics in areas such as accounting, economics, finance, marketing and quantitative methods. You can also read publications on leadership development, which will prepare you for one of the key themes of your MBA programme; admissions directors will be happy to recommend some titles.
- Take the opportunity to boost your IT skills if you feel that you are not entirely up to speed with them.

Disappointing outcomes

Wait-list or pending decisions

A wait-list decision is one of the possible outcomes of the interview process. After the interview, schools sometimes make pending (or holding) decisions in which they state when your candidacy will be reconsidered. Although this is a common decision used by schools, it is not widely discussed or mentioned on their websites.

Business schools use pending or wait-list decisions for different reasons, such as:

- to manage student numbers; admissions staff make an estimate of their yield (the number of candidates holding an offer who will accept it and enrol onto the programme) and they keep a certain number of candidates on hold to fill any available places if some decline their offers
- to select the strongest candidates and to keep some places for later application rounds: they usually make offers to the most competitive candidates and wait-list others to benchmark them against the application pool
- to ensure that they recruit a diverse and balanced class if they realise that some categories could be over-represented at the expense of others.

Occasionally, business schools may wait-list candidates if they think their first choice is another school and they do not want to receive a decline, which has a detrimental impact on their conversion statistics for the rankings.

Wait-list or pending decisions may give you a specific timeline for the final say on your candidacy. However, there are cases in which there is no timeline and you may hear from the school just a few weeks or days before the programme starts, which makes things very hectic if you need to relocate for the MBA. It can also become stressful if you are holding offers from other schools that are not your top choice. In this instance you have to make the decision to either accept a place on a programme at another school or wait to hear back on the wait-list decision.

Most schools will ask you to confirm that you are accepting a place on the wait-list and ask you to pay a deposit or commitment fee. Wait-listed candidates may obtain an offer for the following intake if no places become available for the intake they have applied; however, often wait-listed candidates are unfortunately rejected. In this instance your commitment fee is usually refunded. If the school wants to offer you a place for the following intake, your deposit will go towards securing your place. Since each school has its own wait-list guidelines, it is better to clarify this at the time.

Do schools rank wait-listed candidates?

Business schools will not tell you if you are number 1 or number 20 on their wait-list as generally they do not rank wait-listed candidates. When places become available, the admissions committee usually look at the wait-list against the overall class profile and make offers to the candidates who will contribute additional or different perspectives, for example, under-represented categories. A strong academic record, application, references, GMAT® score, and feedback from your interviewers may help your case when you are on the wait-list.

What to do if you have been wait-listed or held

Your promptness in addressing a wait-list or pending decision will also depend on your circumstances (for example, have you received offers, wait-list decisions or reject letters from other schools? Is this programme your preferred choice?). Before doing anything else, you need to read the letter that you have received and try to understand the underlying reason for being wait-listed. Here are some tips to address wait-list decisions.

- If the school has requested additional information, make sure that you submit it as soon as possible.
- Read your application and think about your interview and any feedback that you may have received; if you find any weak spots, think about how you can address them in the following communication with the school.
- If the school has not asked for any extra evidence, you can still provide other documents, but you need to be strategic and thoughtful about the ways in which you do it.
- First of all, think about the school's messaging regarding wait-listed candidates: some schools openly say that committed candidates should let them know that they are interested and they welcome additional communication and materials. Others seem to discourage you from sending extra information
- If the school encourages you to keep in touch, send a short letter emphasising your interest and commitment, the areas in which you will be a strong contributor and how you will benefit from their programme.
- If you are aware that you will be on the wait-list for a long time, you can

occasionally call or email (perhaps once every four to six weeks) the member of the admissions team you have built a good relationship with. For example, enquire or comment on something that you have heard about the school (published articles, alumni or students' achievements, etc.). This may give you the opportunity to drop a few nice lines, communicating any new achievements and reiterating that you are hoping to hear from them soon.

- Even if the school seems unwilling to receive unsolicited materials, you can still find tactful ways of letting them know about your interest and any promotions, increased responsibilities and achievements in your role. For instance, you could ask another recommender to submit a reference for you; or a member of the school community to write an email or letter of support highlighting the key areas of your contribution to the school.

What not to do

Avoid being too persistent. Frequent and long emails or calls to the admissions team will be seen as inappropriate behaviour and could lead to a reject decision.

Reapply decisions

A reapply decision is another possible outcome from the interview process. In some instances schools decide to give reapply decisions to those candidates whom they see as a strong potential candidate for the programme but with a significant aspect of their candidacy not hitting the mark. Possible reasons include the following.

- Candidates need to consolidate their experience, sometimes for a specific time period; possibly one to two years, or typically for an EMBA programme they need to gain further management exposure.
- There may be a need to undertake further research into the programme or school; a candidate's experience may be at the right level; however, he or she might not have done enough research on the programme or the school and this has clearly been highlighted at the interview stage.

What to do if you are given a reapply decision

Before doing anything, read the correspondence to understand exactly the reason for the reapply decision, then contact the admissions team to clarify the feedback and ensure that you are clear on what is lacking in your candidacy. You should also think carefully about how you will put into action the feedback from the school. For instance if the feedback is relating to your management experience, how will you gain this? You may need to discuss this with your manager (if they are aware of your MBA application) to give you more managerial responsibility. If the feedback is about research, tactfully ask the admissions team what else you can do to help in your research. Did you speak to many students or alumni or attend an open day or sit in on a taster lecture? Go along to a school event and speak to other candidates to find out what they did when researching the programme.

Mountbatten Institute

Mountbatten teaches you how the world does business

Who we are

The Mountbatten Institute combines one-year international work placement with major companies in New York or London with MBA degree study in a cutting-edge educational experience. Graduates from around the world gain practical business experience in a real work environment, earn a monthly stipend and enjoy shared furnished accommodation in New York or London. MBA or Postgraduate Certificate study is scheduled around the working day, either during the evening or over weekends, and is linked to and designed to enhance the student's professional development.

Students who choose the MBA option follow their year in London or New York, with a four-month fieldwork experience in the emerging markets of Asia, centred in Bangkok. Both programmes are validated by our academic provider, St Mary's University College, Twickenham, School of Management and Social Sciences.

St. Mary's was established in 1850 and is the oldest Catholic based institution of higher education in London. The University College offers a full range of undergraduate and postgraduate courses in a variety of subject disciplines.

What we offer

- **The work placement:** The Mountbatten Institute places great emphasis on personal and professional development. Hands-on practical training in an authentic business setting is a central feature of the Mountbatten experience. You will spend 12 months working for a leading global company in New York or London, immediately immersed in a business culture and challenged from day one. Here you will gain insight into the inner workings of a professional environment, learn to adapt to new situations, develop key transferable skills and competencies, all while fast-tracking your career.
- **The MBA and Postgraduate Certificate:** The programme asks you to take an international perspective and understand the ways in which your work placement operates within a global economy. In an interdependent world where cross cultural understanding is essential at all levels of operations and management, the academic programme gives you the context and knowledge to appreciate the complexities and possibilities of international business. In addition to the knowledge base that you will develop in New York or London, if you pursue the MBA, you will be challenged as you complete your degree with a semester of intensive field work and Asian regional study in Bangkok, Thailand.

Case study

Erica Davies (MBA, Class of 2011)

Prior to joining the 2011 Mountbatten class, I completed my undergraduate degree in Information Systems with Arizona State University, having worked for two and a half years with American Express. I had come to a point where I desired an opportunity that would foster optimum growth by moving me outside my boundaries and challenging me in different ways.

Many would ask why I decided to choose an unconventional programme such as the Mountbatten Institute to achieve my goals. My answer is that Mountbatten provided much more than just a degree. It provided a valuable all around experience that challenged and developed me in ways that conventional MBA programmes could not. The Mountbatten Institute is a multidimensional experience consisting of three fundamental elements; formal education, international residency and educational travel, and professional work experience.

The thing I most appreciated about my experience with the formal education, provided through Mountbatten and St Mary's University College, was the classroom and assignment format which led to the development of critical thinking skills and the application of academic theory. The design and delivery of the courses was different from typical formats and fostered more than just fact memorisation. The concepts presented in each course were aligned with real-life business scenarios, many of which were experienced each day. These elements made for an exceptional and valuable educational experience.

My work placement was with Deutsche Bank, a large German global investment company, on the foreign exchange (FX) trading floor as a Middle Office FX analyst. This opportunity in itself was a very prestigious professional experience, but the following semester in Asia further enriched my understanding of global business and set me apart from the crowd.

Upon my return home to the US, many prospective employers and human resource recruiters took positive note of my experience with Mountbatten and were very impressed. I was told that my time in Europe and Asia had set me apart from many other applicants. This is a testament to the value of the programme. I am now employed as a Business Analyst – IT Consultant with CGI, a Canadian based global IT and business process services consulting firm. My Mountbatten experience not only assisted me in obtaining my next career move but provided invaluable personal and professional skill sets.

Rejection

Rejection at any stage in the admissions process is always a tough outcome to deal with, even when you are aware that something did not go too well and perhaps you were expecting it. If you are applying to five or six top schools for an FT MBA, you need to be mentally prepared to receive rejection letters from some of your choices.

Obviously if you have already received offers from some of your preferred schools, a rejection will not cause much disappointment or need for further understanding. It will perhaps show that you are a better fit with some schools than others. If you still have not completed the application process for your preferred choices, exploring the rejection will probably help you learn what to improve for the other schools.

If you are a diligent EMBA or PT MBA candidate, you will have usually sought out and received the school's feedback on your experience and suitability for the programme months before applying. A rejection needs to trigger careful reflection on what went wrong.

What should you do if you are not offered an interview?

If your candidacy has not been taken forward to interview, it is highly unlikely that you will receive any feedback. In these situations you could perhaps ask a friend to read your application and to point at any evident flaws; it will be even more helpful to obtain feedback from someone who has done an MBA.

What should you do if you are rejected after an interview by your preferred school or all your choices?

First of all, explore the reason for your rejection. Usually schools provide some feedback to candidates who are rejected after interview. The feedback is usually provided in writing, but sometimes admissions teams are also open to have a quick chat over the phone.

The level of feedback that rejected candidates receive varies significantly from one school to another as not all schools have resources to dedicate to give candidates feedback. Normally the feedback pinpoints the areas in which you are not competitive in comparison with other candidates (for example, career progression; management experience; international exposure; academic record; ability to contribute through outside interests and community involvement), or the areas of concern where you were unable to persuade the admissions committee that you are at the required level (for example, self-awareness, team skills, intercultural awareness, leadership, academic abilities). Other aspects which may be addressed in feedback letters are career goals and motivation for doing the MBA; the admissions committee will express concerns regarding weak motivations or career goals that are not considered to be realistic, achievable or aligned with what the school can offer.

Schools may be unable to enter in detailed discussion with you for different reasons including confidentiality towards your referees or interviewers; they are also very busy and are less inclined to enter into a lengthy dialogue providing feedback to all rejected candidates. Remember that business schools will be more willing to give you feedback outside peak periods of the admissions cycle.

Do business schools consider appeals?

Not all business schools consider appeals and often the rejection letter makes clear that the decision is final. Even when business schools are open to appeals, appealing a rejection makes sense only if you are able to provide a strong reason for them to reconsider their decision. Presenting the same information again or stating that the school has made a mistake does not give your appeal a solid foundation.

An appeal may have solid grounds if there is new significant information that has not been considered before (for example, you obtain a promotion or an award; you retook the GMAT® and you achieve a much stronger score); or if there has been a major procedural error in the admissions process (for example, you had to read preparation materials before the interview but you never received the information and only learnt about it long after your interview).

What not to do when appealing a rejection

We strongly advise you to avoid being disrespectful when you liaise with admissions staff following a rejection. It may seem obvious, but sometimes disappointment takes its toll and frustrated candidates react and behave in a rude or inappropriate manner.

In addition, do not insist on obtaining an immediate response. Admissions committees need time to look at the application file and sometimes may not be able to enter in phone discussions during busy times. Show some patience!

Do I reapply if I have been rejected by my preferred choice or all my top choices?

To answer this question you need to carry out a candid, critical evaluation of your credentials, your application file and your performance at interview and the possible reasons for the rejection. Certainly feedback from the schools will be helpful in assessing your situation and you should try to obtain it before reapplying. It is worth reapplying *only* if a school has given you this specific decision and feedback or you believe that you are able to present a significantly stronger candidacy for a future intake.

Sometimes you may be aware that your application essays were not as strong as they should have been or your interview performance was not outstanding; or perhaps your referees did not write compelling recommendations. In these cases you need to ensure that you address and substantially improve your application: ask your referees to rewrite the recommendations and provide them with guidance on what the references should include, or choose new referees if necessary; draft fresh essays, possibly including new information which shows the progress that you have made after what you have learnt from your previous application.

It is also important that you time your reapplication well; for example, if the weak area was your level of experience, you may need to wait longer than one year to ensure that you have more solid experience and track record of professional achievements.

Be realistic on your chances of being admitted to one of the top-tier schools – unfortunately, admission to these schools is incredibly competitive.

Don't give up on your MBA aspirations

Not obtaining an offer from the schools that are your top choices should in no way discourage you from obtaining an MBA if you really want to achieve your objectives. As discussed in Chapter 4, there are schools with a strong reputation and recognition within specific business communities; they would be able to meet your needs and offer you a superb educational experience despite not being in the top spots of the rankings. In addition, most institutions partner with top-tier schools for their exchange programmes so you may have the opportunity to take some electives and get exposure to the community of your preferred school. Keep positive: if you are willing to learn and determined to undertake an MBA, you will find the right programme and school for you.

ALBA Graduate Business School at The American College of Greece (www.alba.edu.gr)

ALBA Graduate Business School at The American College of Greece was founded in 1992 and operates under the auspices of the business community, an association of corporations and institutional organisations, currently numbering more than 90 members. ALBA strives for excellence, quality and continuous innovation in research and teaching.

ALBA's vision is to become one of the leading research-driven graduate business schools in Europe, on the basis of excellence in teaching and its intellectual impact on the business world, attracting outstanding faculty and students from all over the world. ALBA offers the following academic programmes, most of which are internationally accredited by AMBA or EFMD.

MBA programmes

As a student at an ALBA MBA programme you will develop not only your skills and competencies but also your perspective on the world. Business is facing complex challenges, demanding not just sound and timely decisions, but, primarily, managerial judgement in taking a holistic view on business and social problems, and the ability to mobilise others in order to make a difference.

The EMBA is designed for accomplished managers of at least 10 years of work experience, a significant part of which has involved profit and loss responsibility and leading teams. It is a modular programme offered every second weekend for 18 months.

The ALBA MBA is designed for early career professionals with a minimum of three years' substantive work experience. The MBA in Shipping and the MBA in Banking follow the same backbone as the generic ALBA MBA, with a certain number of specialised core and elective courses. All three are available in both full-time (12 months) or part-time (24–48 months) mode of study.

The ALBA MBA holds the largest number of awards in the prestigious European Business Plan of the Year Competition over the last 10 years, next to the top business schools of Europe.

- EMBA
- The ALBA MBA
- MBA in Shipping
- MBA in Banking (under the auspices of the Hellenic Bank Association)

MSc programmes

All ALBA MSc programmes are designed for individuals with a commitment to the respective professional field, regardless of previous work experience. All programmes are available in both full-time and part-time study mode, with the exception of the MSc in Business for Lawyers and the MSc in International Shipping and Finance. The MSc in International Business and Management is designed for young graduates who wish to launch their careers in international companies and/or in fast growing export oriented business:

- MSc in Finance
- MSc in Marketing
- MSc in Strategic Human Resources Management
- MSc in International Business and Management
- MSc in Business for Lawyers
- MSc in International Shipping and Finance (in collaboration with the University of Reading).

The ALBA **Career Office** provides world-class support to students and alumni. Through personal coaching, more than 10 focused workshops, career panels, job shadowing, internships and countless company visits, students get prepared to seek the best jobs internationally. The annual career forum attracts more than 110 recruiters and is the ground for more than 1,500 interviews in less than a week. ALBA subscribes and offers to students and alumni all major international recruitment/placement services.

In addition to its academic programmes, ALBA offers high-quality **executive education** in order to meet the needs of large domestic and international corporate clients. These programmes range from open enrolment seminars to customised solutions. More than 11,000 executives have attended executive development programmes at ALBA.

The ALBA **faculty** consists of a core team of resident scholars with extensive teaching, research and consulting experience at an international level. It is the ALBA's strategic choice to engage leading scholars from top business schools worldwide as visiting professors in all programmes, for a large proportion of teaching.

The ALBA **alumni** body comprises approximately 3,000 distinguished individuals who form a group of young and dynamic managers in the process of building challenging careers, while at the same time enhancing ALBA's reputation in the Greek and international business communities.

In October 2011, The American College of Greece (ACG) and ALBA Graduate Business School (ALBA) officially announced their strategic alliance that will lead to the creation of a top international educational institution in Greece. This alliance will set new standards in higher education and will become a catalyst for positive change in Greek society and beyond.

ALBA is a not-for-profit educational association and operates as a Centre of Post-Secondary Education Center (KEME) under the provisions of Law 3848/2010.

Conclusion

We hope that, as you have worked your way through this book, you have gained an insight into the decision-making process to help you select the right MBA programme and school. To end, we have summarised the key phases in the decision-making process for you.

Initial research

In the first chapter we took a closer look at the different components that make up an MBA programme, giving you a comprehensive overview, while discussing who it is aimed at. At this point, you should be looking at the different types of programme available, using handy tips from the first chapter to help you choose the right programme format.

Introspection

The next stage is introspection. In order to establish whether an MBA is right for you at this stage in your career, think critically about your objectives and motivations. The key question to ask yourself is "What can an MBA do for me?" There are numerous reasons why people decide to undertake an MBA, and in Chapter 2 we looked at this in some detail. At this point you need to be clear about what you want to achieve in the short and long term.

Pre-plan and research

Once you have decided that an MBA is for you, think about what you need to do to make it happen. Identify schools and programmes that might be of interest to you and start compiling your research. If you are not at the right level currently, then establish what you need to do to get there. It might be something to do with enhancing your leadership skills or gaining more international exposure.

Financing is a major consideration, you need to be realistic in terms of how much you are willing to spend, how much you need to budget not just for tuition cost but all the other costs too. Furthermore, you need to see what sources of funding are available to you. Explore any opportunities to secure financial aid, loans or scholarships; ideally you want to have some sort of support rather than completely taking on the financial burden yourself. Remember that in most cases you will fund your MBA through a combination of different sources, including personal savings.

When you prepare yourself for a top business school you need to take the GMAT®. Chapter 8 gives you some tips on how to tackle this test; it also includes some sample questions so you can start cracking the test. With advanced preparation you can aim to ensure a competitive GMAT® score hopefully eliminating the need to spend additional time on a re-take.

Research and schools selection

There are countless MBA programmes offered by hundreds of schools, finding the right one for you can at times be a daunting prospect. At this stage you need to be carrying out in-depth research, looking into schools and programmes with the aim of short-listing five to six schools. Your research should assess rankings, location, and fees among other factors covered in Chapter 4.

You need to consider schools that not only give you an extraordinary life experience but also give you the skills, knowledge, brand and lifelong networks to take your career to the next level and beyond. However, it is important that you strike a balance between all those areas and select schools that you really want to be a part of, in terms of culture and fit.

An MBA can be a springboard to bigger and better things; what you need to bear in mind is that success is dependent on how you leverage the MBA after you have completed the programme. To take full advantage of its true value, you need to be clear about your career plan and have a strategic approach to utilise the careers services, the network and school.

Application

Prior to completing any applications it is worthwhile taking some time out to understand the admissions process for each of the schools you are applying to and also to develop a strategy for your applications.

It is crucial that you understand your unique selling points and are able to convey the message in an impactful way within the different elements of the application package such as essays, references, CV, etc. Your success as an MBA candidate depends on your ability to articulate your uniqueness, competitive advantage and how well you connect "who you are", "what you do" and "what you want to do" to the mission and vision of your short-listed schools.

The interview will give you an opportunity to reiterate your passion for the school and demonstrate your knowledge and understanding of the programme. In the book we have given you examples of questions you may be asked at interview and what to expect so that you are fully prepared.

Acceptance

The final stage in the decision-making process is the outcome of your application. In Chapter 10 we covered some of the terminology that you will come across at this point while also giving you advice on how to deal with disappointing outcomes and what options you have going forward.

Take all this into consideration and you are well on your way to being a successful MBA applicant!

After the MBA

An MBA will push you beyond your limits and can transform your future. With newfound confidence and a refreshed toolkit, many MBA students go on to become functional or general managers who drive businesses around the world; take up leadership roles in governments and global companies; others go on to become entrepreneurs who have founded start-ups big and small. An MBA does not limit you to the corporate world either; successful MBA students also choose to apply their new or enhanced management skills to non-profit organisations. There is a range of possibilities to consider during the MBA and after graduation, with access to a strong alumni network and a brand that you draw on for years to come – the world really will become your oyster.

Best of luck!

Directory

For this directory, we calculated the total tuition fees for each programme based on information from the schools' websites. For an FT MBA programme in the US we have reported tuition fees for non-residential international students only. For the two-year FT MBA programmes, we have not taken into account any tuition fee rise for the second year. For example, if the tuition fees for year 1 were US$50,000, we have reported the total fees as US$100,000. The figures provided in this directory should be used as a reference point only and are as accurate as possible as of September 2011. You should check with the school for up-to-date tuition fees for your programme of choice.

US schools

Anderson School of Management, University of California in Los Angeles (UCLA)

FT MBA Admissions: B201, Box 951481, Los Angeles, CA, 90095-1481 USA
Tel: +1 310 825 6944
Web: www.anderson.ucla.edu
Email: mba.admissions@anderson.ucla.edu

Fully Employed MBA Admissions: A307, Box 951481, Los Angeles, CA, 90095-1481 USA
Tel: +1 310 825 2632
Web: www.anderson.ucla.edu
Email: femba.admissions@anderson.ucla.edu

EMBA Admissions: A-101f, Box 951481, Los Angeles, CA, 90095-1481 USA
Tel: +1 310 825 2032
Web: www.anderson.ucla.edu
Email: emba.admissions@anderson.ucla.edu

UCLA – NUS Global EMBA: NUS Business School, National University of Singapore, Mochatar Riady Building, Level 4, 15 Kent Ridge Drive, Singapore, 119245
Tel: +65 6516 1351
Web: http://ucla.nus.edu
Email: ucla@nus.edu.sg

Programme	Length	Start	Tuition fees
FT MBA	22 months	September	US$105,160
Fully Employed MBA	27 (accelerated) or 33 months	September	US$107,397
EMBA	22 months	September	US$118,560

Programme	Length	Start	Tuition fees
UCLA – National University of Singapore (NUS) Global EMBA for Asia Pacific (dual degree)	15 months	May	US$92,222
UCLA – Universidad Adolfo Ibéñez (UAI) Global EMBA for the Americas (dual degree)	15 months	October	US$82,700

Boston University

595 Commonwealth Avenue, Boston, MA, 02215 USA
Tel: +1 617 353 9720
Web: http://management.bu.edu
Email: mba@bu.edu

Programme	Length	Start	Tuition fees
General MBA (FT MBA)	21 months	August	US$81,696
Health Sector MBA (FT and PT MBA)	21 months	August	US$81,696
Public and No Profit MBA (FT and PT MBA)	21 months	August	US$81,696
One-Year International MBA	12 months	August	US$66,832
Professional Evening MBA	36–60 months	January, September	US$81,664
EMBA	18 months	December	US$87,000
Dual degree options available	–	–	–

Broad College of Business, Michigan State University (MSU)

MBA: 215 Eppley Center, East Lansing, MI, 48824 USA
Tel: +1 517 355 7604
Web: http://broad.msu.edu
Email: mba@msu.edu

Weekend MBA: The James B. Henry Center for Executive Development, 3535 Forest Road, Lansing, MI, 48910 USA
Tel: +1 517 355 7603
Web: http://broad.msu.edu
Email: wmba@msu.edu

Programme	Length	Start	Tuition fees
FT MBA	24 months	August	US$79,170
Weekend MBA (executive-style MBA)	19 months	June	US$61,500
Dual degree options available	–	–	–

Carlson School of Management, University of Minnesota

321 19th Ave S, suite 1-110, Minneapolis, MN, 55455 USA
Tel: +1 612 625 0027
Web: www.csom.umn.edu/MBA
Email: mba@umn.edu

Programme	Length	Start	Tuition fees
FT MBA	22 months	August	US$89,136
PT MBA	24–84 months	January, September	US$61,740
EMBA	24 months	September	US$95,000
Dual degree options available	–	–	–

College of Business, University of Illinois at Urbana-Champaign

MBA Admissions: 3019 Business Instructional Facility, 515 East Gregory Drive, Champaign, IL, 61820 USA
Tel: +1 217 244 7602
Web: http://business.illinois.edu
Email: illinoisptmba@illinois.edu

EMBA Admissions: Illini Center, Fourth Floor, 200 South Wacker Drive, Chicago, IL, 60606 USA
Tel: +1 312 575 0900
Web: www.execmba.illinois.edu
Email: emba@illinois.edu

Warsaw EMBA: International Management Center, Faculty of Management, University of Warsaw, ul. NowySwiat 4 00-497 Warszawa, Poland
Tel: +22 625 31 26
Web: www.mba.uw.edu.pl
Email: mba@mail.wz.uw.edu.pl

Programme	Length	Start	Tuition fees
FT MBA	21 months	August	US$113,024
Professional PT MBA	30 months	January	US$76,623
EMBA	20 months	September	US$94,000
Warsaw-Illinois EMBA	16 months	September	€18,200
Joint MBA degree options available	–	–	–

Columbia Business School

216 Uris Hall, 3022 Broadway, New York, NY, 10027 USA
Tel: +1 212 854 1961
Web: www4.gsb.columbia.edu
Email: apply@gsb.columbia.edu

Programme	Length	Start	Tuition fees
FT MBA	20 months	January, August	US$111,736
EMBA New York	20 months	May, August, January	US$154,320
EMBA Global Americas and Europe (in partnership with London Business School)	20 months	May	US$147,723
EMBA Global Asia (in partnership with London Business School and HKU Business School)	20 months	May	US$133,080
Berkeley-Columbia EMBA	19 months	May	US$157,440

Cox School of Business, Southern Methodist University (SMU)

6212 Bishop Blvd, Dallas, TX, 75275-0333 USA
Tel: +1 214 768 1214
Web: www.cox.smu.edu
Email: mbainfo@cox.smu.edu

Programme	Length	Start	Tuition fees
FT MBA	22 months	August	US$91,616
Professional PT MBA (PMBA)	24 months	January, August	US$84,312
EMBA	21 months	August	US$101,325
Joint degree options available	–	–	–

Darden School of Business, University of Virginia

100 Darden Boulevard, Charlottesville, VA, 22903 USA
Tel: +1 434 924 3900
Web: www.darden.virginia.edu
Email: Darden@virginia.edu

Programme	Length	Start	Tuition fees
FT MBA	21 months	August	US$104,000
EMBA (MBA for Executives)	21 months	August	US$119,500
Global EMBA (Global MBA for Executives)	21 months	August	US$139,500
Dual and joint degree options	–	–	–

Davis Graduate School of Management, University of California

Gallagher Hall, One Shields Avenue, Davis, CA, 95616 USA
Tel: +1 860 486 2872
Web: http://gsm.ucdavis.edu

Programme	Length	Start	Tuition fees
Daytime MBA	21 months	September	US$99,924
Sacramento Working Professionals MBA	36 months	September	US$73,440
Bay Area Working Professionals MBA	36 months	September	US$93,672
Dual degree options available	–	–	–

Duke – The Fuqua School of Business

US Office: 100 Fuqua Drive, Box 90120, Durham, NC, 27708-0120 USA
Tel: +1 919 660 7700
Web: www.fuqua.duke.edu
Email: admissions-info@fuqua.duke.edu

London Office: 165 Fleet Street, First Floor, London EC4A 2DY, UK
Tel: +44 20 79366078
Web: www.fuqua.duke.edu
Email: Europe@fuqua.duke.edu

China Office: Suite 730, West Office Building, Shanghai Center, 1376 West Nanjing Road, Shanghai 200040 China
Tel: +86 021 6289 8365
Web: www.fuqua.duke.edu
Email: Asia@fuqua.duke.edu

Johannesburg Office: Duke Corporate Education Africa, The Campus, Augusta Building, Bryanston, Johannesburg, South Africa 2021
Tel: +27 011 575 6241
Web: www.fuqua.duke.edu
Email: Africa@fuqua.duke.edu

Programme	Length	Start	Tuition fees
Daytime MBA	22 months	August	US$100,600
Cross Continent MBA (PT MBA)	16 months	July	US$127,200
Global EMBA	15 months	April	US$152,500
Weekend EMBA	19 months	June	US$109,200
Specialist and joint degree programmes in Health Sector Management (HSM), Medicine (MD), Law (JD), Environmental Management (MEM), forestry (MF), Public Policy (MPP), Science Nursing (MSN)	–	–	–

Fisher College of Business, Ohio State University

100 Gerlach Hall, 2108 Neil Avenue, Columbus, OH, 43210 USA
Tel: +1 614 292 8511
Web: http://fisher.osu.edu
Email: mba@fisher.osu.edu

Programme	Length	Start	Tuition fees
FT MBA	21 months	September	US$85,560
MBA for Working Professionals	30–33 months	January, August	US$80,370
EMBA	18 months	December	US$78,500
Dual degree options available	–	–	–

Georgia Tech College of Management

800 West Peachtree Street, Atlanta, GA, 30308-0520 USA
Tel: +1 404 894 2600
Web: http://mgt.gatech.edu
Email: mba@mgt.gatech.edu

Programme	Length	Start	Tuition fees
FT MBA	22 months	August	US$72,492
Evening MBA	15 months	January, August	US$75,924
Global EMBA	17 months	August	US$75,000
EMBA in Management of Technology	17 months	August	US$73,000

Goizueta Business School, Emory University

1300 Clifton Road, Atlanta, GA, 30322 USA
Tel: +1 404 727 6311
Web: www.goizueta.emory.edu
Email: admissions@bus.emory.edu

Programme	Length	Start	Tuition fees
Two-year FT MBA	22 months	August	US$88,196
One-year FT MBA	12 months	May	US$65,991
Evening MBA	27-32 months	August	US$70,200
Modular EMBA	21 months	August	US$95,600
Weekend EMBA	16 months	January	US$91,700
Joint degree options available	–	–	–

Haas School of Business, University of California Berkeley

FT MBA and Evening and Weekend MBA: 430 Student Services Building #1902, Berkeley, CA, 94720-1902 USA
Tel: +1 510 642 1405
Web: www.haas.berkeley.edu
Email: mbaadm@haas.berkeley.edu

Berkeley-Columbia Executive MBA Admissions: 440 Student Services Building #1912, Berkeley, CA, 94720-1912 USA
Tel: +1 510 643 1047
Web: www.haas.berkeley.edu
Email: emba@haas.berkeley.edu

Programme	Length	Start	Tuition fees
FT MBA	21 months	January, March, October, December	US$102,492
Evening and weekend MBA	36 months	August	US$106,260
Berkeley-Columbia EMBA	19 months	May	US$157,440

Harvard Business School

Soldiers Field Road, Boston, MA, 02163 USA
Tel: +1 617 495 6128
Web: www.hbs.edu
Email: admissions@hbs.edu

Programme	Length	Start	Tuition fees
FT MBA	24 months	September	US$102,400
Joint programmes in law, dental medicine, medicine and public policy	–	–	–

Hult International Business School

Boston Campus: 1 Education Street, Cambridge, MA, 02141 USA
Tel: +1 617 746 1990
Web: www.hult.edu
Email: admissions@hult.edu

San Francisco Campus: 1355 Sansome Street, San Francisco, CA, 94111 USA
Tel: +1 415 869 2900
Web: www.hult.edu
Email: admissions@hult.edu

Dubai International Academic City Campus: PO Box 502988, Dubai, UAE
Tel: +971 4 375 3088
Web: www.hult.edu
Email: admissions@hult.edu

London Campus: 46-47 Russell Square, Bloomsbury, London WC1B 4JP, UK
Tel: +44 20 7341 8555
Web: www.hult.edu
Email: admissions@hult.edu

Shanghai Campus: Jinling Hai Xin Building, 666 Fu Zhou Road, Shanghai, China
Tel: +852 2111 2370
Web: www.hult.edu
Email: admissions@hult.edu

Programme	Length	Start	Tuition fees
One-year MBA	12 months	September	US$64,500 (Boston and San Francisco); £44,600 (London); AED 236,700 (Dubai); CNY 464,400 (Shanghai)
Weekly or monthly EMBA	24 months	September	£44,600 (London); AED 236,700 (Dubai); CNY 464,400 (Shanghai)

Johnson, Cornell University

Sage Hall Cornell University, Ithaca NY, 14853-6201 USA
Tel: +1 607 255 4526
Web: www.johnson.cornell.edu
Email: mba@johnson.cornell.edu

Programme	Length	Start	Tuition fees
Two-Year MBA	21 months	August	US$102,960
Accelerated MBA	12 months	May	US$86,620
Cornell EMBA	22 months	July	US$145,380
Cornell-Queens EMBA	16 months	June	US$106,890
Dual MBA degree options available	–	–	–

Jones Graduate School of Business, Rice University

6100 Main Street, MS-531 109 McNair Hall, Houston TX, 77005 USA
Tel: +1 713 348 4918
Web: http://business.rice.edu
Email: ricemba@rice.edu

Programme	Length	Start	Tuition fees
FT MBA	22 months	August, January	US$88,000
PT MBA for Executives	22 months	July	US$99,000
PT MBA for Professionals	22 months	August	US$92,500
Dual MBA degree options available	–	–	–

Kelley School of Business, Indiana University

Godfrey Center, 1275 East Tenth Street, Suite 2010, Bloomington IN, 47405-1703 USA
Tel: +1 812 855 8006
Web: http://kelley.iu.edu
Email: mbaoffice@indiana.edu

Evening MBA: 801 West Michigan Street, Indianapolis, IN, 46202-5151 USA
Tel: +1 317 274 4895
Web: http://kelley.iupui.edu
Email: mbaindy@iupui.edu

Kelley Direct Online MBA Program: 777 Indiana Avenue, Indianapolis, IN, 46202-5151 US
Tel: +1 317 278 1566
Web: http://kelley.iupui.edu
Email: kdirect@iupui.edu

Programme	Length	Start	Tuition fees
FT MBA	21 months	August	US$90,700
Evening MBA	24 months	September	US$38,000
Online MBA	24–60 months	September	US$41,220
Joint degree options available	–	–	–

Kellogg School of Management, Northwestern University

Evanston Campus – FT MBA, PT MBA and EMBA: 2001 Sheridan Road, Evanston, IL, 60208 USA
Tel: + 1 847 491 3308
Web (FT MBA): www.kellogg.northwestern.edu/Programs/FullTimeMBA.aspx
Web (EMBA): www.kellogg.northwestern.edu/Programs/EMBA.aspx
Email (FT MBA): MBAadmissions@kellogg.northwestern.edu
Email: emba@kellogg.northwestern.edu

Chicago Campus – PT MBA: Wieboldt Hall, 340 East Superior Street, 2nd Floor Mezzanine, Chicago, IL, 60611-3008 USA
Tel: +1 312 503 0385
Web (PT MBA): www.kellogg.northwestern.edu/Programs/PartTimeMBA.aspx
Email (PT MBA): PartTimeMBA@kellogg.northwestern.edu

Miami Campus – EMBA: 95 Merrick Way, Suite 100, Coral Gables, FL, 3313 USA
Tel: +1 305 442 7780
Web (EMBA): www.kellogg.northwestern.edu/Programs/EMBA.aspx
Email (EMBA): emba-miami@kellogg.northwestern.edu

Kellogg-HKUST EMBA: Room 6549 Annex Building, Business School, Hong Kong University of Science and Technology, Clear Water Bay, Kowloon, Hong Kong
Tel: +852 2358 4180
Web: www.bm.ust.hk/emba
Email: emba@ust.hk

Kellogg-Recanati International EMBA: Faculty of Management, The Leon Recanati Graduate School of Business Administration, Tel Aviv University, Ramat Aviv, Tel Aviv 69978 Israel
Tel: +972 3 6406312
Web: http://kr-emba.tau.ac.il
Email: kremba@tauex.tau.ac.il

Kellogg-Schulich EMBA: Suite X212A, Executive Learning Centre, Schulich School of Business, W262P York University 4700 Keele Street, Toronto, ON, M3J 1P3 Canada
Tel: +1 416 736 5486
Web: http://emba2.schulich.yorku.ca
Email: emba@schulich.yorku.ca

Kellogg WHU EMBA: Burgplatz 2, 56179 Vallendar, Germany
Tel: +49 261 6509 333/334
Web: http://kellogg.whu.edu/index.php?id=1399
Email: emba@whu.edu

Programme	Length	Start	Tuition fees
Two-year FT MBA	24 months	September	US$108,000
One-year FT MBA	12 months	June	US$72,000
PT MBA (evenings or Saturdays)	24–60 months	Autumn (Fall), Winter, Spring, Summer	US$106,640
EMBA	24 months	January, September	US$79,950
Kellogg-HKUST EMBA	15 months	January	US$143,300
Kellogg-Recanati International MBA	24 months	September	US$59,000
Kellogg-Schulich EMBA	18 months	January	CAN$110,000
Kellogg WHU EMBA	24 months	September	€70,000
Joint and dual degrees available	–	–	–

Kenan-Flagler Business School, University of North Carolina at Chapel Hill

FT MBA Admissions: Campus Box 3490, McColl Building, Chapel Hill, NC, 27599-3490 USA
Tel: +1 919 962 3236
Web: www.kenan-flagler.unc.edu
Email (FT MBA): mba_info@unc.edu
Email (EMBA): emba@unc.edu

Programme	Length	Start	Tuition fees
FT MBA	21 months	August	US$100,480
Evening MBA	24 months	August	US$74,300
Weekend MBA	20 months	January	US$89,000
Global OneMBA®	21 months	September	US$99,500
MBA@UNC (online)	24 months	January, April, August	US$89,000

Marriott School of Management, Brigham Young University

W437 Tanner Building, Provo, UT, 84602 USA
Tel: +1 801 4223500
Web: http://marriottschool.byu.edu
Email: mba@byu.edu

Programme	Length	Start	Tuition fees
FT MBA	21 months	August	US$21,200
EMBA	24 months	July	US$45,000
Joint degree options available	–	–	–

Marshall School of Business, University of Southern California

USC Marshall MBA Admissions, 630 Childs Way – JKP 308, Los Angeles, CA, 90089-2633 USA
Tel: +1 213 740 7846
Web: www.marshall.usc.edu
Email: marshallmba@marshall.usc.edu

Programme	Length	Start	Tuition fees
FT MBA	22 months	July	US$110,000
PT MBA	33 months	August	US$108,000
EMBA	21 months	August	US$116,000
Global EMBA Shanghai	20 months	May	US$82,800
One-year international MBA	12 months	August	US$83,000
Dual degree options available	–	–	–

Mays Business School, Texas A&M University

390 Wehner Building, 4117 TAMU, College Station, TX, 77843-4117 USA
Tel: +1 888 551 9998
Web: http://mays.tamu.edu
Email: ftmba@tamu.edu or emba@tamu.edu

Programme	Length	Start	Tuition fees
FT MBA	16 months	August	US$46,399
Professional MBA	22 months	August	US$74,500
EMBA	21 months	August	US$74,500

McCombs School of Business, University of Texas

1 Univ. Station B6004, Austin, TX, 78712-0205 USA
Tel: +1 512 471 7698
Web: www.mccombs.utexas.edu
Email: TexasMBA@McCombs.utexas.edu

Programme	Length	Start	Tuition fees
FT MBA	21 months	August	US$94,972
Evening MBA	33 months	August	US$88,000
Texas PT MBA at Dallas/Fort Worth	24 months	August	US$81,000
Texas PT MBA at Houston	24 months	August	US$86,000
Texas EMBA	21 months	August	US$85,000
Texas EMBA at Mexico City	21 months	August	US$60,000
Dual degree options available	–	–	–

McDonough School of Business, Georgetown University

37th and O Streets, NW Rafik B. Hariri Building, Suite 462, Washington, DC, 20057-1223 USA
Tel: +1 202 687 4200
Web: http://msb.georgetown.edu
Email (FT MBA): georgetownMBA@georgetown.edu
Email (Evening MBA): mbaeprogram@georgetown.edu
Email (EMBA): emba@georgetown.edu
Email (Georgetown-ESADE Global EMBA): globalemba@georgetown.edu

Programme	Length	Start	Tuition fees
FT MBA	21 months	August	US$94,276
Evening MBA	34 months	August	US$93,555
EMBA	20 months	August	US$114,000
Georgetown-ESADE Global EMBA	14 months	June	US$142,000
Dual degree options available	–	–	–

Mendoza College of Business, University of Notre Dame

Top of Form, Notre Dame, IN, 46556-5646 USA
Tel: +1 574 631 8488
Web: http://business.nd.edu
Email: mba.business@nd.edu

Programme	Length	Start	Tuition fees
Two-year FT MBA	21 months	May, August	US$88,000
One-year FT MBA	12 months	August	US$61,600
EMBA	21 months	August	US$90,000
Joint MBA options available	–	–	–

Michael G. Foster School of Business, University of Washington

110 Mackenzie Hall, Box 353200, Seattle, WA, 98195 USA
Tel: +1 206 543 4661
Web: www.foster.washington.edu
Email (FT and Evening MBA): mba@uw.edu
Email (EMBA): emba@uw.edu
Email (Technology Management MBA): tmmba@uw.edu
Email (Global EMBA): gemba@uw.edu

Programme	Length	Start	Tuition fees
FT MBA	21 months	September	US$76,818
Evening MBA	36 months	September	US$63,952
Technology Management MBA (PT MBA)	18 months	January	US$65,977
EMBA	21 months	August	US$83,700
Global EMBA	12 months	June	US$58,700

Olin Business School, Washington University in St Louis

Campus Box 1133, One Brookings Drive, St Louis, MO, 63130-4899 USA
Tel: +1 314 935 7301
Web: www.olin.wustl.edu
Email: mba@olin.wustl.edu

EMBA St. Louis and Kansas City:
Email: emba@wustl.edu

EMBA Shanghai: Starr Building, Room 710, 7th Floor, 670 Guoshun Road, Shanghai, China, PRC 200433
Tel: +8621 5566 4788
Web: www.olin.wustl.edu/executiveeducation/ExecutiveMBA
Email: Shanghai@olin.wustl.edu

Programme	Length	Start	Tuition fees
FT MBA	22 months	August	US$92,000
Professional MBA	36 months	January, August	US$72,900
EMBA – St Louis and Kansas City	20 months	April, September	US$99,000
EMBA Shanghai (with Fudan University)	18 months	April	RMB 478,000
Dual MBA degree options available	–	–	–

Owen Graduate School of Management, Vanderbilt University

Management Hall, 401 21st Avenue South, Nashville, TN, 37203 USA
Tel: +1 615 322 2534
Web: www.owen.vanderbilt.edu/vanderbilt
Email (FT MBA): MBA@owen.vanderbilt.edu
Email (Healthcare MBA): HealthCareMBA@owen.vanderbilt.edu
Email (EMBA): EMBA@owen.vanderbilt.edu

Programme	Length	Start	Tuition fees
FT MBA	21 months	August	US$87,804
Healthcare MBA (FT MBA)	21 months	August	US$87,804
EMBA	24 months	August	US$87,804
Americas MBA for executives	24 months	August	US$87,804
Joint MBA options available	–	–	–

Robert H. Smith School of Business, University of Maryland

Van Munching Hall, College Park, MD, 20742 USA
Tel: +1 301 405 2189
Web: www.rhsmith.umd.edu
Email: mba_info@rhsmith.umd.edu or: embainfo@rhsmith.umd.edu

Programme	Length	Start	Tuition fees
FT MBA	24 months	August	US$94,986
Evening or weekend MBA	30–36 months	August	US$80,577
EMBA	19 months	January	US$98,500
Dual MBA degree options available	–	–	–

Simon Graduate School of Business, University of Rochester

305 Schlegel Hall, Rochester, NY, 14627 USA
Tel: +1 585 275 3533
Web: www.simon.rochester.edu
Email: admissions@simon.rochester.edu

Programme	Length	Start	Tuition fees
Two-year FT MBA	24 months	January, September	US$91,866
Accelerated FT MBA	18 months	January	US$91,866
PT flexible MBA	Flexible	January, March, June, September	US$90,360
Accelerated professional MBA	30 months	January, March, June, September	US$90,360
EMBA	22 months	September	US$86,500
International EMBA – Rochester-Bern EMBA	18 months	January	CHF65,500
Joint and specialised MBA degree options available	–	–	–

Sloan School of Management, Massachusetts Institute of Technology (MIT)

MBA Admissions Office: 50 Memorial Drive, Suite E52-126, Cambridge, MA, 02142-1347 USA
Tel: +1 617 258 5434
Web: http://mitsloan.mit.edu/academic
Email: mbaadmissions@sloan.mit.edu

MIT Executive MBA Program: E52-325, 50 Memorial Drive, Cambridge, MA, 02139 USA
Tel: +1 617 253 5033
Web: http://mitsloan.mit.edu/executivemba
Email: executivemba@mit.edu

Programme	Length	Start	Tuition fees
FT MBA	24 months	September	US$105,800
EMBA	20 months	September	US$132,000
Dual degree options available	–	–	–

Smeal College of Business, Penn State University

220, Business Building, University Park, PA, 16802 USA
Tel: +1 814 863 0474
Web: www.smeal.psu.edu/mba
Email: smealmba@psu.edu

Programme	Length	Start	Tuition fees
FT MBA	21 months	August	US$69,942
EMBA	21 months	August	US$93,000
Joint MBA degree options available	–	–	–

Stanford Graduate School of Business

Knight Management Center/McClelland Bldg, 655 Knight Way, Stanford, CA, 94305-7298 USA
Tel: +1 650 723 2766
Web: www.gsb.stanford.edu/mba
Email: mba@gsb.stanford.edu

Programme	Length	Start	Tuition fees
FT MBA	24 months	September	US$111,000

Stephen M. Ross School of Business, University of Michigan

701 Tappan Street, Ann Arbor, MI, 48109 USA
Tel: +1 734 763 7804
Web: www.bus.umich.edu
Email: Rossmba@umich.edu

Programme	Length	Start	Tuition fees
FT MBA	21 months	September	US$105,888
Evening MBA	30–54 months	January, September	US$105,000
Weekend MBA	24 months	May	US$105,000
EMBA	20 months	August	US$136,000
Global MBA	16 months	February	US$113,100
Dual degree options available	–	–	–

Stern School of Business, New York University (NYU)

Henry Kaufman Management Center, 44 West Fourth Street, Suite 6-70, New York, NY, 10012-1126 USA
Tel: +1 212 998 0600
Web: www.stern.nyu.edu
Email: sternmna@stern.nyu.edu

The TRIUM Global Executive MBA Program: 44 West Fourth Street, Suite 4-100
New York, NY, 10012-1126 USA
Tel: +1 212 998 0442 or +33 1 3967 7094
Web: www.triumemba.org
Email: info@trium.org

Programme	Length	Start	Tuition fees
FT MBA	22 months	August	US$103,884
PT MBA	24–72 months	January, September	US$98,400
EMBA	22 months	January, August	US$149,000
TRIUM Global EMBA (NYU Stern, LSE and HEC Paris)	17 months	September	US$149,500
Dual degree options available	–	–	–

Tepper School of Business, Carnegie Mellon University

5000 Forbes Avenue, Pittsburgh, PA, 15213 USA
Tel: +1 412 268 2268
Web: http://tepper.cmu.edu
Email (FT MBA): mba-admissions@andrew.cmu.edu
Email (EMBA): Exec-Director@andrew.cmu.edu

Programme	Length	Start	Tuition fees
FT MBA	21 months	August	US$107,300
FlexTime: PT MBA	33 months	August	US$104,544
EMBA in Asset and Wealth Management (dual degree with HEC at the University of Lausanne)	20 months	May	US$80,000

The Paul Merage School of Business, University of California, Irvine

FT MBA: SB 220, Irvine, CA, 92697-3125 USA
Tel: +1 949 824 4622
Web: http://merage.uci.edu/FullTimeMBA
Email: mba@merage.uci.edu

Fully Employed MBA: SB 202, Irvine, CA, 92697-3125 USA
Tel: +1 949 824 7505
Web: http://merage.uci.edu/FullyEmployedMBA
Email: mcoburn@uci.edu

EMBA and Healthcare EMBA: MPAA 101, Irvine, CA, 92697-3130 USA
Tel: +1 949 824 0561
Web: http://merage.uci.edu
Email: emba@merage.uci.edu or hcemba@merage.uci.edu

Programme	Length	Start	Tuition fees
FT MBA	21 months	September	US$91,835
Fully employed MBA (PT MBA)	27 or 33 months	March, September	US$88,596
EMBA	21 months	September	US$99,625
Healthcare EMBA	24 months	September	US$99,624
Dual MBA degree options available	–	–	–

The University of Chicago Booth School of Business

US Campus: 5807 South Woodlawn Avenue, Chicago, IL, 60637 USA
Tel: +1 773 702 7743
Web: www.chicagobooth.edu
Email: admissions@ChicagoBooth.edu

Europe Campus: Woolgate Exchange, 25 Basinghall Street, London EC2V 5HA, UK
Tel: +44 207 070 2200
Web: www.chicagobooth.edu
Email: europe.inquiries@ChicagoBooth.edu

Asia Campus: International Executive MBA Program at Singapore, 101 Penang Road, Singapore, 238 466
Tel: +65 6835 64 82
Web: www.chicagobooth.edu
Email: asia.inquiries@chicagobooth.edu

Programme	Length	Start	Tuition fees
FT MBA, US Campus	21 months	September	US$112,140
Evening and Weekend MBA – Chicago Campus	30–36 months	January, March, June, September	US$110,586
EMBA – Chicago, London and Singapore Campuses	21 months	June	Chicago US$148,000; London £80,000; SG$180,000

The University of Connecticut School of Business

2100 Hillside Road Unit 1041, Storrs, CT, 06269-1041 USA
Tel: +1 860 486 2872 / +1 860 728 2400
Web: www.business.uconn.edu
Email: contact@business.uconn.edu

Programme	Length	Start	Tuition fees
FT MBA	21 months	August	US$56,876
PT MBA	30–60+ months	August	US$38,760
EMBA	20 months	September	US$58,000
Dual degree options available	–	–	–

The University of Texas at Dallas, Navin Jindal School of Management

SM 42, 800 West Campbell Road, Richardson, TX, 75080-3021 USA
Tel: +1 972 883 2705
Web: http://som.utdallas.edu
Email: mba@utdallas.edu

Programme	Length	Start	Tuition fees
FT MBA	16 months	August	TBC
Professional PT MBA	36 months	January, May, August	TBC
Online MBA	36 months	January, May, August	TBC
EMBA	21 months	August	US$82,000
Global Leadership EMBA	23 months	January	US$67,500
Healthcare Management EMBA for Physicians	16–72 months	Classes may be started at any time	US$46,800
Project management EMBA (on campus or online)	21 months	February (online), September (on campus)	TBC
Joint degree options available	–	–	–

Thunderbird School of Global Management

Admissions Office, 1 Global Place, Glendale, AZ, 85306-6000 USA
Tel: +1 602 978 7000
Web: www.thunderbird.edu
Email: admissions@thunderbird.edu

Programme	Length	Start	Tuition fees
FT MBA	15–20 months	January and August	US$86,160
Accelerated MBA	11 or 16 months	January and August	US$66,774
Distance Learning MBA	19 or 28 months	January, April, September	US$68,800
Distance Learning MBA – Latin America	21 months	August	US$45,800 (in Mexico); US$60,400 (in North America)

Programme	Length	Start	Tuition fees
EMBA US	21 months	August	US$88,700
EMBA Europe	19 months	October	US$88,700
Dual degree options available	–	–	–

Tippie School of Management, University of Ohio

108 John Pappajohn Business Building, Iowa City, IA, 52242-1994 USA
Tel: +1 319 335 0862
Web: http://tippie.uiowa.edu
Email: tippiemba@uiowa.edu

Italy MBA: CIMBA, Via Collegio 40, 31011 Asolo, TV, Italy
Tel: +39 0423 9511004
Web: www.cimba.it
Email: info@cimba.it

Programme	Length	Start	Tuition fees
FT MBA	21 months	August	US$68,624
MBA for professionals and managers	30–120 months	January, August	US$27,000
EMBA	21 months	August	US$51,000 (Cedar Rapids and Iowa City); US$55,000 (Des Moines)
International MBA Hong Kong (PT MBA)	21 months	July	HK$258,000
Italy FT MBA	11 months	September	US$26,275
Italy PT MBA	24 months	September	€15,000
Dual MBA degree options available	–	–	–

Tuck School of Business at Dartmouth

100 Tuck Hall, Hanover, NH, 03755 USA
Tel: +1 603 604 8825
Web: www.tuck.dartmouth.edu
Email: tuck.admissions@tuck.dartmouth.edu

Programme	Length	Start	Tuition fees
FT MBA	21 months	August	US$106,988

Weatherhead School of Management, Case Western Reserve University

10900 Euclid Avenue, Cleveland, OH, 44106-7235 USA
Tel: +1 216 368 2030
Web: www.weatherhead.case.edu
Email: weatherhead@case.edu

Programme	Length	Start	Tuition fees
FT MBA	21 months	August	US$85,000
PT MBA	36 months	June	US$97,200
EMBA	21 months	August	US$95,000
Dual degree options available	–	–	–

Wharton School, University of Pennsylvania

420 Jon M. Huntsman Hall, 3730 Walnut Street, Philadelphia, PA, 19104 USA
Tel: +1 215 898 6183
Web: www.wharton.upenn.edu
Email: mbaoperations@wharton.upenn.edu

San Francisco campus: Wharton School, University of Pennsylvania, 101 Howard Street, Suite 500, San Francisco, CA, 94105 USA
Tel: +1 415 777 1000
Web: www.wharton.upenn.edu/sanfrancisco
Email: mbaexecwest-admissions@wharton.upenn.edu.

Programme	Length	Start	Tuition fees
FT MBA	21 months	August	US$114,488
EMBA	24 months	May	US$173,940 (San Francisco) or US$167,160 (Philadelphia)
Joint programme options available	–	–	–

Wisconsin School of Business, University of Wisconsin-Madison

2450 Grainger Hall, 975 University Avenue, Madison, WI, 53706 USA
Tel: +1 608 262 4000
Web: www.bus.wisc.edu
Email: MBA@bus.wisc.edu

Programme	Length	Start	Tuition fees
FT MBA	21 months	August	US$53,512
Evening MBA	32 months	September	US$66,000
EMBA	21 months	August	US$73,000
Corporate EMBA (customised EMBA)	21 months	August	Varies by custom design

WP Carey School of Business, Arizona State University

BA 160, PO Box 874906, Tempe, AZ, 85287-4906 USA
Tel: +1 480 965 3332
Web: http://wpcarey.asu.edu/mba
Email: wpcareymba@asu.edu

Programme	Length	Start	Tuition fees
FT MBA	22 months	August	US$75,000
Evening Accelerated MBA	19 months	January	US$59,000
Evening MBA	21 months	August	US$58,600
EMBA	22 months	August	US$76,600
Online MBA	23 months	January, July	US$53,200
Dual degree options available	–	–	–

Yale School of Management, Yale University

135 Prospect Street, PO Box 208200, New Haven, CT, 06520 USA
Tel: +1 203 432 5932
Web: http://mba.yale.edu
Email: mba.admissions@yale.edu

Programme	Length	Start	Tuition fees
FT MBA	21 months	August	US$105,500
Leadership in Healthcare MBA for executives	22 months	July	US$149,100

Canadian schools

Desautels Faculty of Management, McGill University

Bronfman Building, 1001 Sherbrooke Street West, Montréal, Quebec, H3A 1G5 Canada
Tel: +1 514 398 4066
Web: www.mcgill.ca/desautels
Email (FT MBA): mba.mgmt@staff.mcgill.ca
Email (EMBA): info@embamcgillhec.ca

Programme	Length	Start	Tuition fees
FT MBA	20 months	August	CAN$69,500
Professional PT MBA	32 months	August	CAN$69,500
Desautels-HEC Montréal EMBA	15 months	September	CAN$78,000
MBA Japan (PT MBA)	20 months	April	YEN 4,800,000 plus tax
Double degree options available	–	–	–

Haskayne School of Business, University of Calgary

Scurfield Hall, 2500 University Drive NW, Calgary, T2N 1N4 Canada
Tel: +1 403 220 5685
Web: www.haskayne.ucalgary.ca
Email: mbarequest@haskayne.ucalgary.ca

Programme	Length	Start	Tuition fees
FT MBA	16 to 20 months	September	CAN$56,230
Evening MBA	32 months	September	CAN$56,230
Early evening MBA	32 months	January	CAN$56,230
EMBA	20 months	August	CAN$58,000
Global energy EMBA	15 months	September	US$105,000
Combined MBA options available	–	–	–

HEC Montréal

Côte-Sainte-Catherine Building, 3000 Côte-Sainte-Catherine Road, Montréal, Quebec, H3T 2A7 Canada
Tel: +1 514 340 6000
Web: www.hec.ca
Email: mba@hec.ca

International Office – Europe: 15, rue du Louvre, Boîte 131, Paris, 75001 France
Tel: +33 1 4233 4340
Web: www.hec.ca/europe

Programme	Length	Start	Tuition fees
FT MBA	12 months	August	CAN$30,000
Desautels-HEC Montréal EMBA	15 months	September	CAN$78,000

John Molson School of Business, Concordia University

1450 Guy Street, Montréal, Quebec, H3H 0A1 Canada
Tel: +1 514 848 2424
Web: http://johnmolson.concordia.ca
Email: gradprograms@jmsb.concordia.ca. This email address is being protected from spambots. You need JavaScript enabled to view it.

Programme	Length	Start	Tuition fees
MBA	12 months	August	CAN$39,282
Accelerated MBA	15 months	September	CAN$31,096
EMBA	20 months	June	CAN$68,000

Queen's School of Business

143 Union Street, Kingston, Ontario, K7L 3N6 Canada
Tel: +1 877 533 2330
Web: http://business.queensu.ca
Email: queensmba@business.queensu.ca

Programme	Length	Start	Tuition fees
FT MBA	12 months	May	CAN$75,000
EMBA	16 months	August	CAN$88,000
Cornell – Queen's EMBA	16 months	June	CAN$100,000
Accelerated MBA for business graduates	12 months	January	CAN$75,000
Accelerated MBA for business graduates – India	12 months	September	CAN$58,238
Dual degree options available	–	–	–

Richard Ivey School of Business, University of Western Ontario

1151 Richmond Street North, London, Ontario N6A 3K7 Canada
Tel: +1 519 661 3206
Web: www.ivey.ca
Email: mba@ivey.ca

Programme	Length	Start	Tuition fees
FT MBA	12 months	April	CAN$88,500
EMBA	17 months	February, September	CAN$90,000
Dual degree options available	–	–	–

Rotman School of Management, University of Toronto

105 St. George Street, Toronto, Ontario, M5S 3E6 Canada
Tel: +1 416 978 5703
Web: www.rotman.utoronto.ca
Email: mba@rotman.utoronto.ca

Programme	Length	Start	Tuition fees
Two-year MBA	20 months	September	CAN$99,001
Morning or evening MBA	36 months	September	CAN$99,000
One-year EMBA	13 months	September	CAN$88,000
Rotman – St Gallen Omnium Global EMBA	18 months	August	CAN$89,000
Dual degree options available	–	–	–

Sauder School of Business, University of British Columbia

2053 Main Mall, Vancouver, BC, V6T 1Z2 Canada
Tel: +1 604 822 8422
Web: www.sauder.ubc.ca
Email: mba@sauder.ubc.ca

Programme	Length	Start	Tuition fees
FT MBA	16 months	August	CAN$52,541
PT MBA	28 months	January	CAN$41,352
International MBA	20 months	March	US$40,000
EMBA in Healthcare	16 months	January	CAN$65,000
Joint and combined degree options available	–	–	–

Schulich School of Business, York University

4700 Keele Street, Toronto, Ontario, M3J 1P3 Canada
Tel: +1 416 736 5059
Web: www.schulich.yorku.ca
Email: admissions@schulich.yorku.ca

Programme	Length	Start	Tuition fees
FT MBA	16 or 20 months	January, May, September	CAN$60,000
PT MBA	40–72 months	January, May, September	CAN$120,000
Accelerated MBA (FT or PT MBA)	8–48 months	January, May, September	CAN$45,000
International MBA (FT MBA)	20 months	January, September	CAN$60,000
Kellogg-Schulich EMBA	18 months	January	CAN$110,000
India MBA (FT MBA)	15 months	January	TBC
Joint programme options available	–	–	–

Asian schools

China Europe International Business School (CEIBS)

Shanghai Campus: 699 Hongfeng Road, Pudong, Shanghai, 201206 China
Tel: +86 21 2890 5890
Web: www.ceibs.edu
Email: admissions@ceibs.edu

Beijing Campus: Building 20, Zhongguancun Software Park, 8 Dongbeiwang West Road, Haidian District, Beijing, 100193 China
Tel: +86 10 8296 6600
Web: www.ceibs.edu
Email: admissions@ceibs.edu

Shenzhen Campus: 8/F, Block A, Rongchao Business Center, No.6003, Yitian Road, Futian CBD, Shenzhen, 518026 China
Tel: +86 755 33378111
Web: www.ceibs.edu
Email: admissions@ceibs.edu

Programme	Length	Start	Tuition fees
FT MBA	18 months	August	US$49,800
EMBA	18 months	April	RMB 458,000

Indian Institute of Management, Ahmedabad (IIMAHD)

Vastrapur, Ahmedabad, Gujarat, 380015 India
Tel: +91 79 66323456
Web: www.iimahd.ernet.in
Email: dmission@iimahd.ernet.in

Programme	Length	Start	Tuition fees
FT MBA (Postgraduate Programme in Management – PGP)	22 months	June	INR 12,60,000
One-year FT MBA for executives (Postgraduate Programme in Management for Executives – PGPX)	12 months	August	INR 21,00,000

Indian School of Business (ISB)

Gachibowli, Hyderabad, 500 032 India
Tel: +91 40 2300 7000
Web: www.isb.edu
Email: pgpadmissions@isb.edu

Programme	Length	Start	Tuition fees
FT MBA (Postgraduate Programme in Management – PGP)	12 months	April	INR 12,50,000
EMBA for senior executives (Postgraduate Programme in Management for Senior Executives – PGPMAX)	18 months	May	INR 27,50,000

International University of Japan, Graduate School of International Management (GSIM)

777 Kokusai-cho, Minami Uonuma-shi, Niigata-ken, 949-7277 Japan
Tel: +81 25 779 1111
Web: http://gsim.iuj.ac.jp
Email: admgsim@iuj.ac.jp

Programme	Length	Start	Tuition fees
FT MBA	21 months	September	YEN 3,800,000

Korea Advanced Institute of Science and Technology (KAIST) Business School

207-43 Cheongyangri 2 – Dong, Dongdaemun-gu, Seoul, 130-722 Korea
Tel: +82 42 869 4114
Web: www.kaist.ac.kr
Email: admission@kaist.ac.kr

Global MBA Office: 87 Heogiro, Dongdaemun-gu, Seoul, 130-722, Korea
Tel. +82 2 958 3668
Web: www.business.kaist.ac.kr/kgsm/index.asp?klang=ENG
Email: hslee0526@business.kaist.ac.kr

Programme	Length	Start	Tuition fees
Techno MBA	24 months	February	TBC
Global MBA	24 months	February, September	WON 16000000
IMBA (Junior EMBA)	12 months	January	TBC
EMBA	22 months	February	TBC
Dual degree options available	–	–	–

Nanyang Business School, Nanyang Technological University

Nanyang Avenue, Singapore 639798
Tel: +65 6790 6033
Web: www.nbs.ntu.edu.sg
Email: nbsmba@ntu.edu.sg

Programme	Length	Start	Tuition fees
FT MBA	16 months	August	SG$55,000
PT MBA	24–32 months	August	SG$55,000
Nanyang-Waseda Double MBA	12–24 months	August	SG$63,000
Nanyang-St Gallen Double MBA	24 months	August	SG$24,500 (plus tuition fees to St Gallen)
EMBA in English	16–30 months	July	SG$94,815

National University of Singapore (NUS) Business School

Mochtar Riady Building, Graduate Studies Office, 15 Kent Ridge Drive, Level 4 Singapore, 119245 Singapore
Tel: +65 6516 2068
Web: http://bschool.nus.edu.sg
Email: mba@nus.edu.sg

Programme	Length	Start	Tuition fees
FT MBA	17 months	August	SG$52,000
PT MBA	24–30 months	August	SG$52,000
Asia-Pacific EMBA	15 months	June	SG$95,000
UCLA-NUS EMBA	15 months	May	US$92,222
NUS-Peking University (PKU) FT MBA	12 months	August	SG$54,000
NUS-Peking University (PKU) PT MBA	24–48 months	August	SG$54,000
NUS-HEC Paris MBA	29 months	August	SG$88,000
Dual degree options available	–	–	–

SP Jain Center of Management Dubai, Singapore and Sydney

Dubai Campus: Block 5, Dubai International Academic City, P. O. Box 502345, Dubai, UAE
Tel: +971 4 4291234
Web: www.spjain.org
Email: emba@spjain.org

Singapore Campus: 10, Hyderabad Road, Off Alexandra Road, Singapore 119579
Tel: +65 62704748
Web: www.spjain.org
Email: admissionssg@spjain.org

Programme	Length	Start	Tuition fees
Global MBA	12 months	April, November	US$21,775
EMBA in Dubai	24 months	January	AED58,800
EMBA in Singapore	15–24 months	November	SG$32,530

The Hong Kong University of Science and Technology (HKUST)

Clear Water Bay, Kowloon, Hong Kong
Tel: +852 2358 7533
Web: www.bm.ust.hk
Email (FT MBA): mba@ust.hk
Email (EMBA): emba@ust.hk

Programme	Length	Start	Tuition fees
FT MBA	12 or 16 months	August	HK$525,000
PT MBA (Hong Kong and Shenzhen)	24 months	August	HK$315,000
Kellogg-HKUST EMBA	15 months	January	US$143,300

European schools

Aalto University School of Economics

PO Box 21210 (Runebeginkatu 14-16), FI-00076 Aalto, Finland
Tel: +358 9 47001
Web: www.aaltoee.fi/en
Email: info@aaltoee.fi

EMBA: Aalto University Executive Education Ltd, Mechelininkatu 3 C, FI-00100 Helsinki
Tel: +358 10 837 3700
Web: www.aaltoee.fi/en
Email: info@aaltoee.fi

Programme	Length	Start	Tuition fees
EMBA (Finland, South Korea, Singapore and Poland)	20 months	February	€41,500*
PT EMBA	24 months	January	€28,000**
Kellogg-HKUST EMBA	15 months	January	US$143,300

*Plus VAT.
**Plus VAT and €3,000 VAT for books.

ALBA Graduate Business School at The American College of Greece

6–8 Xenias Street, 11528, Athens, Greece
Tel: +30 210 8964531–8
Web: www.alba.edu.gr
Email: mba@alba.edu.gr

Programme	Length	Start	Tuition fees
FT MBA	12 months	September	€19,750
PT MBA	24–48 months	September	€19,750
EMBA	18 months	September	€28,000

Ashridge Business School

Berkhamsted, Hertfordshire HP4 1NS, UK
Tel: +44 1442 841061
Web: www.ashridge.org.uk
Email: mba@ashridge.org.uk

Programme	Length	Start	Tuition fees
FT MBA	12 months	September	£32,500
EMBA	24 months	March, September	£32,500

Aston Business School

MBA Office, Aston University, Aston Triangle, Birmingham, B4 7ET
Tel: +44 121 204 3100
Web: www.aston.ac.uk
Email: mba@aston.ac.uk

Programme	Length	Start	Tuition fees
FT MBA	12 months	October	£23,300
EMBA	27 months	October	£24,750
PT MBA	27 months	October, January, April	£17,000
DL EMBA	27 months	October, January	£17,000

Athens University of Economics and Business

47a Evelpidon Street, GR-113 62, Athens, Greece
Tel: +30 210 82 03 659 /662
Web: www.imba.aueb.gr
Email: imba@aueb.gr

Programme	Length	Start	Tuition fees
FT MBA	14 months	September	€12,000
PT MBA	24 months	September	€12,000

Audencia Nantes School of Management

8 route de la Jonelière, B.P. 31222 – 44312, Nantes Cedex 3, France
Tel: +33 2 40 37 34 34
Web: www.mba.audencia.com
Email: mba@audencia.com

EMBA:
Email: emba@audencia.com

Programme	Length	Start	Tuition fees
International MBA	12 months	September	€29,000
EMBA	18 months	March	€26,000

Bath School of Management

University of Bath, Bath BA2 7AY, UK
Tel: +44 122 538 3431
Web: www.bath.ac.uk/management
Email: mbaapps@management.bath.ac.uk

Programme	Length	Start	Tuition fees
FT MBA	12 months	September	£22,500
PT EMBA	24 months	October, January	£22,500

Birmingham Business School

University of Birmingham, Edgbaston, Birmingham B15 2TT UK
Tel: +44 121 414 3344
Web: www.business.bham.ac.uk
Email: admissions@bham.ac.uk

FT MBA and The Birmingham MBA in Singapore:
Tel: +44 121 414 6693
Email: mba@bham.ac.uk

MBA Strategy and Procurement Management and EMBA programmes:
Tel: +44 121 414 4378
Email: v.l.harold@bham.ac.uk

MBA Public Services:
Tel: +44 121 414 7489
Email: j.r.sanderson@bham.ac.uk

Programme	Length	Start	Tuition fees
MBA International Business	12 months	September	£17,700 (UK/EU and overseas)
	21 months	January	Year 1: £2,400 (UK/EU) £5,400 (overseas) Year 2: £17,100 (UK/EU and overseas)
	24 months	September	Year 1: £5,100 (UK/EU) £10,800 (overseas) Year 2: £17,100 (UK/EU and overseas)
MBA Corporate Governance and Responsibility	12 months	September	£17,700 (UK/EU and overseas)

Programme	Length	Start	Tuition fees
MBA Global Banking and Finance	12 months	September	£17,700 (UK/EU and overseas)
MBA Strategy and Procurement Management (FT)	15 months	September	£18,000
MBA Strategy and Procurement Management (PT)	24–72 months	Mid-October*	£18,000
UK EMBA	24–72 months	Mid-October*	£18,000
The Birmingham MBA in Singapore	12 months	September	SG$27,600**
MBA Public Service	24–72 months	Mid-October**	£18,000

*Although entry is also possible at other times during the year when a module is being delivered.
**Excluding GST (Goods and Services Tax).

Bradford School of Management

Bradford University, Emm Lane, Bradford BD9 4JL, UK
Tel: +44 1274 234321
Web: www.brad.ac.uk
Email: management@bradford.ac.uk

Dubai MBA: Dubai Office, University of Bradford Middle East Regional office, Block 13, G39, Dubai Knowledge Village
Tel: +04 439 3694
Email: dubaienquiries@bradford.ac.uk

Bradford MBA in Manila: AIS, Ground Floor, Makati Stock Exchange Building, Ayala Avenue Metro, Makati City, Metro Manila
Tel: +632 501 9347
Email: contact@bradfordmanila.com

EMBA: Postgraduate Recruitment Office, Bradford University School of Management, Emm Lane, Bradford BD9 4JL, UK
Tel: +44 1274 234321
Web: www.brad.ac.uk/management/programmes/research/dba/ataglance/
Email: dba@bradford.ac.uk

Tilburg University: TiasNimbas, Tias building, Warandelaan 2. 5037 AB, Tilburg, The Netherlands
Tel: +49 228 259 0030
Web: www.tiasnimbas.edu
Email: information@tiasnimbas.edu

Programme	Length	Start	Tuition fees
FT MBA	12 months	September	£22,450
Accelerated FT MBA	10 months	January	£24,950
EMBA PT	30–72 months	January, September	£18,950
Dubai MBA	24 months	September	TBC
Bradford Perugia MBA	12 months	October	£22,000
Bradford MBA in Manila	24–72 months	January, April, July, October	£14,000
EMBA (in collaboration with TiasNimbas Business School in Tilburg or Utrecht)	24 months	September	€40,000

Cambridge Judge Business School

University of Cambridge, Trumpington Street, Cambridge CB2 1AG, UK
Tel: +44 1223 339700
Web: www.jbs.cam.ac.uk
Email: mba-enquiries@jbs.cam.ac.uk

EMBA:
Tel: +44 1223 766329
Email: emba-enquiries@jbs.cam.ac.uk

Programme	Length	Start	Tuition fees
The Cambridge MBA FT	12 months	September	£36,000 plus £2,289 Average college membership
The Cambridge EMBA	20 months	September	£52,000

Cass Business School

106 Bunhill Row, London EC1Y 8TZ, UK
Tel: +44 20 7040 8600
Web: www.cass.city.ac.uk
Email: info@city.ac.uk

FT MBA:
Tel: +44 20 7040 5277
Email: viola.papiez.1@city.ac.uk

EMBA:
Tel: +44 20 7040 5276
Email: timothy.navin-jones.1@city.ac.uk

EMBA in Dubai:
Tel: +9714 401 9316
Email: ehsan.razavizadeh.1@city.ac.uk

Programme	Length	Start	Tuition fees
FT MBA	12 months	September	£34,500
EMBA evening	24 months	September	£42,000
EMBA weekend	24 months	March	£42,000
EMBA in Dubai	24 months	September	£34,500

Copenhagen Business School

Solbjerg Plads 3, DK 2000 Frederiksberg, Denmark
Tel: +45 3815 3815
Web: www.cbs.dk
Email: cbs@cbs.dk

CBS Full-time MBA Programme:
Tel: +45 3815 3016
Email: info.mba@cbs.dk

Flexible EMBA:
Tel: +45 3815 6002
Email: lrb@mba@cbs.dk

Programme	Length	Start	Tuition fees
FT MBA	12 months	September	DKK 290,000
CBS Flexible EMBA	–	September	DKK 400,000

Cranfield School of Management

Cranfield, Bedford MK43 0AL, UK
Tel: +44 1234 754431
Web: www.som.cranfield.ac.uk
Email: MBAadmissions@cranfield.ac.uk

Cranfield MBA (Defence):
Tel: +44 1793 785922
Email: odavies.cmt@defenceacademy.mod.uk

Programme	Length	Start	Tuition fees
FT MBA	12 months	September	£33,000
PT EMBA	24 months	January	£33,000
Modular EMBA	24 months	January	£33,000
The Cranfield MBA (Defence) PT and Modular	24 months	January	*

*Contact directly to confirm fees

Durham Business School

Durham University, Mill Hill Lane, Durham DH1 3LB, UK
Tel: +44 191 334 5533
Web: www.dur.ac.uk
Email: pg.bus@durham.ac.uk

Global MBA:
Global Learning Centre, Durham Business School, Durham University, Mill Hill Lane, Durham DH1 3LB, UK
Tel: +44 191 334 5533
Email: global.mba@durham.ac.uk

Programme	Length	Start	Tuition fees
FT MBA	12 months	September	£19,500 EU £23,250 non-EU
PT EMBA	24 months	January	£17,500
Global MBA various options	24–60 months	April, October	£14,500
Programme	**Length**	**Start**	**Tuition fees**
Global MBA (Caribbean)	24 months	October	BDS$49,200 Flexible option BDS$45,000 lump sum

EADA

Aragó 204, 08011 Barcelona, Spain
Tel: +34 934520844
Web: www.eada.edu
Email: mba@eada.edu

Programme	Length	Start	Tuition fees
FT MBA	10 months	September	€30,500

EDHEC Business School

Lille-Nice, 58 Rue du Port, 59046 Lille, Cedex, France
Tel: +33 3 20 15 45 00
Web: www.edhec.edu
Email: communication@edhec.edu

MBA Admissions: 393, Promenade des Anglais, BP3116, 06202 - Nice - Cedex 3, France
Tel: +33 4 93 18 45 66
Email: mba.admissions@edhec.edu

EMBA PT: 24 Avenue Gustave Delory, CS 50411, 59057 Roubaix Cedex 1, France
Tel: +33 3 20 15 45 16
Email: executive-mba@edhec.edu

Programme	Length	Start	Tuition fees
Global MBA FT	12 months	January, September	€36,000
EMBA PT	18 months	TBC	€30,000

EM Lyon Business School

23, av. Guy de Collongue, BP 174, 69132 Ecully Cedex, France
Tel: +33 4 78 33 78 00
Web: www.em-lyon.com
Email: info@em-lyon.com

International MBA:
Tel: +33 4 78 33 77 83
Email: imba@em-lyon.com

Programme	Length	Start	Tuition fees
International MBA	12 months	September	€35,900

ESADE Business School

Avenue d'Esplugues, 92-96, 08034 Barcelona, Spain
Tel: +34 934 952 088
Web: www.esade.edu
Email: mba@esade.edu

EMBA: Madrid
Email: exedMAD@esade.edu

Barcelona:
Email: exedBCN@esade.edu

Global EMBA: Georgetown University, 37th and O Streets, NW Rafik B. Hariri Building, Suite 462, Washington, D.C. 20057-1223 USA
Tel: +1 202 687 2691
Web: www.globalexecmba.com
Email: globalemba@georgetown.edu

ESADE Business School, Admissions Office – Executive Education, Av. d'Esplugues, 92-96 08034 Barcelona, Spain
Tel: +34 93 495 3843
Email: Pollyanna.nethersole@esade.edu
Web: www.globalexecmba.com

Programme	Length	Start	Tuition fees
FT MBA	15–18 months	September	€57,000
EMBA Barcelona or Madrid	18 months	January	€55,900
Global EMBA (in partnership with Georgetown's McDonough School of Business)	14 months	June	US$142,000

ESCP Europe

79, avenue de la République, 75011 Paris, France
Tel: +33 1 49 23 22 70
Web: www.escpeurope.eu
Email: miranda@escpeurope.eu

Berlin: Heubnerweg 6, 14059 Berlin, Germany
Tel: +49 30 32 00 71 71
Email: mba.de@escpeurope.eu

Madrid: Arroyofresno 1, 28035 Madrid, Spain
Tel: +34 91 386 25 11
Email: solicitudes@escpeurope.eu

London: 527 Finchley Road, London NW3 7BG, UK
Tel: +44 207 443 8800
Email: ukexeced@escpeurope.eu

Torino: Corso Unione Sovietica, 218 bis, 10134 Torino, Italy
Tel: +39 347 78 51 211
Email: infomba@escpeurope.eu

Programme	Length	Start	Tuition fees
European EMBA (France/UK/ Germany/ Spain/Italy)	18 months	January	€51,000

ESSEC Business School

Avenue Bernard Hirsch B.P. 50105, 95021 Cergy-Pontoise Cedex, France
Tel: +33 1 34 43 30 00
Web: www.essec.edu
Email: essecinfo@essec.fr

Global MBA:
Email: globalmba@essec.edu

ESSEC and Mannheim MBA:
France
Tel: +33 146 92 17 94
Web: www.essec-mannheim.com
Email: loi@essec.fr

Mannheim:
Tel: +49 621 181 3721
Web: www.essec-mannheim.com
Email: vatansever@mannheim-business-school.com

Programme	Length	Start	Tuition fees
Global MBA	12 months	September	€45,000
ESSEC MBA ('double degrees offered with various partnership schools)	11 months 23 months	August	€29,500–€37,000 €16,000
ESSEC and MANNHEIM EMBA			
Modular track	18 months	October	€47,000
Paris Weekend	18 months	April	€44,000
Mannheim Weekend	18 months	April	€44,000

European Business School London, Regent's College

Admissions Department, European Business School London, Regent's College London, Regent's Park, Inner Circle, London NW1 4NS, UK
Tel: +44 20 7487 7505
Web: www.regents.ac.uk/ebsl
Email: EBSL@regents.ac.uk

Programme	Length	Start	Tuition fees
FT MBA	12–16 months	September, January	£17,995

Grenoble Graduate School of Business

12, rue Pierre Sémard, BP 127, 38003 Grenoble Cedex 01, France
Tel: +33 4 76 70 61 87
Web: www.grenoble-em.com
Email: admissions@ggsb.com

Programme	Length	Start	Tuition fees
FT MBA	12 months	September	€27,000

HEC Paris

1, rue de la Libération, 78351 Jouy en Josas, France
Tel: +33 1 39 67 70 00
Web: www.hec.edu
Email: admissionmba@hec.fr

Programme	Length	Start	Tuition fees
FT MBA	16 months	January September	€45,000 €48,000
PT MBA	24 months	January	€48,000

Henley School of Management

University of Reading, Whiteknights, PO Box 217, Reading, Berkshire RG6 6AH, UK
Tel: +44 1491 418 803
Web: www.henley.reading.ac.uk
Email:mba@henley.com

Programme	Length	Start	Tuition fees
High potential MBA	12 months	October	£25,000
EMBA	24 months	October	£39,950
MBA by flexible learning	36 months	March, June, October	£20,000

Hult International Business School

1 Education Street, Cambridge, MA, 02141 USA
Tel: +1 617 746 1990
Web: www.hult.edu
Email: info@hult.edu

Programme	Length	Start	Tuition fees
One-year MBA (USA, UK, UAE, China)	12 months	September	Boston/San Francisco US$64,500; London £44,600; Dubai AED 236,700; Shanghai CNY 464,400
Programme	**Length**	**Start**	**Tuition fees**
EMBA (UK, UAE, China)	24 months	September	London £23,500; Dubai AED 124,500; Shanghai CNY 244,000

IE Business School

María de Molina, 11 28006 Madrid, Spain
Tel: +34 91 568 96 00
Web: www.ie.edu
Email: admissions@ie.edu u

IE Admissions Department: María de Molina, 13 28006 Madrid, Spain
Email: IXMBA.admissions@ie.edu

Global MBA:
Tel: +34 915 689 610
Email: blended.programs@ie.edu

Programme	Length	Start	Tuition fees
International MBA	13 months	November, April	€58,200
Global MBA (blended)	15 months	TBC	€39,200
Global EMBA	13 months	November	€64,200
International EMBA bi-weekly	13 months	November	€55,200

IESE

Avenida Pearson, 21, 08034 Barcelona, Spain
Tel: +34 93 253 42 00
Web: www.iese.edu
Email: mbainfo@iese.edu

EMBA: EMBA Admissions, IESE Business School, Av. Pearson, 21, 08034 Barcelona
Tel: +34 93 253 40 72/42 00
Email: embabcn@iese.ed

Programme	Length	Start	Tuition fees
FT MBA	19 months	September	€57,500
EMBA	15 months	January	€63,500
Global EMBA	15 months	January	€92,000

IMD

Ch. de Bellerive 23, PO Box 915, CH-1001 Lausanne, Switzerland
Tel: +41 21 618 0111
Web: www.imd.org
Email: info@imd.ch

MBA:
Tel: +41 21 618 0298
Web: www.imd.org/mba

EMBA:
Tel: +41 21 618 0700
Web: www.imd.org/emba

Programme	Length	Start	Tuition fees
FT MBA	11 months	January	CHF 60,000
EMBA	15 months	January	CHF 126,000

Imperial College London

South Kensington Campus, London SW7 2AZ, UK
Tel: +44 20 7589 5111
Web: www.imperial.ac.uk

FT MBA and EMBA:
Tel: +44 20 7594 9206
Email: mba@imperial.ac.uk

Programme	Length	Start	Tuition fees
FT MBA	12 months	October	£35,850
EMBA Weekday EMBA Weekend	24 Months 21 months	December April	£39,500 £41,000

INSEAD

Europe Campus: Boulevard de Constance, 77305 Fontainebleau, France
Tel: +33 1 60 72 00
Web: www.insead.edu/home
Email: mba.info@insead.edu

Global Executive MBA: INSEAD GEMBA Admissions Office, Boulevard de Constance, F-77305 Fontainebleau, France
Email: emba.candidates@insead.edu

Tsinghua-INSEAD EMBA: INSEAD, Executive MBA Office, 1 Ayer Rajah Avenue, Singapore 138676
Tel: +65 6799 5356
Web: www.tsinghua.insead.edu
Email: tiemba@insead.edu

Tsinghua SEM, EMBA Programme: Room 311 Shunde Building, Beijing, China 100084
Tel: +86 10 6279 5799
Web: www.tsinghua.insead.edu
Email: tiemba@sem.tsinghua.edu.cn

Programme	Length	Start	Tuition fees
FT MBA	10 months	January	€56,000
Global EMBA 3 sections: Asia Europe Middle East	 17 months 15 months 14 months	 August October November	 S$145,000* €95,000 US$95,000
Dual degree MBA (in collaboration with Tsinghua in Singapore, France and UAE)	18 months	June	€90,000

*Including 7% GST (Goods and Services Tax).

International Institute of Business

8a, Brest-Litovskyi Highway, Kyiv, 03179 Ukraine
Tel: +38 044 585 00 33
Web: www.iib.com.ua
Email: info@iib.com.ua

Programme	Length	Start	Tuition fees
PT EMBA*	22 months	October	€17,000
PT International MBA**	18 months	March	€16,500

*Taught in Russian.
**Taught in English.

International University of Monaco

2, Avenue Albert II, Principality of Monaco, MC 98000 Monte-Carlo
Tel: +37797 985727
Web: www.monaco.edu/international-university-monaco.cfm

Online EMBA:
Web: www.embaonline.monaco.edu/executive-mba-program
Email: emba@monaco.edu

Programme	Length	Start	Tuition fees
FT MBA	10 months	September+	€27,450*
Online EMBA	24 months	February, September	€21,000*

*Plus €150 for Student Association Fee and €600 for International University of Monaco Life Fee that gives lifelong access to alumni services.

Kingston University

Kingston Hill, Kingston Upon Thames, Surrey KT2 7LB, UK
Tel: +44 844 855 2177 (UK callers only); +44 208 328 1148 (callers outside the UK only)
Web: http://business.kingston.ac.uk
Email: businesspgenquiry@kingston.ac.uk

Programme	Length	Start	Tuition fees
FT MBA	12 months	September, February	£18,560
PT MBA	24 months	September, February	£9,650 (Year 1)

Lancaster University Management School

Lancaster University, Bailrigg, Lancaster LA1 4YX, UK
Tel: +44 1524 510753
Web: www.lums.lancs.ac.uk
Email: management@lancaster.ac.uk

Programme	Length	Start	Tuition fees
FT MBA	12 months	October	£25,000
PT EMBA	24 months	October	£18,500
Global MBA Jordan	24 months	October	TBC
Global MBA Zambia	24 months	December	TBC
Global MBA Singapore	24 months	March	TBC

Leeds University Business School

MBA Admissions Office, Leeds University Business School, Maurice Keyworth Building, University of Leeds, Leeds LS2 9JT, UK
Tel: +44 113 343 2610
Web: www.business.leeds.ac.uk
Email: mba@lubs.leeds.ac.uk

Programme	Length	Start	Tuition fees
FT MBA	12 months	September	£17,000 UK/EU £20,500 Non UK/EU
EMBA	24 months	October	£17,000

London Business School

Regent's Park, London NW1 4SA, UK
Tel: +44 20 7000 7000
Web: www.london.edu

FT MBA: MBA Information Office, London Business School, Regent's Park, London NW1 4SA, UK
Tel: +44 20 7000 7500
Email: mbainfo@london.edu

EMBA London: London Business School, Regent's Park, London NW1 4SA, UK
Tel: +44 20 7000 7514
Email: emba@london.edu

EMBA Dubai: DIFC Centre of Excellence, DIFC Dubai International Financial Centre, Gate Village, Building 2, Level 3, PO Box 506630, Dubai, UAE
Tel: +971 440 193 01
Email: embadubai@london.edu

EMBA Global Americas and Europe:
London Business School
Tel: +44 20 7000 7511
Web: www.emba-global.com
Email: embaglobal@london.edu

Columbia Business School
Tel: +1 212 854 1961
Web: www.emba-global.com
Email: apply@gsb.columbia.edu

EMBA Global Asia: HKU Business School
Tel: +852 3962 1262
Web: www.emba-global.com
Email: asia@emba-global.com

Programme	Length	Start	Tuition fees
FT MBA	15–21 months	August	TBC
EMBA London	20 months	January, August	£57,775
EMBA Dubai	20 months	January, August	US$89,950
EMBA Global A&E (in partnership with Columbia Business School)	20 months	May	US$147,723
EMBA Global Asia (in partnership with Columbia Business School and HKU Business School)	20 months	June	US$133,080

LSE (London School of Economics)

The TRIUM Global Executive MBA Program, 44 West Fourth Street, Suite 4-100, New York, NY 10012-1126 USA
Tel: USA Number +1 212 998 0442; Europe Number +33 1 39 67 70 94
Web: www.triumemba.org
Email: info@triumemba.org

Programme	Length	Start	Tuition fees
TRIUM Global EMBA	17 months	September	€149,500

Manchester Business School

Booth Street West, Manchester M15 6PB, UK
Tel: +44 161 306 1320
Web: www.mbs.ac.uk

FT MBA:
Tel: +44 161 275 6414
Email: mba_admissions@mbs.ac.uk

Global MBA:
Tel: +44 161 275 7212
Email: global@mbs.ac.uk

Programme	Length	Start	Tuition fees
FT MBA	18 months	September	£37,400
PT Global MBA	36 months	January, July	£23,100
PT Global MBA Accelerated	24 months	September	TBC

Mannheim Business School

L 5, 6, D68161 Mannheim, Germany
Tel: +49 621 181 3721
Web: www.mannheim-business-school.com
Email: info@mannheim-business-school.com

FT MBA:
Web: www.mannheim-mba.com

ESSEC and Mannheim MBA:
France
Tel: +33 146 92 17 94
Web: www.essec-mannheim.com
Email: loi@essec.fr

Mannheim:
Tel: +49 621 181 3721
Web: www.essec-mannheim.com
Email: vatansever@mannheim-business-school.com

Mannheim and Tongji EMBA:
Shanghai
Tel: +86 21 659 80875
Web: www.mannheim-tongji.com
Email: vickiexu.sem@tongji.edu.cn

Mannheim:
Tel: +49 621 181 3721
Web: www.mannheim-tongji.com
Email: vatansever@mannheim-business-school.com

Programme	Length	Start	Tuition fees
FT MBA (5 tracks: German; Eurasian; Transatlantic; European; Global	12 months	September	€33,000
ESSEC and MANNHEIM EMBA			
Modular track	18 months	October	€47,000
Paris Weekend	18 months	April	€44,000
Mannheim Weekend	18 months	April	€44,000
Mannheim and Tongji EMBA	18 months	March	€38,000

Mountbatten Institute

Web: www.mountbatten.org

NY Office: 50 East 42nd Street, Suite 2000, New York, NY, 10017-5405 USA
Tel: +1 212 557 5380
Email: info@mountbatten.org

UK Office: Michael House, 5th floor, 35-37 Chiswell Street, London EC1Y 4SE, UK
Tel: +44 845 370 3535
Email: info-uk@mountbatten.org

Bangkok Office: 1 GlasHaus Building, Suite 1404, Sukhumvit 25, Sukhumvit Road, Wattana, Bangkok 10110, Thailand
Tel: +66 2661 7081-84
Email: info-ap@mountbatten.org

Sydney Office: 107-115 Pacific Highway, Suite 2, Hornsby NSW 2077, Australia
Tel: +612 9476 8744
Email: mountbatten@itm.co

Programme	Length	Start	Tuition fees
FT International Business Practice MBA			
New York and Bangkok	16 months	March, August	$32,000/£2,500*
London and Bangkok	16 months	March, August	$36,000

*As of 21 Feb 2012. Tuition in GBP based on current exchange rate. Accommodation and monthly living allowance are included in the fees.

Newcastle University Business School

Newcastle University Business School, 5 Barrack Road, Newcastle upon Tyne NE1 4SE, UK
Tel: +44 191 208 1500
Web: www.ncl.ac.uk/nubs

Programme	Length	Start	Tuition fees
FT MBA	12 months	September	£19,800

Nottingham Business School

Nottingham Trent University, Burton Street, Nottingham NG1 4BU, UK
Tel: +44 115 848 4460
Web: www.ntu.ac.uk/mba
Email: nbs.enquiries@ntu.ac.uk

Programme	Length	Start	Tuition fees
FT MBA	12 months	September	£15,000*
EMBA	24 months	January	£15,000*

*Subject to change. For the latest fee information, please visit www.ntu.ac.uk/mba.

The Open University

PO Box 197, Milton Keynes MK7 6BJ, UK
Tel: +44 845 366 6035
Web: www.oubs.open.ac.uk

MBA: Student Registration and Enquiry Service, The Open University Business School, PO Box 197, Milton Keynes MK7 6BJ, UK
Email: oubs@open.ac.uk

Programme	Length	Start	Tuition fees
MBA	3–7 years	May, November	£14–£16,000

Politecnico di Milano School of Management

Via Lambruschini 4C - building 26/A - 20156 Milano
Tel: +39 02 2399 2820
Web: www.english.polimi.it

FT MBA:
Tel: +39 02 2399 9194
Email: imba@mip.polimi.it

EMBA:
Tel: +39 02 2399 2878 or +39 02 2399 2830
Email: embadmissions@mip.polimi.it

Programme	Length	Start	Tuition fees
FT MBA	14 months	October	€26,000 plus €1,700 university tax and admin fee
PT evening and PT weekend format also available	–	–	–
EMBA formats also available	–	–	–
PT EMBA	20 months	June	€26,000
EMBA Evening	20 months	November	€26,000

Rotterdam School of Management

Erasmus University, Burgemeester Oudlaan 50, 3062 PA Rotterdam, PO Box 1738, 3000 DR Rotterdam, The Netherlands
Tel: +31 10 408 22 22
Web: www.rsm.nl
Email: mba.info@rsm.nl

International FT MBA:
Tel: +31 10 408 1077 or +31 10 408 2884
Email: msteenkamp@rsm.nl or acammen@rsm.nl

EMBA:
Tel: +31 10 408 2857
Email: jwitteveen@rsm.nl

Global Executive One MBA:
Tel: +31 10 408 2857
Email: jwitteveen@rsm.nl

Programme	Length	Start	Tuition fees
International FT MBA	12 months	January	€39,000
EMBA	24 months	January	€44,000
Global Executive OneMBA	21 months	September	€53,000

Saïd Business School

University of Oxford, Park End Street, Oxford OX1 1HP, UK
Tel: +44 1865 278804
Web: www.sbs.oxford.edu/mba
Email: mba-enquiries@sbs.ox.ac.uk

FT MBA: MBA Office, Saïd Business School, Park End Street, Oxford OX1 1HP, UK
Tel: +44 1865 278804

EMBA: Executive MBA Office, Saïd Business School, Park End Street, Oxford OX1 1HP, UK
Tel: +44 1865 288901

Programme	Length	Start	Tuition fees
FT MBA	12 months	October	£37,750 plus £3,200 college fees
EMBA	21 months	January	£52,000

SDA Bocconi School of Management

SDA Bocconi, Masters Division – Recruiting and Admissions Service, Via Balilla 18 – 20136, Milan, Italy
Tel: +39 02 5836 3228/3297/3299
Web: www.sdabocconi.it/en
Email: admissions@sdabocconi.it

Programme	Length	Start	Tuition fees
FT MBA	12 months	October	€43,500
Global EMBA	20 months	March	€51,000

Stockholm School of Economics

Sveavägen 65, SE-113 83 Stockholm, Sweden
Tel: +46 8 736 9000
Web: www.hhs.se
Email: info@hhs.se

Programme	Length	Start	Tuition fees
EMBA	24 months	January	SEK 395, 000*

*Exclusive of VAT (25%).

Strathclyde Business School

University of Strathclyde, 199 Cathedral Street, Glasgow G4 0QU, UK
Tel: +44 141 553 6118/6119
Web: www.strath.ac.uk/business
Email: sbs.admissions@strath.ac.uk

Programme	Length	Start	Tuition fees
FT MBA	12 months	September	£22,000 TBC
PT evening MBA	24–36 months	September	£14,500
PT MBA via international centres	24–72 months	September	TBC
Flexible learning MBA	24–36 months	September	£12,700

TiasNimbas Business School

Tilburg University, TiasNimbas, Tias building, Warandelaan 2. 5037 AB, Tilburg, The Netherlands
Tel: +31 13 466 86 00
Web: www.tiasnimbas.edu
Email: information@tiasnimbas.edu

International MBA:
Tel: +31 13 466 3941

International EMBA:
Tel: +31 13 466 3963

EMBA:
Tel: +31 13 466 39 46

Programme	Length	Start	Tuition fees
International MBA	12 months	September	€37,500
International EMBA (IMM)	18 months	March	€52,500
EMBA (in collaboration with Bradford School of Management in Tilburg or Utrecht)	24 months	September	€40,000

UCD Michael Smurfit Graduate Business School

Carysfort Avenue, Blackrock, County Dublin, Ireland
Tel: +353 1 716 8934
Web: www.smurfitschool.ie
Email: smurfitschool@ucd.ie

FT MBA and EMBA:
Tel: +353 1 716 8862
Email: mba@ucd.ie

Programme	Length	Start	Tuition fees
FT MBA	12 months	August	€29,500
EMBA	24 months	August	€29,000

University of Edinburgh Business School

Postgraduate Admissions, University of Edinburgh, Business School, 29 Buccleuch Place, Edinburgh EH8 9JS, UK
Tel: +44 131 650 9663
Web: www.business-school.ed.ac.uk
Email: mba@business-school.ed.ac.uk

Programme	Length	Start	Tuition fees
FT MBA	12–16 months	September	£24,500–£26,100

Southampton Management School

University of Southampton, Highfield, Southampton SO17 1BJ, UK
Tel: +44 23 8059 7677
Web: www.southampton.ac.uk/management
Email: StudentOffice.FBL@soton.ac.uk

FT/PT MBA:
Tel: +44 23 8059 5341
Email: MBAapply.FBL@soton.ac.uk

Programme	Length	Start	Tuition fees
FT MBA	12 months	September	£18,000
PT MBA	24 months	September, February	£9,000 per year

University of St Gallen

University of St Gallen, Blumenbergplatz 9, CH-9000 St Gallen, Switzerland
Tel: +41 71 224 24 78
Web: www.mba.unisg.ch
Email: www.unisg.ch

Programme	Length	Start	Tuition fees
FT MBA	12 months	September	CHF 63,000
PT MBA	24–36 months	February, August	CHF 70,000
Double degree MBA (in partnership with (Nanyang Technological University)	14 months	September	CHF 69,400

Vlerick Leuven Gent Management School

Ghent Campus: Reep 1, 9000 Gent, Belgium
Tel: +32 9 210 97 11
Web: www.vlerick.com
Email: info@vlerick.be

FT MBA:
Tel: +32 16 24 88 86
Email: yolanda.habets@vlerick.com

Modular MBA:
Tel: +32 16 24 88 09
Email: gladys.vannuffel@vlerick.com

EMBA in Moscow:
Tel: +7 921 938 99 23
Email: anastasia.korshunova@vlerick.ru

Programme	Length	Start	Tuition fees
FT MBA	12 months	August	€31,500
PT MBA	24 months	September	€30,500
Modular MBA	18 months	January	€30,500
EMBA in Moscow	17 months	October	€45,000

Warwick Business School

Warwick MBA Recruitment, Warwick Business School, University of Warwick, Coventry CV4 7AL, UK
Tel: +44 24 7652 4100
Web: www.wbs.ac.uk
Email: warwickmba@wbs.ac.uk

Global Energy MBA: Graduate Marketing and Recruitment, Warwick Business School, University of Warwick, Coventry CV4 7AL, UK
Tel: +44 24 7652 4100

Programme	Length	Start	Tuition fees
FT MBA	12 months	September	£26,000 TBC
EMBA	24–36 months	March, October	£9,950 per year
Global Energy MBA	36 months	May	£10,400 per year
DL EMBA	30 months	January, July	£6,200 per year

Westminster Business School

35 Marylebone Road, London NW1 5LS, UK
Tel: +44 20 7911 5000
Web: www.westminster.ac.uk
Email: www.westminster.ac.uk/mba

Programme	Length	Start	Tuition fees
FT MBA	12 months	September, January	£19,000
PT MBA	24 months	September, January	£9,540 per year

Whu – Otto Beisheim School of Management

WHU – Otto Beisheim School of Management, Burgplatz 2, 56179 Vallendar, Germany,
Tel: +49 261 6509 0
Web: www.whu.edu/en/home
Email: whu@whu.edu

FT MBA: WHU – Otto Beisheim School of Management, MBA-Office, Burgplatz 2, 56179 Vallendar, Germany
Tel: +49 261 6509 140
Web: www.fulltime-mba.whu.edu
Email: mba@whu.edu

PT MBA: WHU – Otto Beisheim School of Management, Part-time MBA Office, Burgplatz 2, 56179 Vallendar, Germany
Tel: +49 261 6509 670
Email: part-time.mba@whu.edu

Kellogg-WHU Executive MBA Program: WHU – Otto Beisheim School of Management, Kellogg-WHU Executive MBA Program, Burgplatz 2, 56170 Vallendar, Germany
Tel: +49 261 6509 183
Email: emba@whu.edu

Programme	Length	Start	Tuition fees
FT MBA	15 months	April	€35,000
PT MBA	24 months	September	€39,000
Kellogg-WHU EMBA Program	24 months	September	€70,000

Ranking comparison tables

In this section we have provided comparative tables of the main rankings (see Chapter 4) for the top FT MBAs in North America (the US and Canada), Europe and Asia, and the top EMBAs worldwide.

We have also listed the top 30 European business schools according to the *Financial Times* 2010 rankings.

Online MBAs are currently not ranked. The available rankings for PT MBAs refer to US-based programmes, which are not the main focus of this book.

Note: All the schools that appear in these tables are listed in the directory.

North America

Top 30 FT MBAs in the USA

	BusinessWeek (2010)	*Financial Times* (2011)	*The Economist* (2010)	*Forbes* (2009)	*US News* (2011)
1	Chicago Booth	Wharton	Chicago Booth	Stanford	Stanford
2	Harvard	Harvard	Dartmouth – Tuck	Dartmouth – Tuck	Harvard
3	Wharton	Stanford	Berkeley – Haas	Harvard	MIT – Sloan
4	Kellogg	Columbia	Harvard	Chicago Booth	Wharton
5	Stanford	MIT – Sloan	Stanford	Wharton	Kellogg
6	Duke – Fuqua	Chicago Booth	Wharton	Columbia	Chicago Booth
7	Michigan – Ross	NYU – Stern	Virginia – Darden	Cornell – Johnson	Dartmouth – Tuck
8	Berkeley – Haas	Yale	Columbia	Kellogg	Berkeley – Haas
9	Columbia	Dartmouth – Tuck	MIT – Sloan	Virginia - Darden	Columbia
10	MIT – Sloan	Duke	NYU – Stern	Yale	NYU – Stern
11	Virginia – Darden	Kellogg	USC – Marshall	Texas, Austin – McCombs	Yale
12	SMU – Cox	Michigan – Ross	Carnegie Mellon – Tepper	Berkeley – Haas	Duke – Fuqua
13	Cornell – Johnson	Berkeley – Haas	Yale	Duke – Fuqua	Virginia – Darden
14	Dartmouth – Tuck	Cornell – Johnson	Hult	MIT – Sloan	UCLA – Anderson
15	Carnegie Mellon – Tepper	UCLA – Anderson	Duke – Fuqua	UNC Kenan – Flagler	Michigan – Ross

	BusinessWeek (2010)	*Financial Times* (2011)	*The Economist* (2010)	*Forbes* (2009)	*US News* (2011)
16	UNC Kenan – Flagler	Emory – Goizueta	Washington – Foster	Brigham Young – Marriott	Texas, Austin – McCombs
17	UCLA – Anderson	Georgetown – McDonough	Cornell – Johnson	NYU – Stern	Carnegie Mellon – Tepper
18	NYU – Stern	Maryland – Smith	Indiana – Kelley	Michigan – Ross	UNC Kenan – Flagler
19	Indiana – Kelley	Carnegie Mellon – Tepper	Emory – Goizueta	UCLA – Anderson	Washington in St Louis – Olin
20	MSU – Broad	Virginia – Darden	UCLA – Anderson	Iowa – Tippie	Minnesota – Carlson
21	Yale	Rice – Jones	Notre Dame – Mendoza	Michigan State – Broad	USC – Marshall
22	Emory – Goizueta	Texas A&M – Mays	UNC Kenan – Flagler	Emory – Goizueta	Emory – Goizueta
23	Georgia Tech	Illinois at Urbana – Champaign	Rice – Jones	Carnegie Mellon – Tepper	IU – Kelley
24	Notre Dame – Mendoza	Texas at Austin – McCombs	Boston University	Texas A&M – Mays	Georgetown – McDonough
25	Texas at Austin – McCombs	Vanderbilt – Owen	Texas at Austin – McCombs	Indiana – Kelley	Ohio State – Fisher
26	USC – Marshall	Rochester – Simon	Washington in St Louis – Olin	Minnesota – Carlson	Arizona State – Carey
27	Brigham Young – Marriott	California at Irvine – Merage	Vanderbilt – Owen	Connecticut	Georgia Tech
28	Minnesota – Carlson	Penn State – Smeal	Georgetown – McDonough	Penn State – Smeal	University of California Davis
29	Rice – Jones	Hult	Wisconsin-Madison	Maryland – Smith	Wisconsin-Madison
30	Texas A&M – Mays	UNC Kenan – Flagler	Penn State – Smeal	Vanderbilt – Ouen	Vanderbilt – Owen

Top FT MBAs in Canada

	BusinessWeek (2010)	*Financial Times* (2011)	*The Economist* (2010)	*Forbes* (2009) (1-year MBAs)	*Forbes* (2009) (2-year MBAs)
1	Queen's University	University of Toronto – Rotman	York University – Schulich	HEC Montréal	York University – Schulich
2	University of Western Ontario – Ivey	University of Western Ontario – Ivey	University of British Columbia – Sauder	–	University of British Columbia – Sauder
3	University of Toronto – Rotman	York University – Schulich	University of Calgary – Haskayne	–	–
4	York University – Schulich	McGill University – Desautels	Concordia University – John Molson	–	–
5	McGill University – Desautels	University of British Columbia – Sauder	–	–	–
6	HEC Montréal	–	–	–	–

Europe

Top 30 FT MBAs in Europe

	BusinessWeek (2010)	*Financial Times* (2011)	*The Economist* (2010)	*Forbes* (2009) (1-year MBAs)	*Forbes* (2009) (2-year MBAs)
1	INSEAD	LBS	IESE	INSEAD	LBS
2	IE	INSEAD	IMD	IMD	Manchester
3	ESADE	IE	HEC Paris	IE	IESE
4	LBS	IESE	Cranfield	Cambridge – Judge	HEC
5	IMD	IMD	Henley	Oxford – Saïd	ESADE
6	Cambridge – Judge	HEC Paris	LBS	City – Cass	–
7	IESE	ESADE	ESADE	Lancaster	–
8	Cranfield	Cambridge – Judge	IE	–	–
9	HEC Paris	Oxford – Saïd	INSEAD	–	–
10	Oxford – Saïd	SDA Bocconi	Mannheim	–	–
11	Manchester Business School	Manchester Business School	Bath School of Management	–	–
12	SDA Bocconi	City – Cass	Cambridge – Judge	–	–
13	–	Cranfield	UCD – Smurfit	–	–
14	–	Rotterdam, Erasmus	Warwick Business School	–	–

	BusinessWeek (2010)	*Financial Times* (2011)	*The Economist* (2010)	*Forbes* (2009)	*US News* (2011)
15	–	Imperial College	EM Lyon	–	–
16	–	Lancaster University	Vlerick Leuven Gent	–	–
17	–	Joint: Durham and Vlerick Leuven Gent	EDHEC	–	–
18	–	Warwick	International University of Monaco	–	–
19	–	Hult	City University – Cass	–	–
20	–	Birmingham	Durham	–	–
21	–	Strathclyde	Rotterdam – Erasmus University	–	–
22	–	UCD – Smurfit	Manchester Business School	–	–
23	–	EADA	Grenoble Graduate School of Business	–	–
24	–	Edinburgh	SDA Bocconi	–	–
25	–	Bradford/TiasNimbas	Ashridge	–	–
26	–	Leeds	Birmingham Business School	–	–
27	–	Politecnico di Milano	Oxford – Saïd	–	–
28	–	EM Lyon	Audencia Nantes	–	–
29	–	–	Aston Business School	–	–
30	–	–	University of Edinburgh Business School	–	–

Asia

Top FT MBAs in Asia

	Financial Times (2011)	*The Economist* (2010)
1	Hong Kong University of Science and Technology – HKUST (Hong Kong)	University of Hong Kong – HKU (Hong Kong)
2	Indian Institute of Management, Ahmedabad – IIMA (India)	Hong Kong University of Science and Technology – UST (Hong Kong)
3	Indian School of Business (India)	Nanyang Business School (Singapore)
4	China Europe International Business School – Ceibs (China)	Chinese University of Hong Kong (Hong Kong)
5	National University of Singapore School of Business (Singapore)	International University of Japan, Graduate School of Management (Japan)

	Financial Times (2011)	*The Economist* (2010)
6	Nanyang Business School (Singapore)	National University of Singapore School of Business (Singapore)
7	SP Jain Center of Management (Singapore and Dubai)	Indian Institute of Management, Ahmedabad – IIMA (India)
8	Kaist College of Business (South Korea)	China Europe International Business School – Ceibs (China)

Top EMBA programmes globally

	BusinessWeek (2010)	*Financial Times* (2011)	*The Economist* (2010)
1	Kellogg	Kellogg/Hong Kong UST Business School	Wharton
2	Chicago Booth	Trium: HEC Paris/LSE/New York University: Stern	Washington in St Louis – Olin
3	Wharton	Columbia/London Business School	Thunderbird
4	Columbia	INSEAD	USC – Marshall
5	USC – Marshall	University of Chicago: Booth	Kellogg
6	IE	Duke University: Fuqua	Notre Dame – Mendoza
7	Michigan – Ross	University of Pennsylvania: Wharton	NYU – Stern
8	UCLA – Anderson	IE Business School	Cornell – Johnson
9	SMU – Cox	UCLA/NUS	Columbia (NY programme)
10	Duke – Fuqua	London Business School	UNC Kenan-Flagler (weekend)
11	UNC Kenan-Flagler	Joint: Ceibs and Kellogg/York University – Schulich	UCLA – Anderson
12	Emory – Goizueta		Texas, Austin – McCombs
13	IESE	IESE Business School	Arizona State – Carey
14	NYU – Stern	Chinese University of Hong Kong	Illinois at Urbana – Champaign
15	Ohio State – Fisher	Washington University: Olin School of Business/Fudan University School of Management	Michigan – Ross
16	IMD	IMD	Chicago Booth
17	ESADE	Joint: Kellogg/WHU – Otto Beisheim School and Northwestern University – Kellogg	Ohio State – Fisher
18	Georgetown – McDonough		Cornell – Johnson/Queen's University (joint programme)
19	INSEAD	National University of Singapore School of Business	Rice – Jones
20	Notre Dame – Mendoza	Arizona State University – Carey	Boston University
21	Case Western Reserve – Weatherhead	New York University – Stern	Rutgers University

	BusinessWeek (2010)	*Financial Times* (2011)	*The Economist* (2010)
22	Texas – Dallas	UC Berkeley/Columbia	Maryland – Smyth
23	Boston University	JOINT: Korea University Business School and Imperial College Business School	Berkeley – Haas/Columbia
24	LBS		IE
25	Queen's University	Columbia Business School	Vanderbilt – Owen
26		JOINT: Cornell – Johnson and OneMBA:	
27			
28		University of Toronto: Rotman	
29		JOINT: Oxford – Saïd and City – Cass	
30			
31		ESCP Europe	
32		Michigan – Ross	
33		ESSEC/Mannheim	
34		Warwick Business School	
35		Georgetown – McDonough	

Financial Times European business school rankings 2010 (top 30)

	Financial Times (2010)		
1	HEC Paris	16	St Gallen
2	LBS	17	SDA Bocconi
3	INSEAD	18	Imperial College
4	IMD	19	Stockholm
5	IF	20	Strathclyde
6	Rotterdam – Erasmus	21	Warwick
7	ESCP Europe	22	Aalto
8	ESADE	23	Copenhagen
9	IESE	24	Tilburg – TiasNimbas
10	EM Lyon	25	EDHEC
11	Oxford – Saïd	26	LSE
12	City – Cass	27	EADA
13	Vlerick Leuven Gent	28	Grenoble
14	ESSEC	29	Whu – Otto Beisheim
15	Cranfield	30	University College Dublin – Smurfit

Bibliography

AACSB accreditation process
www.aacsb.edu/accreditation/business/standards
www.degree.net/resources/degree-level/mba-degree-guide_201002182375.html

AMBA accreditation process
www.mbaworld.com/accreditationprocess

Della Bradshaw, Securing funding outside studies, *Financial Times*, January 2010.
www.ft.com/cms/s/2/8a9b2f66-ffdc-11de-ad8c-00144feabdc0,dwp_uuid=91a27406-05c5-11df-88ee-00144feabdc0.html#axzz1QlkXV5ZG

BusinessWeek rankings methodology
www.businessweek.com/bschools/content/nov2008/bs20081113_320726.htm#MBA1
www.businessweek.com/bschools/faq/execmba.htm

John A. Byrne, Turning the tables: ranking the MBA rankings.
www.poetsandquants.com/2010/06/28/turning-the-tables-ranking-the-mba-rankings

EQUIS accreditation documents
www.efmd.org/index.php/accreditation-/equis/equis-documents

Forbes MBA rankings and methodology
www.forbes.com/2009/08/05/best-business-schools-09-leadership-careers_land.html

FT EMBA ranking methodology
www.ft.com/cms/s/2/d135c81a-d771-11df-8582-00144feabdc0,dwp_uuid=f92d611a-d77c-11df-8582-00144feabdc0.html#axzz1QtBRfbbQ

FT Global MBA ranking methodology
www.ft.com/cms/s/2/5f2fb300-05c8-11df-88ee-00144feabdc0.html#axzz1QtBRfbbQ

Geoff Gloeckler, The case against case studies, *Bloomberg Businessweek*, January 2008.
www.businessweek.com/magazine/content/08_05/b4069066093267.htm

Francesca Levy, The spread of specialized MBA programs, *Bloomberg Businessweek*, July 2008.
www.ft.com/cms/s/2/8a9b2f66-ffdc-11de-ad8c-00144feabdc0.html#ixzz1bpYRIn5r

A history of the MBA programme and its increasing importance, from *The Economist* Intelligence Unit's "Which MBA?", *The Economist*, October 2003.
www.economist.com/node/2135907

US News ranking methodology
www.usnews.com/education/best-graduate-schools/articles/2011/03/14/business-school-rankings-methodology-2012

Index of advertisers